GENTLE WARRIORS

Clara Ueland and the Minnesota Struggle for Woman Suffrage

Barbara Stuhler

Minnesota Historical Society Press · St. Paul

Cover: Clara Ueland and Women's Suffrage Club at Hamline University, 1913, Minnesota Historical Society; jonquils, the symbol of the suffragists, photographed by Bill Johnson

Publication of this book was supported, in part, with funds provided by the June D. Holmquist Publication Endowment Fund of the Minnesota Historical Society.

Minnesota Historical Society Press
St. Paul 55102

Manufactured in the United States of America
10 9 8 7 6 5 4 3 2 1

International Standard Book Number 0-87351-317-7 (cloth)
0-87351-318-5 (paper)

∞ The paper used in this publication meets the minimum requirements of the American National Standard for Information Sciences—Permanence for Printed Library Materials, ANSI Z39.48-1984

Photographs:
Minnesota Historical Society collections, St. Paul—pages 5 (Hibbard and Potter), 23, 31 Nelson (Phillips), 45, 49 Jaeger (St. Paul Dispatch) Simpson (Lee Brothers) Winter (Sweet Studios), 52, 66, 77 (museum collections), 83 (Minneapolis Tribune), 84, 89, 94 (St. Paul Pioneer Press), 101 (C. J. Hibbard), 108, 126, 127, 149, 153, 158, 179 (St. Paul Dispatch), 188 (Hibbard), 197, 202 (Pacific and Atlantic Photos), 206, 210 (Gene Garrett)
Northeast Minnesota Historical Center, University of Minnesota-Duluth—page 31 Stearns
Andrea Ueland (Mrs. John B.) Brainard and Margaret L. (Mrs. Rolf) Ueland—pages 36, 44, 47, 72, 215
Minneapolis Public Library, Minneapolis Collection—page 95 (Lee Brothers)

Library of Congress Cataloging-in-Publication Data
Stuhler, Barbara
    Gentle warriors : Clara Ueland and the Minnesota struggle for woman suffrage / Barbara Stuhler.
      p.   cm.
    Includes bibliographical references and index.
    ISBN 0-87351-317-7 (cloth : acid free). — ISBN 0-87351-318-5 (paper : acid free)
    1. Women—Suffrage—Minnesota—History. 2. Ueland, Clara, 1860-1927. 3. Suffragists—Minnesota—Biography. I. Title.
    JK1911.M6S78   1995
    324.6'23'09776—dc20   95-19391

GENTLE WARRIORS

For my League friends

CONTENTS

PREFACE

My personal experiences and political interests have produced this tale of a cause and a crusader. The cause is woman suffrage and the crusader is Clara Ueland of Minnesota. I have attempted to help build the fragile edifice of existing state suffrage histories, not by telling the whole of the Minnesota story but by concentrating on the final years and demonstrating once again that individual effort can make a difference. In a happy coincidence of timing and leadership, it was Ueland's good fortune to be able to celebrate the passage by Congress of the Nineteenth Amendment and its ratification by the Minnesota legislature in 1919, the year when she served as the last president of the Minnesota Woman Suffrage Association and as the first president of the Minnesota League of Women Voters.[1]

My interest in the antecedents of the succession of women's movements emerged from my long association with the Minnesota and national organizations of the League of Women Voters. As I dipped into the history books, I became fascinated with the women who first protested their exclusion from the political process. Abigail Adams, Frances Wright, Margaret Fuller, and England's Mary Wollstonecraft and Harriet Taylor are some of those women who were neither queens, saints, or warriors but who—by their rhetoric, influence, and example—began to break down the stereotypes of womankind as the lesser sex.

Pioneering suffragists—Lucretia Mott, Elizabeth Cady Stanton, Susan B. Anthony, and Lucy Stone—followed in their footsteps. They built the commitment to change women's lives for the better by focusing on the cause of women's rights and by forming organizations to achieve the vote. Leaving aside that notable quartet, most readers, I suspect, would be hard pressed to name other suffrage leaders who possess through no fault of their own an anonymity they did not necessarily seek. Even Carrie Chapman Catt, who was twice president of the National American Woman Suffrage Association and who masterminded the final suffrage victory, has been forgotten over the years. Few could name suffrage leaders in other states. Few would even know who Clara Ueland was or what she did. Persons familiar with the Minnesota writer, Brenda Ueland, frequently ask, "Are they related?" Yes, Clara was Brenda's mother. She was also the wife of a prominent Norwegian-American attorney and the mother of two other enterprising daughters and four successful sons. Clara Ueland's claim to fame, however, is neither as a spouse or mother (though she apparently did both very well) but as a civic activist whose achievements should appear with greater frequency in the pages of Minnesota's history. This book, concentrating as it does on the suffrage experience and Ueland's leadership, attempts to repair some of those omissions.

While consideration of Ueland's private life helps to make her a whole person, the primary focus in these pages is about the issues, personalities, activities, and politics relating to twentieth-century suffrage efforts in Minnesota. Because the suffrage movement originated elsewhere and sprang up everywhere, some attention must be paid to the national scene which provides a context for the Minnesota experiences. Because there are striking parallels as well as differences between nineteenth- and twentieth-century women's movements, some space has been given to a description of issues, attitudes, and coalitions of the earlier period. And because there are similarities between the Minnesota efforts to gain votes for women and those of other states, this account may serve to reinforce those common bonds.

The early suffragists, who were the object of relentless ridicule and merciless mockery, had to be made of stern stuff. "War horses" they were sometimes called, and probably with good reason.

Professional women, who broke ground for the "second sex" in law, medicine, and religion, populated the suffrage movement. They understood that the enfranchisement of women was the necessary prelude to their liberation. Twentieth-century suffragists, typified by Clara Ueland, brought another dimension to suffrage and recruited new women to the cause. This second generation, many more of them gaining advantage through their experience as club members and college graduates, constituted the core of trained, articulate advocates who assumed the organizational responsibilities necessary to make suffrage a reality. While Ueland had reservations about the style and manner of some of her predecessors, she respected the early suffrage leaders for their courage, their ability to withstand ridicule, and—above all—because they were not meek in spirit or in action. She maintained those same qualities of diligence and persistence, but she also brought to the suffrage campaign efficiency, money, organization, and—above all—a shrewd political acumen that finally won votes for women in Minnesota.

Ueland did not include herself among the women who feared to exert power or experience conflict (so long as disagreements were contained by civil behavior and good manners). In *Writing a Woman's Life*, Carolyn G. Heilbrun observes that "however unhappy the concept of power and control may make idealistic women, they delude themselves if they believe that the world and the condition of the oppressed can be changed without acknowledging it." And later she says:

> Because many women would prefer (or think they would prefer) a world without evident power or control, women have been deprived of the narratives, or the texts, plots, or examples by which they might assume power over—take control of—their own lives.[2]

The skills Clara Ueland acquired from her brief career as a teacher, her longer stint managing a large household, and her apprenticeship as a community activist may have helped her to learn the kindly use of power. She was a feminist who believed, in the words of Frederick Douglass, that "no man, however eloquent, can speak for woman, as a woman can for herself." She understood that women must make and take opportunities to do for themselves and speak for themselves in achieving fuller lives and larger liberties. She possessed the primary attributes of political leadership: a quiet eloquence, conviction, organizational and administrative skills, and an aptitude for fundraising and lobbying. She was a new woman of her time, politically important, enormously competent, highly influential, and widely respected. The measure of Clara Ueland's leadership was her ability to ask more of others because she gave so much of herself.[3]

Knowledge about the suffrage movement has been tremendously enriched by the explosive magnitude of feminist scholarship in the last few decades. For a time, the subjects of woman suffrage and notable women were overshadowed as scholars attempted to write all women back into history, not just a privileged few. Nancy F. Cott, in her keynote address during Women's History Week in 1985, explained some of the reasons. Suffragists suffered from visibility at a time when scholars were searching for the invisible women who also constituted history and political reality. Suffrage was viewed as an upper-middle-class elite social movement at odds with the concerns of less privileged women and—until recently—overlooked as a pioneering effort by women to free themselves from oppression. Furthermore, the ratification of the Nineteenth Amendment was discounted as a legal, formal achievement, producing no significant change in the institutions of work and family (thereby failing to benefit women) and with no significant political payoff. But a second look has suggested that suffrage left enduring legacies and should be rightly regarded as a major accomplishment opening the door of political citizenship to the women of the United States.[4]

Clara Ueland and company did not believe that winning the vote would change the world—or Minnesota—overnight, but they knew what they wanted to do with their newly acquired power. After gaining the vote, women created a vast number of voluntary organizations and engineered the passage of an extraordinary number of economic and social reforms. Those contributions, together with the new feminist movement that emerged in the 1960s and the recent accomplishments of women in business, the professions, and politics, derive from the suffrage heritage. While seeing that injustices and inequities still remained, Ueland and her allies would have been pleased that succeeding generations in Minnesota have brought so much to the table of women's progress: the first program of pay equity in public employment; the first battered women's shelter; the first private foundation solely devoted to women and girls; and the first state supreme court with a majority of women. These accomplishments have been matched by individual women of Minnesota who have broken new ground in fields ranging from diplomacy to exploration to journalism.[5]

The lessons of the Minnesota experience illustrate the difficulties and divisions that characterized the national suffrage movement. Despite a long and arduous struggle, a powerless class won power by dint of their own efforts and without violence. The ultimate success of the suffrage campaign is an extraordinary story of colorful and diverse personalities whose leadership changed the life of a nation. The women's movement in the last half of the twentieth century has experienced the joy of victories and the pain of defeat. As women continue the struggle for equality into the twenty-first century, they need to remember—and emulate—the continuing commitment and civic courage of leaders like Clara Ueland of Minnesota.

ACKNOWLEDGMENTS

A happy collaboration with the resources and staff of the Minnesota Historical Society has produced this book. A two-year research grant helped get it under way. The archival collections yielded the complete records of the Minnesota Woman Suffrage Association, the League of Women Voters of Minnesota, and papers of many of the leading lights of the suffrage period. Although I was privileged to occupy an office in the Knight Foundation's Research Suite of the Society's handsome new History Center, I did most of my writing at home where my occasional computer frustrations and anxieties were greatly eased by friend and neighbor Karon Schmitt.

Local historian Mary C. Pruitt of Minneapolis Community College and independent scholar Linda Lounsbury generously shared with me unpublished products of their research. I am also indebted to women—and men as well—of diverse disciplines who have in recent years contributed so significantly to the accounts and interpretations of the history of American women, including the suffrage and post-suffrage eras which are the focus of this book.

I am grateful to many members of the Ueland family for their interest in this effort and for their patience and cooperation in response to my requests for photographs, anecdotes, and remembrances. Especially helpful have been Margaret Ueland (widow of Rolf), the late Harriet Ueland (widow of Sigurd), Gabrielle

(Gaby) McIver (Brenda's daughter), Andrea Brainard (Arnulf's daughter), and Clara Ueland (daughter of Rolf and Margaret).

I want to thank the professional men and women who work as reference specialists in the History Center. Among those who helped me find answers to questions like "Where can I find . . . ?" and "How do I . . . ?" were Ruth Bauer Anderson, Tino Avaloz, Pat Harpole (before her retirement), Dallas Lindgren, Alissa Rosenberg, and Steve Nielsen. Tracey Baker found many of the illustrations that embellish the book.

My closest colleagues in this endeavor came from the staff of the Publications and Research Division. I cannot name them all, but I must recognize Jean A. Brookins, the division's director, who was always encouraging and enthusiastic. Production Manager Alan Ominsky, whom I had known from previous publication years, was good humored and good company. Others, whom I had known slightly or not at all—like Research Supervisor Deborah Miller—were always friendly and supportive. She also made it possible for me to employ the impressive talents of intern Rachel Wheeler, then a recent graduate of Carleton College, to do biographical research on most of the women who appear in these pages. I am grateful to Holly Elliot for her editing assistance and to Deborah Swanson whose careful verification of my assertions saved me from grievous errors. Ann Regan, the managing editor of the Minnesota Historical Society Press, orchestrated with considerable elan the complexities of the final process. I do not know whether to call Elaine Carte my alter ego or my guiding light, but she is the editor who made this book go, and it is to her that I extend my deepest appreciation.

PROLOGUE

The suffrage activists from twenty-six states who gathered for their annual convention in Minneapolis on May 30, 1901, had little to celebrate. In the fifty-three years since a group of women had resolved in Seneca Falls, New York, "to secure for themselves their sacred right to the elective franchise," the tally revealed a piteous few suffrage successes. Only Wyoming, Colorado, Utah, and Idaho had achieved the status of full suffrage states. There was, to be sure, limited suffrage elsewhere: Minnesota women, for example, could vote in school and library elections. By the turn of the century, however, stagnation had settled on the suffrage movement. From 1894 to 1913 Congress ignored the issue, and fourteen years passed—from 1896 to 1910—before Washington broke the dry spell and became the fifth state to enfranchise women. Had the assembled women known of the bleak years ahead, they would have been dismayed but not deterred. They were endowed with extraordinary determination, optimism, and persistence.[1]

The high-spirited suffrage leaders who congregated in Minneapolis were responding to a convention call that sounded their sentiments: "Believers in this cause are legion, but many,

satisfied that victory will come without their help, do nothing.
. . . If the final victory is long in coming, the responsibility rests
with those who believe but do not act."[2]

Leaders spanning nearly the entire period of the suffrage
movement—from 1848, when the first Women's Rights Convention was held in Seneca Falls, New York, to 1920, when the
Nineteenth Amendment was finally ratified—were present for
this thirty-third convention. The first women's rights organizations were not formed until 1869, twenty-one years after Seneca
Falls. Another twenty-one years passed before the two existing
associations merged, with Stanton serving as the first president of
the National American Woman Suffrage Association (NAWSA)
and Susan B. Anthony as its second president from 1888 to 1900.
Of the early leaders, only Anthony was there in Minneapolis
among the 144 gathered. Infirm in body but healthy in mind and
spirit, Stanton sent a message to the Minneapolis gathering reaffirming her crusade to pin responsibility for the bondage of
women on church law.[3]

Carrie Chapman Catt, who had served an impressive apprenticeship as chair of NAWSA's organization committee in the final
five years of the nineteenth century, had been elected in 1900 as
the new (and third) president of the national association. She
proved to be an obvious, if contested, choice to succeed Susan B.
Anthony, and Catt brought to the presidency not only a new
generation of leadership (she was only forty-one) but a new kind
of suffrage leadership. Four years later when Catt—worn down
by her own exertions and the precarious health of her husband
and mother (he died in 1905, her mother in 1907)—decided not
to continue, she was succeeded by Anna Howard Shaw, a physician, minister, and compelling speaker for the cause. Shaw, also
present at the Minneapolis convention, was a throwback to the
older generation of suffragists, a proselytizer in the earlier tradition of suffrage campaigning but lacking in organizational skills.
It was not until Catt once again assumed the presidency of the
national association in 1915 that suffrage got back on track. She
and other like-minded twentieth-century leaders—including

Clara Ueland of Minnesota—merged organizing sensibilities with political realities and steered suffrage to victory.[4]

As the suffragists came together in Minneapolis, a new politics of reform was making its debut in the United States. The populism of the farmers gave way to the progressivism of the urban middle class, signaling the transformation of the still-youthful nation from an agrarian to an industrial society. The high-minded concerns of morality, honesty, and accountability in both business and government articulated by the burgeoning Progressive movement proved to be a comfortable fit for women whose lifestyles were changing. As the nation's economy shifted from a rural to an industrial base, the range of options for working women widened. They left the field for the factory; they constituted a rich source of supply for the sales forces of new department stores in the cities; and they proved to be more skillful than the men they replaced as secretaries and clerks in business offices. Parents encouraged their daughters to take advantage of these opportunities to support themselves, thereby contributing to the family income. In the early 1900s more working women could be found occupying rented rooms in Minneapolis than in most other cities, a fact that underscored the magnitude of the migration from rural to urban communities. With the establishment of women's colleges and the growth of coeducational universities, increasing numbers of female high school graduates had greater access to educational opportunities. Many mothers who had been intellectually stimulated in women's literary societies encouraged their daughters to take advantage of higher education. Many of these same women moved from literary societies that served as means for self-improvement to clubs for women, where they acquired managerial skills and began to put their moral convictions into action, doing good things to improve their communities, making them better places to live and to work.[5]

As growing numbers of these middle-class women became independent, educated, and active, they inevitably hitched their figurative wagons to the suffrage star, recognizing that the right to vote was the gateway to political power and to their ability to right the wrongs of society. Unlike their predecessors in the last half of the nineteenth century, they were not content to rely solely on persuasion and propaganda, the sacrifices of many, and the generosity of a few. The suffragists of the new century marshaled a more organized campaign, benefiting from improvements in transportation and communication. This enabled them to sustain and nourish local societies, which had often languished and died from benign neglect. They also learned the language and the ways of politics. Consider, for example, a Mrs. Ellis Meredith of Denver, speaking to the Minneapolis convention about pretenders to politics: "They have read Bryce's American Commonwealth and have an intellectual understanding of the theory and form of our government but they do not know what ward they live in, they are vague as to the district, have never met their Congressman and do not know a primary from a kettle drum."[6]

The new suffragists became effective lobbyists, skilled at public relations, and enthusiastic fund-raisers. They knew what they had to do. Laura Clay of Kentucky spoke directly to the delegates about the need to win the active support of not just a few but literally millions of other women: "We have learned that the apathy of women to their own political freedom is as great an obstacle to our success as the unwillingness of men to grant our claims. It is of the same importance to us to educate women out of their indifference as it is to educate men out of their unwillingness."[7]

As the number of suffragists grew, the earlier ridicule was replaced with a growing respect by the public and by decision makers. Slowly but inexorably the suffrage movement would enter the mainstream of political debate.

The women of the convention city proved to be genial and efficient hosts. They entertained delegates in their homes, handled the complex logistical arrangements, and attended to all the amenities that provide aid and comfort to visitors. The First Baptist Church, which featured "the largest audience room in Minneapolis," was rented for the weekly fee of $250. Leading merchants and businessmen contributed money to cover the cost. Delegates and national officers stayed at the fashionable West

Hotel, and a carriage transported the dignitaries to and from the church. Delegates toured the city on chartered streetcars and sometimes absented themselves from duller business meetings to visit the city's stores and shops. Carrie Chapman Catt spoke eloquently of Cora Smith Eaton, who chaired the arrangements committee, describing her energy, executive ability, tact, and enthusiasm as reasons enough to meet in Minneapolis. (Eight years later, the same intrepid physician—then Dr. Cora Smith King—carried a "Votes for Women" banner to the summit of Mount Ranier.) Anthony paid the local organizers the highest compliment when she called the convention the "best arranged" and noted, "I do not see how it could have been bettered."[8]

At the first evening session the speakers were reportedly witty and wise. Governor Samuel R. Van Sant gave the first of many welcoming speeches and cordially counseled the delegates

The West Hotel, about 1900

to convert more women, admitting that, as a former legislator, he was often convinced by numbers. Mayor Albert A. Ames applauded the women's efforts and approved their cause. Former Mayor William Henry Eustis, speaking for the Commercial Club, joked that the Falls of St. Anthony had been named in Susan B. Anthony's honor, and he stated more seriously that organizations like his were temporary, "but a great movement like this is eternal." In her evening keynote address, "The Invisible Foe," Anna Howard Shaw effectively discredited opponents who had refused her invitation to a debate.[9]

In her presidential address Carrie Chapman Catt specified three obstacles to the achievement of suffrage: militarism, which held people to "the old ideals of force in government and headship in the family"; prostitution, which revealed "the estimate in which women as a whole" are regarded; and the "inertia" or backlash stemming from the "ill-advised" and "hasty" enfranchisement of "the foreigner, the negro, and the Indian." These influences, Catt insisted, "shape every opinion of the opponents of woman suffrage." The first two obstacles were self-evident, but the third one—part of the prevailing prejudice of the time—reflected the resentment of suffragists that immigrant men and freedmen had the vote while that right of citizenship continued to be denied to women.[10]

On May 31 Nellie Sowle Gregory, whose husband was a prominent grain merchant and civic leader, entertained the delegates at a glittering reception in her Park Avenue home. One newspaper reported "a crush" of hundreds of beautifully clad women. "Society leaders" and the "brightest businesswomen of Minneapolis" turned out in force, eager to see and meet these legendary heirs of Seneca Falls. One of the emerging "society leaders" (although that would not have been her term of choice) was the forty-year-old Clara Hampson Ueland, a woman of considerable talents and achievements, who was beginning to relate her own interests to the suffrage movement.[11]

Ueland's experience in helping to establish kindergartens in the Minneapolis public schools, her insistence on avoiding sexual stereotypes in rearing her own children, her earlier career as a teacher, and her growing reputation as a woman of substance made her a likely suffrage supporter. But Clara, as one friend noted, "was not with us at first," having been repelled "by the acrid bitterness, the cranky eccentricity of those early war horses" in the movement. As more mainstream women, many of them close friends of hers, began to sign up for suffrage, Ueland must have decided to give it another look. Although the cause began to "stir her feelings" in 1901, another decade would pass before she became fully committed and on her way to leadership of the movement in Minnesota.[12]

The delegates returned to their homes from Minneapolis with renewed hope that woman suffrage would one day be achieved. Little did they realize that they would cross the threshold of the new century hand in glove with progressive reformers, which would give a big boost to their cause. Nor could those suffragists have predicted in 1901—however optimistic they might have been—that the four suffrage states would grow to forty-eight in less than twenty years. Nor could they have possibly known that the movement they started with a demand for the vote would be resurrected long after they were all gone and would forever change the lives of women and the life of a nation.

In 1914 Clara Ueland would become the state suffrage leader in Minnesota, working closely with Carrie Catt and equally resolute women in other states to manage the final successful campaign and to celebrate the day when votes for women became a reality. The ratification of the Nineteenth Amendment on August 26, 1920, represented a triumph for women who had originally protested their "injuries and usurpations" in the Seneca Falls Declaration of Sentiments seventy-two years before—and all those who followed, seeking to repair in a formal and organized way those injustices. Of the twelve resolutions approved at Seneca Falls, the right of women to the elective franchise had emerged as the core issue, the essential remedy that would give women the political power from which other powers derived. Never in the history of this young nation had such a large group been excluded from full citizenship for so many years. Never before had a single issue occupied so much space in the lives of a remarkable band of women. By the end, two million American women—mostly white, well-to-do, well educated, and prominent in their communities—had been mobilized on behalf of suffrage, attracted by the power of an idea and by the skills of leaders like Clara Ueland, who knew how to put those women to work.[13]

1

THE GENESIS
OF A MOVEMENT

A woman ought to meddle in politics.
JANE GREY SWISSHELM, 1858

 From the nation's infancy, American women came together in times of war and peace not only to serve others but to help themselves. The nineteenth century witnessed the emergence in the United States of a quartet of issues that attracted women's interest and commitment—moral reform, temperance, the abolition of slavery, and suffrage.

Moral reform, an effort to control prostitution and other vices that undermined the sanctity of home and church, was an appropriate task for women who were confined by society's expectations of their piety, purity, submissiveness, and domesticity. Temperance was closely allied to moral reform, even as leaders like Frances Willard tried to stretch the movement to encompass a broader agenda. Although abolition grew out of the same tradition of pietistic female benevolence, it became secularized and politicized.[1]

Suffrage represented the pinnacle of these reforms, fueled by women's experiences as wives, mothers, or single women exceedingly frustrated by their inability to get off the pedestal of reverence that camouflaged the abuses they suffered. Many women who had the means chose to organize to repudiate, in the words of one historian, "the social shibboleth . . . that 'woman's place' was in the home" and to affirm their rightful place in the public arena pursuing social and political reform. Jane Addams, recognizing that the well-being of families depended on a healthy society, observed that it was "necessary that woman shall extend her sense of responsibility to . . . things outside of her own home, if only in order to preserve the home in its entirety."[2]

The suffrage movement took root on American soil eight years after the initial meeting of Lucretia Mott and Elizabeth Cady Stanton in London, England. The occasion was the first World Anti-Slavery Convention; the date was June 1840. Mott was there as a delegate from the Female Anti-Slavery Society in Philadelphia (abolitionist organizations were segregated by sex). Elizabeth Cady was there as the newly wedded spouse of delegate Henry Stanton. Early in the proceedings, the convention voted not to seat the women delegates, thereby excluding them from participation. That decision prompted the resolve of Lucretia Mott, who experienced the exclusion, and Elizabeth Cady Stanton, who witnessed it, to join forces in combating the oppression of women.

Described as "both serene and vivacious," Lucretia Coffin Mott was a Quaker minister, abolitionist, and feminist. Born on Nantucket Island in 1793, she came by her convictions from strong parents. Her father was a ship's captain plying the China trade, and her mother an independent merchant. Although Mott was diminutive in stature, she was large in conviction, boycotting goods such as cotton cloth and sugar cane that came from the labor of slaves, founding the Philadelphia Female Anti-Slavery Society in 1833, and organizing the Anti-Slavery Convention of American Women in 1837. Mott encouraged the feminism and independence of her new young and exuberant friend. When later asked what she found to be the most impressive thing about England, Stanton is said to have replied, "Lucretia Mott." A Stanton biographer noted that the "impact on Elizabeth Cady Stanton of weeks of companionship and conversation with Lucretia Mott cannot be underestimated. At last

Stanton had found a suitable female role model and a willing mentor." The two agreed that, on their return to America, they would form a society to advance the rights of women.[3]

That good intention was delayed for Stanton by the birth of sons in 1842, 1844, and 1845 and by Mott's involvement with various Quaker sectarian differences. In July 1848 Mott, who was attending a contentious Quaker conclave in New York State, invited Stanton to meet with her in Waterloo, a twin town to Seneca Falls, where Stanton and her family had moved the year before. They were joined by three other women—their hostess, Jane Hunt; Mott's sister, Martha Coffin Wright; and Mary Ann McClintock. Stanton took the occasion to pour out "the torrent of my long-accumulating discontent with such vehemence and indignation that I stirred myself, as well as the rest of the party, to do and dare anything." Her indignation over the limitations imposed on the lives of women, limitations that stifled any opportunities for individual fulfillment, enjoyed a sympathetic hearing from Stanton's four listeners. In short order they wrote an unsigned "call" in the *Seneca County Courier* to a "convention to discuss the social, civil, and religious condition and rights of women." The date was set for July 19–20, 1848.[4]

In the eight-day interval between call and convention, Stanton took the leading role in writing a "Declaration of Rights and Sentiments," declaring that "all men *and women* are created equal," describing specific economic, political, social, domestic, and religious grievances and demanding "immediate admission to all rights and privileges" belonging to women as citizens of the United States. Anticipating "no small amount of misconception, misrepresentation, and ridicule," the declaration proclaimed the intention of women to petition, to enlist the pulpit and the press in their behalf, and to replicate this convention in "every part of the country." A Philadelphia newspaper obligingly complied with the expectations of "misrepresentation and ridicule": "A woman is a nobody. A wife is everything. A pretty girl is equal to 10,000 men, and a mother is, next to God, all powerful. . . . The ladies of Philadelphia, therefore, under the

influence of the most serious 'sober second thoughts' are resolved to maintain their rights as Wives, Belles, Virgins, and
Mothers, and not as Women."[5]

On July 19 nearly three hundred "Wives, Belles, Virgins,
Mothers," *and* "Women"—along with husbands, brothers, and
fathers—filled the Wesleyan Methodist Church in Seneca Falls
to capacity. They examined the litany of injustices against
women. Women, for example, had no right to hold property or
keep any wages they may have earned. They could not attend
college, and consequently "all the avenues to wealth and distinction" were closed to them. Women were compelled to obey their
husbands and, in the event of divorce, could not claim guardianship of their children. They were subjected to different codes of
conduct and condemned to separate spheres of life. Delegates
adopted resolutions proposing that women be regarded as the
equal of men, that women be assertive about their rights, that
men be expected to exhibit the same "virtue, delicacy and refine-
ment of behavior that is required of women in the social state,"
and that women be accepted in every sphere of activity, including that of religion. They also approved a comprehensive plea
calling for "the zealous and untiring efforts of both men and
women, for the overthrow of the monopoly of the pulpit, and for
securing to woman an equal participation with men in the various trades, professions, and commerce."[6]

The women and men at the convention passed all the proposed resolutions without opposition except for one—the plank
demanding for women the "inalienable right to the elective franchise." Such a radical proposition gave the convention pause—
the idea of women voting remained the most controversial of all
the proposed remedies. Three months before Seneca Falls,
Stanton and others had succeeded in persuading the New York
state legislature to pass an act permitting married women to own
property. This proved to be an acceptable and fairly tame reform
because it enlarged women's rights only within the domestic
sphere, and it no doubt influenced the delegates' acceptance of
the other resolutions. The demand for the franchise, however,

represented a difference not simply in degree but in kind, because it extended women's sphere into the realm of public life. Henry Stanton, who was otherwise supportive, fretted that it would make a farce of the occasion and declined to attend the convention. Even Lucretia Mott was apprehensive. "Why Lizzie," she said, "thou will make us ridiculous." Nevertheless Stanton persisted, and with a persuasive second by Frederick Douglass, the former slave and then editor of the antislavery *North Star* newspaper in Rochester, the resolution passed.[7]

No one—much less "Lizzie," who continued to contend for broad sweeping reforms on all fronts—anticipated that the elective franchise would become the centerpiece of the woman's movement well into the twentieth century. The call for suffrage threatened to replace male authority with female autonomy, implying that women's interests could be in conflict with those of men, that women should be in a position to protect themselves, and that the traditional dependency of women would be transformed into independence of thought and action. In the minds of many, suffrage challenged the centrality of the family with the father as its head, representing and protecting his wife and children in the wider world. To grant suffrage to women would fracture that fundamental precept of American politics. "It is well known," said one New York legislator, "that the object of these unsexed women is to overthrow the most sacred of our institutions." No wonder that Henry Stanton absented himself and that Lucretia Mott was momentarily dismayed.[8]

Although they did not meet until 1851, three years after Seneca Falls, Elizabeth Cady Stanton and Susan B. Anthony emerged as the leaders of the suffrage movement throughout the nineteenth century. The meeting of these two women marked the start of a durable, if occasionally fractious, collaboration that provided the substance and form of the suffrage movement for the next fifty years. Strangely, the Stanton-Anthony imperfect partnership was a perfect alliance. Stanton possessed the facile pen, the oratorical skills, and a winning personality. Anthony was persistent and pragmatic, and her organizational abilities provided a useful counterpart to the sometimes wayward ideological spurts of her friend and coworker. One writer has said of the two:

> Dogged, persistent, capable, and hard-working, the spinster Susan tramped up and down in New York in all weathers, organizing, circulating petitions, speaking, and in general fanning the breath of life into a movement that might otherwise have died from opposition or from lack of interest from the rank and file. Mrs. Stanton had a little more of genius and tact, a touch of humor and zest, and an invaluable compound of charm and magnetism. . . . Both were vital to the cause.[9]

Stanton, tied down by pregnancies and continuing maternal responsibilities, was frequently visited by Anthony, who helped by holding the baby and stirring the pudding. Together they were able to sustain each other and plot their next moves on behalf of votes for women. Stanton wrote of these encounters: "We never met without issuing a pronunciamento on some question. . . . She supplied the facts and statistics, I the philosophy and the rhetoric, and, together, we have made arguments that stood unshaken through the storms of long years. . . . Our speeches may be considered the united product of our two brains."[10]

An early collaboration important to the emancipation of women was the alliance with the abolitionists. Sarah and Angelina Grimké, two young women from South Carolina who had freed their own slaves, came north in 1828 to critique the practice of slavery. They found an eager listener in Abby Kelly, a Massachusetts Quaker, who became a leader of the radical wing of the antislavery movement. Kelly, along with the Grimkés and Lucretia Mott, was one of two hundred delegates gathered on May 9, 1837, in what is now Greenwich Village, for the Anti-Slavery Convention of American Women, "the first public political meeting of women in the United States." Her ardent support of abolition extended in time to gender as well as race, and Lucy Stone said of her, "Abby Kelly earned for us all the right of free speech. The movement for equal rights of women began directly and emphatically with her." The Grimkés also spoke on the concerns of women, and with the publication of Sarah Grimké's *Letters on Equality of Sexes and the Condition of Women* in 1838, the first significant American treatise on the subject was in print. The theme was succinctly stated: "I ask no favors for my sex. . . . All I ask my brethren is that they will take their feet from off our necks, and permit us to stand upright on that ground which God designed us to occupy."[11]

The Grimké sisters were the first but by no means the only young white women who publicly identified with the plight of the slaves. Lucy Stone, a graduate of Mount Holyoke Female Seminary and Oberlin College, started out as a speaker for anti-slavery but often spoke to the inequities, indignities, and injustices endured by women. "I was a woman before I was an abolitionist. I must speak for the women," she would reply to critics of her alleged mixed messages. When Stone married Henry Blackwell in 1855, they read their prenuptial agreement at the ceremony, a statement protesting the husband's custody of the wife's person, control over their children, ownership of her property and wages, and the "whole system by which the legal existence of the wife is suspended during marriage." Stone also kept her own name (she was the first American woman known to have done so), much to the delight of Elizabeth Stanton and the ultimate acceptance of Lucretia Mott, who commented, "Seeing there are so few to advocate woman's whole cause, it is needful for some of us to be ultra."[12]

With the outbreak of the war between the North and the South in 1861, more than forty years of work to reach some political compromise over the divisive issue of slavery went up in the smoke of cannon fire. At war's end, Republicans hastened to make emancipation a part of the Constitution (the Thirteenth Amendment, 1865), to provide full-scale citizenship to Negroes (Fourteenth Amendment, 1868), and to bar states from interfering with the freedmen's right to vote (Fifteenth Amendment, 1870). The desire of the Republican party to ensure these constitutional guarantees was based not just on principle but on politics as well. It needed the Negro vote to prevent slaveowners from returning to power both in the Congress and in state legislatures.[13]

The Reconstruction amendments had another, perhaps unintended, result, as conflicts over the insertion of the word *male* in the Fourteenth Amendment and the exclusion of women from the Fifteenth Amendment shattered the long-standing partnership between men and women on behalf of human rights. The position articulated in 1865 by Wendell Phillips, a prominent abolitionist and the movement's most talented orator, prevailed: "I hope in time to be as bold as Stuart Mill and add to that last clause 'sex'!! But this hour belongs to the negro." Even suffrage's good friend, Frederick Douglass, stood with Phillips, saying, "The woman's hour will come."[14]

Division extended to the ranks of women as well, with Lucy Stone finally supporting the Fifteenth Amendment without the inclusion of "sex" in the belief that half a loaf was better than none and that it represented a step in the right direction. Neither Susan B. Anthony nor Elizabeth Cady Stanton subscribed to that compromise. In their view an amendment establishing universal manhood suffrage was tantamount to creating an "aristocracy of sex." Both Anthony and Stanton, who had previously worked for the abolition of slavery, resorted to arguments tinged with racial and elitist overtones. Anthony icily remarked that she would "cut off this right arm of mine before I will demand the ballot for the Negro and not the woman." Stanton, who had come from a background of wealth, privilege, and power, resented—and said so—that women like herself had to take second place to unschooled and politically ignorant men. The debate over the Fifteenth Amendment in 1869–70 marked the overt beginning of a nativism and racism that infected the suffrage movement for another fifty years.[15]

The issues of gender and race also became tangled in the web of partisan politics and produced a division of opinion within the woman suffrage movement that led to the great schism of 1869. The faction led by the more militant New Yorkers, Stanton and Anthony, became the National Woman Suffrage Association

(NWSA). The other faction—the American Woman Suffrage Association (AWSA)—was organized by cautious Bostonians Lucy Stone, Henry Ward Beecher, and Julia Ward Howe. Strangely, the division benefited the suffrage cause because it provided not just one but two organizational bases.[16]

The reasons for the schism were fundamental and complex, involving not only tactics and politics but philosophy as well. NWSA's reply to AWSA's position summed up the difference between the two groups: "The ballot is not even half the loaf; it is only a crust—a crumb. . . . Woman's chief discontent is not with her political, but with her social, and particularly her marital bondage." The Stanton-Anthony camp's commitment to an independent women's movement intensified, as historian Ellen DuBois has written, "the feminism that underlay their demand for woman suffrage." The Stone-Beecher-Howe group adopted the more modest, single goal of winning the vote for women.[17]

Amid these quarrels in 1869 came a landmark victory— approval of suffrage for women in the new Wyoming Territory. Opinions about women took a new turn in frontier communities, where women were valued because they were few in number and because they made recognizable contributions to the process of settlement and survival. Early settlers in Minnesota had experienced that same mutual dependency imposed by life on the frontier. One woman wrote:

> One of the great advantages of pioneer life is the necessity to man of woman's help in all the emergencies of these new conditions in which their forces and capacities are called into requisition. She thus acquires a degree of self-reliance, courage and independence, that would never be called out in older civilizations, and commands a degree of respect from the men at her side that can only be learned in their mutual dependence.[18]

Compelling as the reality of interdependence between men and women may have been, it could not offset the prevailing views and conventional attitudes of most decision makers. Conse-

quently suffragists made only small and marginal gains throughout the 1870s and 1880s.[19]

A few years after it emerged from the shadow of the abolitionist movement, suffrage found an ally in the temperance
movement in the person of Frances E. C. Willard, president of
the Woman's Christian Temperance Union (WCTU). Other mod-
erating influences gave the effort to secure votes for women a
more respectable middle-class mien. One of these was the extraordinary growth in women's clubs in the last three decades of
the nineteenth century. These associations, which sprang up all
over the country, provided training for many members who
would become latter-day suffrage leaders. They built libraries and
playgrounds, improved schools, initiated public health protective measures, and developed social service institutions to work
with the poor and disadvantaged. Women came of age as community leaders—and the club was their vehicle for leadership.[20]

In 1888, nearly twenty years after the rupture, Lucy Stone's
daughter, Alice Stone Blackwell, and other younger women
began efforts to reunite the two suffrage groups. While Elizabeth
Cady Stanton regarded this new alliance as conservative and
not exactly her radical cup of tea, she recognized the merits of
reconciliation and kept her peace. In February 1890 the reuni-
fied National American Woman Suffrage Association (NAWSA)
held its first meeting in Washington, D.C. Stanton held the
presidency until 1892, when she voluntarily stepped down and
was succeeded by Anthony, who served until her eightieth
birthday in 1900. In her final years, Stanton, with her cosmic
view of needed reforms, became increasingly impatient with
Anthony's "suffrage evermore" crusade, and she railed against
the movement's focus on enfranchisement—even though it had
been her own daring initiative. When Stanton died in 1902,
one year after the Minneapolis convention, Susan Anthony said
of her impatient, creative, and nonconforming friend, "It was a
great going out of my life when she went." When Anthony, the
last of the pioneer leaders, died in 1906, it was a great going out
of the life of woman suffrage, but there were women in the wings

who would provide a new kind of leadership for the changing times of the twentieth century.[21]

In Minnesota, suffrage pioneers resembled their sisters elsewhere, being a diverse lot of sometimes notable, occasionally controversial, and almost always persuasive and energetic women. In 1847—two years before Minnesota became a territory—Harriet Bishop arrived from Vermont to become St. Paul's first full-time public school teacher. Although she dwelt less on the oppression of women and more on their achievements and potential in effecting moral reform, religious benevolence, improved education, and temperance, she also supported equal suffrage and became one of the founders of the state suffrage society in 1881. There was much to do in this infant territory, and Bishop reminded women of the diverse roles they might play. In 1849 the whole of Minnesota had 4,131 white residents (and about 10,000 Dakota and Ojibway residents). Of that modest total, St. Paul could claim 910 and Minneapolis, that upstart twin town—a mere village—was home to only 248 individuals. By the time of statehood in 1858, both communities were on the move, their commerce, transport, and manufacturing fostered by the Mississippi River.[22]

In 1857 the Democratic wing of the constitutional convention, meeting in the Capitol building in St. Paul to prepare Minnesota for statehood, introduced a proposition to extend electoral privileges to married women; it was summarily dismissed, however, as too frivolous for notice. A year later Mary J. Colburn, a physician who had the reputation of being a "forceful character," gave what was probably the first public lecture in Minnesota on women's rights and wrongs in her home community of Champlin.[23]

Jane Grey Swisshelm, a nationally known journalist from Pennsylvania, escaped an unhappy marriage to move in 1857 with her six-year-old daughter to her sister's home in St. Cloud, Minnesota. In short order she maintained her reputation by becoming the flamboyant and courageous editor of the *St. Cloud Visiter* and later the owner of the *St. Cloud Democrat* (a Republican newspaper). She was a crusading abolitionist, made more so by her husband's earlier assertion that he was the owner of her "person and services"—she, too, was a slave! While Swisshelm also made effective use of her pen and platform on behalf of women's rights, she was a one-step-at-a-time suffragist, proposing gradual rather than sweeping reforms. But even her restrained approach stunned listeners. On one occasion, the *St. Paul Press* reported that her argument "so heightens the wrongs of women, as to even render almost justifiable the crime of murder to effect deliverance from their wrongs."[24]

Invited in 1860 to be the first of her gender to address the Minnesota House of Representatives, on "Woman and Politics," Swisshelm was relieved that her listeners received her remarks "with a favor beyond my highest hopes" and ecstatic that her "great cry which has been bursting my heart for long, long years" met with approval "by the best of and most honorable of our State." Indeed, one newspaper reported that she had "made many strong hits and good points, which were appreciated and applauded by the audience, and left a favorable impression of herself." Another, commenting on her examples of "women who have mingled in politics without losing their feminine attributes and the respect of men in all ages" and who "have made wise rulers, correct legislators, and even great generals," was impressed with both the style and content of her presentation. Two years later Swisshelm addressed the Minnesota Senate on "Woman's Legal Disabilities," reporting afterward that "the hall was packed and the lecture received with profound attention, interrupted by hearty applause." She left Minnesota in 1863 to work in Washington, D.C., during the Civil War with her reputation preserved and enhanced as an independent fighter for the abolition of slavery and for woman suffrage.[25]

In 1867 Sarah Burger Stearns joined forces with Mary Colburn and other women (Stearns called them "friends of equality") to petition the legislature for an amendment striking the word *male* from article 7, section 1, of the state constitution, which enfranchised "every male person." Stearns had moved the year before with her husband, attorney (later judge) Ozora P.

Stearns, from Michigan to Rochester, Minnesota. Destined to play a prominent role in the early days of suffrage work in Minnesota, Stearns claimed to have been a feminist since she was sixteen. Although Stearns and Colburn secured a hearing before a special committee of the legislature, no action was taken.[26]

Following that initial effort, a petition of 350 citizens ("Mary A. Graves and 349 others") was introduced in the Minnesota House in 1868, reported out favorably from the Elections Committee, greeted with laughter on the floor, and quickly tabled. Nevertheless, petitions to Congress and to the Minnesota legislature became a common mode of demonstrating the extent of public support for suffrage and a means of persuading senators and representatives to introduce legislation calling for the enfranchisement of women.[27]

In 1864, after winning first prize in a state-sponsored essay contest on "Minnesota as a Home for Emigrants," Colburn had written a friend declaring impatiently, "I will not stoop longer to ask of any congress or legislature for that which I know to be mine." Rhetoric to the contrary, she had participated in that first petition effort in 1867; and in 1869 she once again joined forces with Stearns in forming the state's first suffrage societies in their home communities of Rochester and Champlin.[28]

In 1870 suffragists again circulated and presented petitions to the legislature, which responded by proposing that women as well as men be permitted to vote on a constitutional amendment giving women the right of suffrage. Although this might have seemed to indicate some progress, in reality it was a hoax. The House voted approval thirty-three to thirteen and the Senate twelve to nine, but legislators apparently did so in the expectation that it would be defeated by the votes of women and would thereby lay to final rest the vexing question of woman suffrage.[29]

The matter became moot, however, with Governor Horace Austin's veto. He explained in a letter to Stearns that he would have signed the measure had women's votes been counted, not as legal and binding, but only as advisory. In another letter, however, he indicated that his opposition was lodged in the political reality that three-fifths of the Minnesotans who were foreign born were "hostile to the measure to a man." One observer commented, "The Woman's Suffrage bill of the Minnesota Legislature was conceived in jest and born in frivolity. . . . The whole thing was coupled disgracefully with levity and fun. A worthy way for the people's representatives to spend their time and the people's money!" And Jane Grey Swisshelm, then serving as western correspondent for a suffrage paper, exploded, "Must women go down on their knees to ask for that which is unjustly held from them?"[30]

The next year, taking a new tack, Minnesota suffragists organized a campaign that petitioned Congress to grant women "the citizen's right to vote" under the guarantees of the Fourteenth and Fifteenth amendments. Those efforts also failed.

Despite one discouragement after another, small numbers of Minnesota women continued to organize, petition, and press for suffrage. In 1875 they finally enjoyed some success. Whether acting from guilt or an emerging sense of justice, or merely responding to continuing pressure, the Minnesota legislature submitted to male electors a constitutional amendment authorizing the legislature to enable women to vote on school questions and to hold school offices. Stearns and her associates made two tactical decisions resulting in an affirmative vote. First, they determined that they would do nothing that might stir the opposition and refrained from publicizing the issue until just before election day, when Stearns asked the editor of the *Pioneer Press*—Minnesota's leading newspaper—to urge the amendment's adoption. The editor obliged, telling Stearns in a private letter that he "had quite forgotten such an amendment had been proposed." Second, they appealed to the committees of both parties to print their ballots with the following wording: "For the amendment of Article VII relating to electors—Yes." Minnesota historian William Watts Folwell provides a vivid description of the voting process: "Opposers were thus obliged to unbutton their coats, get out their glasses, fumble for a pencil, and cross out 'yes' and write 'no.' There were 19,469 patriots who took the trouble to scratch their tickets, but as 24,340 left them undefaced, the amendment was ratified. . . . There was rejoicing." Although women had to wait another year for the legislature to pass a law affirming the decision, suffrage supporters took solace from this modest victory.[31]

In many respects, Minnesota would have seemed a likely suffrage prospect. For men and women like Andreas and Clara Ueland, Minnesota was a magical place of opportunity in the late 1800s. In addition to its reputation for a healthy—if sometimes overly invigorating—climate, it offered an exceptional environment and a good living to hard workers. The best evidence of its popularity was the extraordinary increase in population of 78 percent in the decade of the 1870s. In 1873 the first of four summers of grasshopper invasions and a national financial crisis (triggered by the collapse of the New York banking house of Jay Cooke and Co.) seemingly dampened this era of buoyant

Minnesota women exercising the vote, about 1908

growth. These proved, however, to be temporary setbacks in a period of sustained prosperity.[32]

Three rich natural resources contributed to the sinew and muscle of Minnesota: bountiful land to be planted and harvested; abundant forests to be cut and milled; and, starting in the 1890s, iron ore to be discovered and mined. Capital derived from the sale of lumber was invested in related industries but also in flour milling and in the expansion of railroads that delivered Minnesota wheat to markets throughout the United States and overseas as well. These were the ingredients that produced what some have described as Minnesota's golden age.[33]

Pioneering settlers in Minnesota came primarily from New England, New York, and Pennsylvania. They became the office-holders, attorneys, doctors, and leading merchants of their time. They were followed by another immigrant wave from Germany, Scandinavia, and the British Isles. By 1880, three of four European Americans in Minnesota were foreign born or had parents who were foreign born. A decade later the state had reached the million mark. Many of the newcomers were farmers. In 1890 Minneapolis had a population of 165,000—representing an increase of 251 percent over 1880—and ranked as the nation's eighteenth largest city. St. Paul, enjoying a similar increase of 221 percent, was twenty-third, with a population of 133,156. Thereafter the rates of increase slowed considerably, with both cities registering a growth of 23 percent over the next decade. Railroads continued to expand, the price of real estate escalated, and speculation was the norm.[34]

Despite an economic slowdown and the end of the population boom, Duluth, Minneapolis, and St. Paul were in the process of becoming urban communities and acquiring the templates of big cities. In Minneapolis and St. Paul streets were paved, sidewalks built, telephones installed, and "massive, vaulted, arched, towered, and profusely ornamented" buildings, like the Metropolitan Building and the massive red granite City Hall in Minneapolis, began to dominate the skylines. Merchants sold their wares in "consumer palaces" like Donaldson's Glass Block.

The electric streetcar was the principal source of urban transportation, reaching the peak of its popularity in 1920 when Minneapolis cars carried 140 million passengers.[35] The cultural accoutrements of the community evolved to include public libraries, musical organizations, art collections open to the public, sports, colleges, parks, and playgrounds. In 1882 the Schubert Club of St. Paul—originally the Ladies Musicale—began its long life as a respected cultural institution in the capital city. Across the river, Thomas B. Walker opened his gallery to the public in 1879; the Minneapolis Society of Fine Arts was established in 1882. In 1903 the Minneapolis Symphony Orchestra (now the Minnesota Orchestra) was founded and soon acquired the reputation of being one of the nation's outstanding musical organizations.

As long ago as 1872 the St. Paul Common Council had invited Chicago landscape architect Horace W. S. Cleveland to outline a city park system; he proposed that Minneapolis and St. Paul be connected by a grand boulevard along the Mississippi River. By 1883 Minneapolis had a board of park commissioners, whose first chairman, Charles M. Loring, stimulated the extensive development of parks in that city.[36]

A number of colleges had opened their doors in the last half of the nineteenth century: the normal school in Winona was replicated in Mankato, Moorhead, St. Cloud, Duluth, and Bemidji; private colleges included Gustavus Adolphus (1862), Carleton (1867), St. Olaf (1874), and Macalester (1885); and the territorial legislature had established the state-supported University of Minnesota in 1851. Minnesotans built country clubs to indulge their interests in golf and tennis, and in a land of so many lakes, boating, fishing, and swimming appropriately caught the fancy of men and women alike—St. Paul had a boat club in 1870. Minnesotans also found ways to make the most of the long winters with Norwegian settlers in Red Wing organizing the nation's pioneering ski group and citizens of St. Paul creating the St. Paul Winter Carnival in 1886.

Although the economic boom had become a boomlet, measures of growth and prosperity remained. The flour-milling firms consolidated into what would ultimately emerge as General Mills, Pillsbury, and International Multifoods and diversified their products. By the turn of the century, Minneapolis's second most important business enterprises were printing and publishing firms. Other kinds of manufactures—among them jute and cotton flour bags and heat regulating devices—had also been firmly established. Construction and the retail trades flourished, with banking and insurance becoming important service industries.[37]

Government and politics were also thriving in the Minnesota milieu. To be sure, Lincoln Steffens, a well-known muckraking journalist of his day, included Minneapolis in *The Shame of the Cities*—a 1904 account of the municipal corruption then prevalent in the nation. His critique was mild, however, speaking more to indifference than to evil. After describing Minneapolis as a city populated by Scandinavians but dominated by Yankee settlers from New England, Steffens characterized their connivance in these words:

> The "Roundhead" takes the "Squarehead" out into the woods, and they cut lumber by forests, or they go out on the prairies and raise wheat and mill it into fleet cargoes of flour. They work hard, they make money, they are sober, satisfied, busy with their own affairs. There isn't much time for public business. Taken together, Miles, Hans, and Ole are very American. Miles insists upon strict laws, Ole and Hans want one or two Scandinavians on the ticket. These things granted, they go off on raft or reaper, leaving whoso will to enforce the laws and run the city.[38]

The "whoso" then running the city was Mayor Albert Ames, who had welcomed the suffrage convention to the city three years previously. While Ames was "a man of ability and engaging manners," vice and graft flourished under his congenial, though undisciplined, administration, and he was forced to flee the state.[39]

Steffens's stereotypical description, while entertaining and in some respects on target, only hinted at the rich political character of Minnesota. Republicans governed from the time of Clara Hampson's arrival in Minnesota in 1869 until the turn of the century. Although the first elected governor was Democrat Henry Sibley, he was followed by twelve Republicans, who occupied that office from 1860 to 1899. That party also controlled the legislature (excepting 1891) and constituted the majority of Minnesota's representation in the U.S. Congress. This robust Republicanism did not go unchallenged, however. From the 1870s on, a number of third parties (Anti-Monopolists, Greenbackers, Farmers' Alliance, Populists, Prohibition), usually grounded in anti-establishment protest and agrarian discontent, made their presence felt. In 1898 the dissidents enjoyed success when a coalition of Populists, Democrats, and Silver Republicans elected Swedish-born John Lind to office, and the incumbency of this second immigrant governor left the state with enduring strains of progressive politics and voter independence. "Middle class rebels," who were dissatisfied with the two major parties, called themselves Progressives, whose "aim was to balance the power of organized money in America by a broader and more vigorous use of the powers of government." Lind served only one term, losing a close vote for reelection in 1900. Despite this defeat, his Republican successor followed in the progressive mode that Lind had initiated, as did all the Republican governors (with varying degrees of commitment and accomplishment) of the early 1900s.[40]

In 1876—the first year of women's eligibility for such offices—women were cheered by the election of Charlotte O. Van Cleve and Charlotte S. Winchell as school directors in East Minneapolis. In a large and enthusiastic rally during the campaign, Sarah Stearns and Mahala Fisk Pillsbury, wife of the new governor, made rousing speeches of support. That same year, retiring Governor Cushman K. Davis took some credit as the first governor to approve the principle that women should have a vote in school management. As Theodore Christianson observed in his history of Minnesota, however, Davis's comments revealed how limited were his views of women's role in public service:

I have regretted . . . that I could not appoint women to positions
which will give them a voice in the management of some of the
state institutions. They are needed in the Institute for the Deaf,
Dumb and Blind, to guide their sisters through the labyrinths of
darkened or deadened senses. They are needed in the Hospital for
the Insane, to aid in the removal of the cloud of delirium or delu-
sion in which so many women walk. They are needed at the State
Reform School, where little girls are to be reclaimed by gentler
means than man knows from the paths of vice or temptation
toward which they have begun to stray.[41]

Despite Davis's benighted outlook, school suffrage had given
women reason to believe that they could build on that first victory and enlarge the arena in which they could cast their votes.

In 1877 reformers—probably stimulated by the organization
that same year of the state chapter of the WCTU in Minnesota—
campaigned for a constitutional amendment giving women the
vote on temperance issues. The measure was defeated by the
strenuous opposition of the liquor interests, who equated woman
suffrage with prohibition, and by a substantial margin of male
voters. According to one account, "When a group of women
appeared before the House in this matter, Mr. Gilman, who was
then speaker became so abusive and insulting in his address that
no paper in reporting the meeting would print what he said."
One might have expected more of Charles Andrew Gilman, who
also served as lieutenant governor and who completed his public
career as the state librarian.[42]

Nevertheless, the suffrage movement in Minnesota began to
grow, to proselytize, and, finally, to organize. Fourteen women in
Hastings (including Harriet Bishop) formed the Minnesota
Woman Suffrage Association (MWSA) in 1881; membership grew
to 124 in the first year, then doubled in the second. Not surprisingly, Sarah Stearns (then a resident of Duluth) was elected president. Stearns, who has rightly been described as a "leading spirit"
of the Minnesota suffrage movement in its early years, also served
on the Duluth school board, and in the early 1880s she estab-

lished a home for women "needing a place of rest and training for self-help and self-protection."[43]

But the MWSA's major struggle was with the legislature. In 1879 the National Woman's Suffrage Association, frustrated by the failure of efforts to amend state constitutions, had suggested that suffrage organizations lobby their legislatures for joint resolutions asking Congress to submit to the states a federal amendment prohibiting the disenfranchisement of women. The resolution failed by five votes in the Minnesota House. Suffrage leaders continued the struggle, trying one tactic after another. At the request of the MWSA, a bill proposing suffrage for women on temperance issues was introduced in 1881; it lost by one vote in the House and was not considered by the Senate. Four years later, the House established a committee on woman suffrage but postponed indefinitely a bill entitling women to vote in presidential elections. (Then as now, voters actually cast their ballots for presidential electors, who later elect the president.) In 1891 the House defeated a bill calling for municipal suffrage for women and two years later the Senate passed a proposal for a constitutional amendment (substituting it for a bill proposing municipal suffrage for women who possessed specified educational qualifications). Although it was supported by a majority of House members, it did not receive the two-thirds required for consideration. In 1895 three bills on liquor suffrage, municipal suffrage, and a state constitution were introduced and failed to pass.[44]

Such support as there was for this suffrage legislation came from a minority of legislators like Ignatius Donnelly, who had read John Stuart Mill's groundbreaking essay on the subjection of women and who had addressed relevant issues in unpublished, fragmentary essays on "Marriage" and "The Woman Question." The colorful Donnelly supported legislation enfranchising women taxpayers, a position reflecting his view that while he did not think "women are ready for the ballot . . . the pear is ripening rapidly."[45]

Even though the MWSA had first chosen to ally itself with the Stanton-Anthony forces in the NWSA, the 1869 rupture seemed remote to Minnesota—some distance away both in place and in time. Stearns urged the new state suffrage association to comply with the principles of the national association, but her successor, Dr. Martha G. Ripley, had received her medical training in Boston and was close to Lucy Stone and Henry Blackwell of the rival AWSA. Ripley, who headed the Minnesota group from 1883 to 1888, may have been responsible for the choice of Minneapolis as the site for the 1885 AWSA convention.[46]

The woman who served as MWSA president for the turbulent, frustrating years from 1890 to 1896 was Julia Bullard Nelson of Red Wing. She had been educated at Hamline University in St. Paul, then in Red Wing, and married a fellow student after his service in the Civil War. When their son died before his first birthday and her husband passed away five months later, the twenty-six-year-old Nelson returned to her career as a school-teacher. An ardent abolitionist, she taught in a freedmen's school in Texas and in Quaker mission schools in Tennessee for seventeen years. She returned to Red Wing periodically, and then in 1888 she moved back to stay in Minnesota, crusading for temperance and suffrage. She secured thousands of signatures on petitions directed to legislators and attributed her success in obtaining those signatures and in the consequent introduction of suffrage measures to the efforts of the WCTU, which she described as "better organized" than the suffrage association.[47]

In 1898 voters approved an amendment permitting women to vote and serve on library boards. It was a second, small victory (after the 1875 amendment allowing them to vote on school questions and to hold school offices), engineered in large part by the state Federation of Women's Clubs. Any celebration, how-ever, had to be tempered by the passage in that same election of another measure that portended hard times ahead for Minnesota women hoping to win full suffrage by amending the state consti-tution. The rules for passing an amendment changed—from requiring a majority of all votes cast on that amendment to requiring a majority of all votes cast at the election itself. Both the library board amendment and the amendment changing the

Sarah Stearns

Julia B. Nelson

amending process would have failed had that second amendment been in effect. The consequences for suffrage strategists were enormous. One suffrage leader would later characterize the document as "One of those old-fashioned, iron bound, copper riveted constitutions. . . . It cannot be amended if there is any sort of organized opposition." In the waning years of the nineteenth century, suffrage had, for all practical purposes, been checkmated in the North Star State.[48]

Despite their limited franchise, Minnesota women began in this period to acquire positions with public responsibilities. They served as school officers and directors, librarians, members of library boards, agents of the Society for the Prevention of Cruelty to Animals, deputies in county offices, police matrons, physicians in state hospitals for the insane, superintendents of a variety of charitable institutions. As early as 1882 Mary G. Hood and Mary T. Whetstone, both physicians, founded and served as administrators of the Northwestern Hospital for Women and Children in Minneapolis. In 1888 Martha Ripley founded the Maternity Hospital for "unfortunate women," also in Minneapolis. In addition to the sixty-eight women doctors registered in the state in the 1890s, professional women could also be found in increasing numbers in the ranks of lawyers, ministers, and, of course, educators, including forty-three county superintendents. Women teachers outnumbered men by 9,811 to 2,306, but the average monthly salary of the men was forty-six dollars while the women earned an average of only thirty-five dollars. According to Julia Nelson, women were "especially conspicuous" in the important industry of farming, and one woman working the fields was reported to have plowed a record of eighty acres in thirteen days with five horses abreast.[49]

As the years passed, leaders from both of the national organizations made their way to Minnesota to motivate and inspire. Stearns wrote in 1885 of "other influences coming like the rays of the morning sun directly from the East where so many noble women are at work for the freedom of their sex." The primary means of persuasion in the 1880s and 1890s was still—as it had been from the beginning—the public lecture. Suffragists of greater or lesser renown traveled great distances from place to place, hoping that women in the communities they visited would be moved to organize. Among the NWSA notables who traveled to Minnesota on more than one occasion were Susan B. Anthony, Elizabeth Cady Stanton, Frances Willard, Anna Howard Shaw, and Carrie Chapman Catt. Julia Nelson, writing about the Minnesota convention that met in Blue Earth City in 1891, noted that "this place had not lost the savor of the salt" scattered by Stanton, Anthony, and others who had been speaking in the vicinity for three years. Julia Ward Howe, one of the original AWSA organizers, was a frequent visitor to Minnesota and often played the piano accompaniment to her famous song, "The Battle Hymn of the Republic." It became a favored musical theme of the suffrage movement all over the country until the vote was won.[50]

Slowly but surely in those early years, the idea of suffrage began to take hold in many Minnesota communities, both large and small. As early as 1883 the MWSA engaged Mrs. L. May Wheeler, an experienced suffrage lecturer and organizer who developed local societies in Excelsior, Farmington, Jordan, Lake City, Mantorville, Red Wing, Rochester, Rockford, Shakopee, and Wayzata. Other communities had committees, a lesser status with probably fewer than ten members; in this category were Anoka, Armstrong, Blakely, Brooklyn Center, Champlin, Frontenac, Long Prairie, Long Lake, and Wabasha. Also in 1883, Luther Bixby, manager of the Minneapolis newspaper *Temperance Review*, authorized Helen E. Gallinger to begin a column on woman suffrage. The column provided the first means of regular communication between the state organization and the local auxiliaries. Wheeler continued her organizing work into the next year, when she produced a collection of temperance and suffrage songs. In 1884, at the Northwestern Industrial Exhibition in Minneapolis, a woman suffrage headquarters was located on Newspaper Row in a tent shared with the WCTU. When Frances Willard stopped by, she assured her listeners of the value of the ballot as well as of the Bible in winning the temperance cause.[51]

In 1895 two national organizers—Emma Smith DeVoe of Illinois and Lara M. Johns of Kansas—came to Minnesota and formed a number of new clubs. When Julia Nelson succeeded to the MWSA presidency in 1890, she devoted an entire month to lecturing and visiting local societies, which often wilted after they were formed, only to be revived again by visitation and communication. Many of these early suffrage clubs and committees appeared in communities close to Minneapolis and St. Paul or in the southeastern quadrangle of the state. Residents of these localities, more likely to be English speaking and native born ("homogeneous," in the MWSA's view), apparently responded more readily to the opportunities and obligations of suffrage than did newer settlers, who were preoccupied with the priorities of carving out a living in a new land.[52]

Even with the best of intentions, local clubs had only a loose relationship with the state organization, in part because state leaders had an ill-defined notion of how to employ the talents and energies of club members. It was not clear at any given moment who was a member in good standing and who was not; consequently, membership totals—if given at all—were probably unreliable. The auxiliaries deferred to the state association to manage suffrage efforts at the legislature and in the Congress, but members of local societies acted as important backups, writing letters to legislators and appearing at the state Capitol to demonstrate their support for suffrage bills. They also gathered signatures on petitions and beseeched other organizations to pass resolutions in favor of suffrage. Frustrated by the persistent opposition of a majority of decision makers whom they had no part in electing, this small band of willful Minnesota women went about the business of creating a climate of opinion to win friends for the suffrage cause. In some respects the national convention held in Minneapolis in 1901 was a prelude to the final effort, and, insofar as it prompted influential women like Clara Ueland to give suffrage greater attention, it proved to be a turning point as well.[53]

2

THE FORMATIVE YEARS

My parents were political idealists, feminists, democrats.
BRENDA UELAND

 When Clara Hampson and Andreas Ueland came to Minnesota—Clara in 1869 and Andreas in 1871—little did they realize that they would cross the threshold of the state's "golden age" and become deeply engaged in the professional and political life of the North Star State. Clara Hampson could likewise not have imagined that she would become a leader among men and women who replaced indifference with civic activism, distinguished by its quality and commitment to the common good.

The Uelands typified upper-middle-class Minnesotans of their day—progressive in thought and conventional in manner. Even among their more conservative contemporaries, they were accepted despite their status as Democrats, Unitarians, and feminists. Andreas was, after all, a successful attorney and a member of the Minneapolis Club, a prestigious citadel of the city's movers and shakers. It may have been Clara, however, even more than Andreas, who made them acceptable to the community of wealthy and influential citizens. She was a reformer who chose to work within the system on behalf of change, a politician who transcended partisanship, and a feminist who gave the term new meaning. Her involvement in a variety of progressive causes was

Andreas Ueland and Clara Hampson Ueland as newlyweds, about 1885

reinforced by her desire for a state of civic virtue characterized by high ethical standards and behavior. In some respects, Clara Ueland was the personification of that civic virtue.[1]

The Uelands were an attractive and prepossessing couple, made more so by their intelligence and manner. Clara had a caring warmth that bespoke graciousness, consideration, and an eclectic curiosity. Andreas had a primitive charm and a slightly comedic air. He took delight in his reputation as a wit and in references to him as a Norwegian Mark Twain.[2]

In her thirties, Clara Ueland's dark hair turned snowy-white. Her slim waist thickened with the births of her children, and she camouflaged it with flowing gowns. Andreas remained trim, his complexion ruddy, his "slouchy" hats worn with notable style. Brenda Ueland, the youngest daughter, described her mother's appearance: "My mother, I heard everybody say, was beautiful. . . . She was always beautifully dressed. I never saw her in anything homely, or in a hurriedly-put-on house-dress. She wore now her summer straw hat with a veil floating about it and she wore brightly clean white shoes and a white linen dress with a jacket. The jacket had much elaborate sewn braid and heavy lace on it." Clara was no slave to fashion, however, refusing to wear either corsets or high heels. She replied with a touch of irony to a friend's question as to what she was wearing to a forthcoming event, "My usual costume with my usual success."[3]

There was no particular reason to believe that Clara Hampson, born in Akron, Ohio, on October 10, 1860, would lead such an extraordinary life. She had a distinguished Yankee lineage on both sides of her family, including a great-grandfather who served as a colonel under George Washington in the Revolutionary War. Her grandfather James Hampson served as master of a packet boat until he resigned after many years by way of protest over the serving of liquor on his ship. James then probably returned to manage his father's farm located on the rich soil of Erie County, Pennsylvania. Clara's maternal grandfather was Random Osborn, whose success enabled him to build a handsome home in Oak Hill, New York.[4]

Clara's parents, Henry Oscar Hampson and Eliza Osborn, were less prosperous than their own parents. Although Hampson was handsome and dashing, he had uncertain success selling reapers and—after the Civil War—working for a brief time as a partner in a foundry. In 1856, the first year after their marriage, Eliza and Henry had a son they named Fred; four years later their daughter, Clara, was born. After the outbreak of the Civil War, Henry Hampson enlisted in the Union army, but by 1863 he was bored, suffering from unidentified ailments, and impatient to quit soldiering and return to his young family. After his discharge from the army, Hampson traveled to Minnesota in search of a more healthful and profitable climate, an expedition that was apparently unsuccessful. Returning home to Ohio, he died at age thirty-five on September 29, 1864, leaving a widow with an eight-year-old son and a nearly four-year-old daughter. When Clara, after twenty-five years, returned to the Akron home that she had left when she was about eight, she expressed some surprise at how cramped and poor it was, even though, as she noted, "I did not find it insufficient as a child."

She could have scarcely known her father in the year or so they were together, yet Clara possessed a somewhat romanticized memory of him. In remarks to the 1923 convention of the Minnesota League of Women Voters, President Marguerite M. Wells referred to Ueland as a "very white flame of devotion for good government," whose father had been "a brilliant young man full of promise." Her mother, "unused to responsibility or to poverty," brought the children to "this distant frontier country," where she struggled to eke out a "frugal" living for the family. Eliza may have supplemented Henry's pension of fourteen dollars a month by working as a seamstress. In one of the last letters that he wrote to his mother, Henry said: "Eliza has a new sewing machine and she keeps clattering away on garments of all Shapes and Sizes."[5]

Eliza Hampson's decision to move to Minnesota was prompted by practical considerations. She was attracted—as Henry had been—by the state's reputed healthful climate and by the fact that she could be with Harriet DeFrate, an older sister then living in Faribault with her family. The trio of Ohio Hampsons arrived in Minnesota in 1869, about six years after Henry had traveled there. Three years later Eliza moved her family from Faribault to Minneapolis to be with a younger sister, Laura Snyder. The Hampsons, who were very poor, lived over a hardware store.[6]

Despite these deprivations Clara was apparently content, interested in her studies at Washington School and popular with her classmates. Most people noted her beauty. Andreas Ueland recalled that at their first meeting, which took place at a church gathering when Clara was only fifteen, she was "the prettiest there and probably in the whole city." Maud Conkey, a schoolmate three years younger than Clara and destined in later life as Maud Stockwell to be a close friend and suffrage colleague, commented: "I can remember thinking how incongruous she was with all the saloons around that district. She was dark and slim, a beauty beyond compare. She wore a brown dress almost all that year . . . and it was quite plain. I knew that her family were not well-to-do at all but I remember thinking how anything she wore made her look wonderful."[7]

Clara Hampson liked learning and proved to be an intellectually adventurous young woman. In some respects she was also unconventional. She refused other invitations to the Junior Ball and went with the only African-American boy in the school. As Brenda Ueland understood the story, Clara felt that he needed friendship and backing. Despite these occasional manifestations of nonconformity, Clara was "socially acceptable from the first to prosperous and fashionable people, in spite of the hardware store and an ailing unknown young mother from Ohio." Brenda believed that Eliza Hampson's preoccupation with ill health prompted Clara at an early age "to build up her protective spiritual shield against such dark thoughts, with good sense, quietness and stoicism." Although she had a "gloomy and sparse childhood," she was apparently determined "not to mind being poor. She was always serenely gay as a little girl, never troubled by social differences nor uneasy in the presence of people richer than herself." Clara's oldest son, Sigurd, made a similar comment: "Notwithstanding her early poverty she was an aristocrat."[8]

Andreas Ueland was born in 1853 in Heskestad Parish, Norway, in a valley within distant sight of the North Sea. Although Andreas came from a farm family of modest means, his father, Ole Gabriel Ueland, became a leading political figure, serving for nearly forty years in the Norwegian Storting (Parliament). When his father died in 1870, Andreas knew that the farm would go to his older brother. Casting about for a vocation and resisting the plea of his mother, Anne Ollestad Ueland, that he become a teacher, he chanced to meet a visiting Norwegian-American farmer from Houston County in Minnesota, who infected him with the "America fever." Taking the inheritance from his father and a modest supplement from his mother—about one hundred dollars in all—he arrived in the United States in 1871 and made his way directly to Minnesota. Although Houston County was the destination of the other

Norwegian immigrants with whom he traveled, Andreas decided to strike out on his own, and he purchased a ticket for Rushford in Fillmore County.[9]

A new land required a new language for this young Norwegian immigrant, and Andreas agonized over the decision to spend the princely sum of three dollars for the book *One Hundred Lessons in English*, so that he could communicate with the succession of farmers in southeastern Minnesota who hired him during his first summer in America. He then went on foot from the Farmington area to Minneapolis, where he got a job constructing the city's first sewer. As Sigurd observed many years later, building that first sewer distinguished his father from other prominent, pioneering Minneapolitans who had not shared the experience. Andreas later wrote that for the next five years, he worked hard in summers and had some schooling in winters "until I got a chance to study law . . . and then the struggle with the law books and poverty."[10]

Andreas preferred to associate with fellow Scandinavians who aspired to "higher culture" in society. He sought out and maintained close contact with well-educated Norwegians such as Paul Hjelm-Hansen, a journalist whose promotion of the lands of the Red River Valley helped to make that region the third major Norwegian settlement area in the state—after the southeastern and the west-central park regions. Another Scandinavian of "higher culture" was Kristofer Janson, a visiting Norwegian author and folk high school teacher, who was shocked by the prevalence of Lutheran orthodoxy in free America (a view shared by Andreas, who rebelled against the fearsome and gloomy rhetoric of the church of his childhood). When Janson arrived in Minneapolis in 1881 as a recently ordained Unitarian minister, he organized five congregations that became known for their liberal views on such matters as socialism and feminism. (Janson's wife, Drude Krog, wrote on social issues, in particular about the condition of women in society.) Andreas also frequented a variety of churches—Norwegian, Swedish, and American—and meetings of the Liberal League, a Minneapolis group where "orthodox dogmas were freely discussed" and apparently criticized.[11]

Andreas was also critical of fellow immigrants who clung to the past, speaking the old language and preserving old traditions. "No people," he once asserted in a speech to the Odin Club, "can live a full life on the past or upon what is borrowed. Either means stagnation. That which is of most value and a contribution to the culture of the world must be evolved from our own lives and surroundings."[12]

Clara and Andreas found themselves together in 1875 at a meeting of the young people's literary society. Andreas later remarked, "I became acquainted with a girl of fifteen . . . destined to become my wife ten years later." He described her as "a brunette with large, black eyes, very dark hair, finely-drawn features, and hands commented on by many for their exceptional beauty." Brenda remembered that her father called Clara "my black-eyed Susan" as a term of endearment.[13]

Although Andreas made it sound as if there were no other woman in his life, he was in fact married for the first time in September 1879 to Anna A. Ohlhouse in Rushford. The local newspaper embellished its announcement of the wedding by describing Anna as being "well known to Rushford people as a handsome, accomplished young lady, who will adorn the home she is soon to preside over." Andreas may have met the Ohlhouse family when he arrived in Fillmore County from Norway. Anna died at the age of twenty in Minneapolis six months after the wedding, and while there is no official record of her death, obituaries ascribed it to "consumption." Her hometown paper said of Anna, "From a child she was unusually attractive, possessing a bright intellect, a gentle and generous nature [with which] she won the kind regard of those with whom she associated."[14]

As a young widower, Andreas probably returned to his earlier haunts and his admiration of Clara Hampson. They had both come from respectable backgrounds but had known what it was like to be poor. They shared interests in intellectual pursuits and enjoyed common ambitions, striving for that "higher culture" in society. Although Clara had undoubtedly wished for a college in her future, she did not dwell on what she could not afford. Following her graduation from Washington School, where she attended both elementary and high school, Clara began her teaching career in about 1877 with seventh- and eighth-grade students at Jefferson School.[15]

That same year, after a long period of arduous study, Andreas was admitted to the bar, the only attorney in Minneapolis of Scandinavian birth. He was generally acknowledged to be—in what he referred to as that "hackneyed phrase"—a rising young lawyer, having established his reputation in a well-publicized case, *Muus* v. *Muus*. Andreas served as the attorney for Oline Muus, who brought suit in 1879 to get her husband to return her inheritance of about $3,700, which he had claimed for himself. A principal argument invoked by Andreas was the unwillingness of Norwegian immigrants to become Americanized, to live by the laws of their new land. Oline and Bernt Muus had lived in Minnesota for twenty years and, therefore, were subject to Minnesota law stipulating that a married woman's inheritance was her property. The judge upheld that view, and in 1882 the Minnesota Supreme Court affirmed the decision.[16]

Following the Muus case, local Republicans chose Andreas as a candidate for probate judge in 1881. They hoped that his candidacy would attract Scandinavian voters and thereby enable them to win at least one office in Hennepin County. Many years later Andreas wrote that his opponent, J. W. Lawrence—a Democrat and "a member of a leading law firm and socially highly connected"—said of Andreas that he was "a nice Norwegian boy, but he couldn't speak English and did not know anything." With customary humor Andreas observed that "this was putting it a little strong and yet there was so much truth in it that I did not resent it." The election proved that he had no cause for concern. Andreas carried every precinct in Minneapolis and nearly all the "country towns" in Hennepin County. As judge of probate he was responsible for determining the authenticity of wills and the legitimacy of the administration of decedents' estates. It was an important position usually held by older, established lawyers. After serving his first two-year term with a yearly salary of $2,500, he was unanimously nominated by Republicans and Democrats for an extended three-year term. With the security of a judgeship in hand, Andreas felt sufficiently emboldened to propose marriage to Clara Hampson, who accepted.[17]

Judge Andreas Ueland and Clara Hampson were married on June 19, 1885, in her brother Fred's home in Ada, Minnesota. The newlyweds spent about two weeks at Lake Geneva, near Alexandria, where they fished and boated and went to dinner at the nearby home of Congressman Knute Nelson (who during his long political career served Minnesota as its first foreign-born governor and as the first Norwegian-born U.S. representative, state senator, and senator). Just as Andreas had been accused by his opponent in his 1881 campaign for probate judge as a nice know-nothing Norwegian, Knute Nelson was branded a "little Norwegian" one year later in his successful election bid for the new fifth congressional seat. Their contemporary, John Lind, born in Sweden, served three terms in Congress from 1887 to 1893 before becoming the second immigrant governor of the state in 1899. The association of Andreas Ueland with both of these men suggests not only the shifting ethnic pattern of Minnesota politics but Andreas's interest in the possibility of higher office.[18]

In 1886 Clara gave birth to Anne, the first of eight children. In the next year Andreas decided to return to his career as a lawyer, a task that proved to be so time-consuming that, he recalled, "I could give but little attention to politics or public affairs—very much less than I ought to have done." The responsibilities of their growing family diverted Andreas from politics to law just as they retarded Clara's civic activism.[19]

In the first years of their marriage Clara and Andreas lived in a little house on Fifteenth Avenue South in Minneapolis, but they were eager to build their own home on three acres of land purchased by Andreas on the south shore of Lake Calhoun (called by the Dakotas the Inland Lake). The Uelands loved the site because of its history and because it featured "all the native

The Ueland home, 3820 West Calhoun Boulevard

trees of Minnesota." When they built their sixteen-room house in 1890, they became pioneer residents of an unpopulated countryside four miles from town.[20]

The house became a landmark, set on a high ridge overlooking the lake. Its sheer size, embellished by curved bay windows and many porches, made it a dominant feature of the landscape. Nevertheless it was limited in its conveniences: Brenda once described the house as having "a thousand rooms and one bath." Downstairs was a library, living and dining rooms, a kitchen, and a great center hall—with low oak paneling and a red-tile fireplace—that served as the social center for family and friends. Upstairs were six bedrooms and a big center hall with a blackboard, where the children could draw pictures, do sums, and play games. The third floor included rooms for two maids and storage areas.[21]

The barn was home to a driving and riding horse, a cow, a pony, black Minorca chickens, and a room for the hired man— "Gus or Alfred or Ole [or] whoever he happened to be," according to Brenda. About an acre was set aside for pasture for the live-

stock and a field for playing football and baseball.
A tennis court that was
added later became the
focus of Ueland social
activities for many years.
After 1913, when Clara
became more intensely
involved in suffrage activities, the property was
used for many fund-raising
"fetes," featuring games,
athletic contests, individual and group perform-
ances, food, fun, and
frolic.[22]

Anne, the first child
of Clara and Andreas,
had been followed by

Brenda Ueland

Elsa in 1888 and Dorothy in 1889. Brenda, the fourth and last
daughter, was the first child to be born (1891) in the new home.
The attending physician was Thomas Roberts, also a noted
ornithologist and author of the classic guide, *Birds of Minnesota*.
He described the newborn girl as having "very dark plumage."
After Brenda, four boys—Sigurd, Arnulf, Rolf, and Torvald—
were born in the house between 1893 and 1902. Seven of the
eight children would grow to adulthood; Dorothy, the third
daughter, died before she was three.[23]

Clara had definite theories about bringing up children. For
one thing, no stimulants were allowed. She considered them to be
deceptive, camouflaging fatigue that could best be remedied with
a daily nap, which Clara took nearly every day. It was a family joke
that the children were not permitted to have coffee or tea until
they were twenty-five. Candy was rationed; apples and oranges
were not. Clara believed in the merits of sunshine, and naked
Ueland children were occasionally seen in the neighborhood.[24]

The Uelands were equally enlightened about the matter of girls and boys. Brenda said of her mother that she was "naturally feministic" and that "Father had not come from Norway or read all of Ibsen for nothing." (A common Ibsen theme was the wife's right to self-fulfillment.) Clara made no distinctions between the girls and boys "in actions, freedom, education or possibilities." The boys were expected to make their own beds. Both Elsa and Brenda were athletically inclined, and Clara let them dress in knee pants when they played baseball and football with the boys in the pasture. One day a passerby was heard to remark of Elsa, "Either that is a boy with braids or a girl with pants on." Clara once observed, "I know a family in which boys sew on their own buttons. The mother very sensibly says that she has not discovered any difference between the masculine and feminine hand." In the summer she limited the children to fifteen minutes of swimming every other day, but when they were in Lake Calhoun, she let them go as far out and as far under as they wished. She preferred daring to prudence: "Our adventurousness was never quashed," Brenda recalled.[25]

Although Clara took a leadership role in the establishment of free kindergartens, she herself taught all the children at home until they were eight, when they then went into the second grade. She may have wished to keep her hand in her former profession, or, more likely, she was determined to see that all the Uelands got off to a good beginning under her high standards of tutelage.[26]

The size of the growing Ueland family was unusual for that era—in the fifty years from 1850 to 1900, the average size of families in the United States had declined from 5.6 persons to 4.7. Brenda, who longed for the distinction of being an only child, once came upon her mother appearing both weary and teary, only to learn that another pregnancy was the cause of Clara's distress. Although not necessarily a consequence of choice, the large family was lovingly cared for by Clara and Andreas. Shortly before his death in 1933, Brenda had teased her father about having too many children, but he responded by saying that "they

The Uelands, about 1898: Sigurd, Anne, Andreas, Clara, Arnulf, Elsa, and Brenda

had lost one child and that was the great sorrow of their lives."
Marguerite Nye, a friend of Elsa—they were the only two girls in
the manual training class at Central High School—described the
home on Lake Calhoun as seeming to have been "wholly devoted to children." The playroom had an upright piano, a large table
stacked with children's books and magazines, and wide window
seats accommodating either games or reading. There were few
don'ts and many invitations to do in the Ueland children's room.
"All this I saw," Nye observed, "without fully comprehending the
keen and loving intelligence that created this setting for a growing family." According to Sigurd, "My mother presided over the
establishment with a gracious dignity, expected to be obeyed,
insisted that clothes and playthings should be put away."[27]

Clara's ideas about motherhood departed from the norm of
that era. There was in fact a tinge of radicalism in her belief, as

Brenda wrote, that she should be involved in "public-spirited work, quite outside her family and children . . . because it contributed to the *freedom* of her children. It was so easy for a woman, a mother, to slump into a haphazard, maternal slovenliness of love, menial work and anxiety. This is called 'self-sacrifice' but too often it is a way of sacrificing others, making others, especially one's children, feel guilty and, alas, bored. A great mistake." The Ueland parents saw to it by precept, example, and opportunity that their children would be encouraged to explore the world of ideas, to appreciate art and music, to test their mental and physical skills, and to be attentive and informed citizens. As a former teacher, Clara had equally firm and sometimes unorthodox ideas about education. In the late 1880s, she and other young mothers came together and formed a club to study "infant welfare." They, too, got caught up in the new opportunities for women to be elected to school boards and chose Jennie C. Crays, a former teacher and a businesswoman, who won the election in 1892 and served for two years as president of the Minneapolis school board. Clara served on the club committee that selected Crays to run for office, and her experience in that campaign prompted her initial interest in suffrage.[28]

The need for kindergartens was another reform taken up by Clara and her friends, among them Nanny Mattson Jaeger, Josephine Sarles Simpson, and Alice Ames Winter. This trio of associates typified the women that Clara worked with in the ensuing years for one good cause or another. Nanny Jaeger's father, Hans Mattson, was a lawyer and newspaper publisher who was active in Minnesota politics and had served as U.S. consul general in India in 1881–83. Although Nanny was born in Red Wing, she attended school in Sweden for about five years before she became the first woman of Scandinavian descent to enter the University of Minnesota, enrolling in 1877. She served in its final years as president of the Minnesota Scandinavian Woman Suffrage Association. Josephine Simpson graduated from the University of Wisconsin, receiving her degree with highest honors and capping her achievement with a prestigious prize for ora-

Nanny Mattson Jaeger, Josephine
Sarles Simpson, and Alice Ames
Winter

tory. Clara and Josephine would follow a parallel path from kindergarten advocacy to work in the Woman's Club of Minneapolis to leadership in the Minnesota Woman Suffrage Association. Alice Winter, originally from New York State, had both a bachelor's and a master's degree from Wellesley College. She spent most of her civic life with the Federation of Women's Clubs, serving as the first president of the Woman's Club of Minneapolis (1907–15) and later as national president of the General Federation of Women's Clubs (1920–24). Although she was an enthusiastic suffrage supporter, Winter never held office in a suffrage organization; apparently she was content with her role as the quintessential clubwoman.[29]

These four women—and many other American women interested in good schooling for their children—were particularly impressed with the writings of Friedrich Froebel, who had established the first kindergarten in Blankenburg, Germany, in 1837. In 1890 Clara Ueland delivered a paper on Froebel's ideas to a group of other young mothers studying child training. One result was the organization of a neighborhood kindergarten in the Ueland library. Children needed kindergartens, Clara argued, because "habits and tendencies are so nearly formed at six years of age that it is not easy to reform them." Hence the need for *free* kindergartens for three hours each day so that all children, rich and poor, could benefit from instruction and encouragement. Clara's concern for the education of all children, not merely her own, prompted her initial foray into the arena of public policy.[30]

With Clara as the moving spirit, the group formed the Minneapolis Kindergarten Association, organizing a number of free kindergartens and establishing a training school for kindergarten teachers in 1892. Stella Louise Wood, a "remarkable glowing young woman, teeming with laughter and ideas," moved, at Clara's invitation, to Minneapolis in the fall of 1896 from Dubuque, Iowa, to head the school. When the young teacher arrived, Clara introduced her to the Ueland children. The children surrounded and captured Stella Wood, leading her to the stable to be introduced to Prince, the pony, and to be shown their swimming beach and their other favorite places. She asked them questions and told them wonderful new stories. In short order she had become a member of the family. Once the children were in bed, Stella and Clara sat together before a glowing log fire and planned the further development of the school. These conversations convinced Stella Wood of her recruiter's "devotion to everything that affected the well-being of children."[31]

By 1905 kindergartens had been integrated with the Minneapolis public school system, and, consequently, the Minneapolis Kindergarten Association disbanded and turned the training school over to its proprietor. Stella Wood operated Miss Wood's Kindergarten-Primary Training School for another forty-three years until her retirement in 1948.[32]

A continuing influence on the life and thought of Clara and Andreas Ueland was the First Unitarian Society, which had been established in Minneapolis in 1881. Although Andreas's friend Kristofer Janson had organized the Free Christian Church one year later, the Uelands stayed with the society. Andreas held Henry Martyn Simmons, the Minneapolis society's first minister, in the highest regard for being "probably better informed on science generally than anybody else in the Northwest" and for "his unbounded toleration for every kind of sincere religious belief." That regard and respect was widely shared. In 1888 Simmons won the balloting in a public contest as the most popular minister in the city.[33]

"Every Sunday," Brenda Ueland recalled, "the large Ueland carriage ambled the long journey downtown" for services in the stone church built by the society in 1887. Simmons often joined the family for the return trip and Sunday dinner. Some years later Clara Ueland described an annual meeting of the church: "Unitarians are cheerful sinners and enjoy their own shortcomings and being scolded. I gave a report for the Music com-

First Unitarian Society, about 1900

mittee. The music in our church is always the cause of great merriment." "Being Unitarian children," Brenda Ueland observed, "we were not christened" and "grew up more light-hearted and untrammeled than Orthodox children, overawed and inculcated with guilt (Original Sin)." She was happy not to have grown up fearful of religion and having to say that "dismal prayer, 'If I should die before I wake. . . .'" Brenda recalled that her parents "were generous to all religions" and that Clara seemed pleased when young Torvald asked, "Is God a bird?"[34]

In 1910 or 1911 Clara and Andreas left the society. (Simmons had died in 1905 after nearly twenty-five years as minister.) "I think I no longer belong there because it is dominated by people who seem to me unsound in views," Clara wrote. The

Uelands were not in sympathy with the new humanistic movement in the Minneapolis society, remaining faithful instead to
the established theism espoused by Ralph Waldo Emerson and
other New Englanders whose ideas had so influenced the substance of American Unitarianism. Along with several of their
friends, they migrated to the Plymouth Congregational Church.
The Plymouth tradition of showing compassion and humanity
while caring for immigrants and the poor was clearly compatible
with the Uelands' interests and values. However, their departure
did not sit well with other Unitarian friends who embraced the
new ideology and chose to remain with their church. "Mr. [Luth]
and Mrs. [Nanny] Jaeger here for dinner. A *heated* discussion
about my having left the church," Clara noted in her journal on
August 25, 1911.[35]

Despite the apparent harmony in the family life of the Ueland
household, one discordant note kept resurfacing—Andreas's
continuing criticisms of the way Clara managed household
expenses. He indulged in colorful language when confronted
with big bills and unforeseen expenses. ("A thousand barrels of
devils!" he would cry.) Angered and humiliated, Clara usually
held her tongue, but occasionally she retaliated, saying that she
"just would not have it!" Andreas immediately became contrite.
According to Brenda, "Mother was certainly not selfishly extrav-
agant, but she built up a good life for us. She quietly held my
father to that. She contended for her children." Clara did not
presume to tell Andreas how to run his law practice, and she
resented his criticisms of decisions that he knew little about.
Sigurd noted that "occasionally when the bills were too high or
there was unnecessary breakage, my father went on the warpath
but normally love and affection and calm prevailed."[36]

Disagreements over household finances could have been the
reason why Clara, when asked in 1917 to be treasurer of a
Mississippi Valley Conference for woman suffrage, replied, "I
think it would be better to call me Chairman of the Finance
Committee rather than treasurer as I do not like accounts, but
never mind about that now." Throughout her life Clara was

indignant about "women being bullied about money" and about the failure to provide a system of monetary rewards for the work of homemakers. When a New York court decided in 1914 that what a woman saved out of the money her husband gave her was not hers—not even half hers—Clara responded: "A good wife and mother has to act in the capacity of trained nurse, seamstress, cook and laundress, and she is distinctly entitled to compensation for her work. She should not be allowed to feel that she is being supported by her husband. It would increase her self respect and raise women in public estimation if the law would recognize a woman's earning capacity in the home and accord her some just proportion of her husband's income."[37]

Sigurd once observed of his parents' relationship that it must have been "trying at times to be married to a rough and rugged, self-made man who held many of the trivia of social life in contempt" but that somehow they managed to surmount these difficulties.[38]

When the Ueland children were young, Clara was understandably occupied with their care and education, and she extended these concerns beyond the boundaries of the home to the school, the community, and the church. Thanks to servants who were available to cook, clean, and watch over the children in her absence, she also had some time for herself. In 1893 Clara joined the Peripatetics, a three-year-old literary society with a growing social and intellectual stature. The Peripatetics was one of numerous women's study clubs that were formed throughout the country after the Civil War. These organizations, which gained momentum and increased in numbers in the early 1890s, represented an effort by small local groups, generally consisting of middle-aged, middle-class women, to inform themselves about art, music, history, geography, and literature.[39]

The Peripatetics topic in Clara's first year as a member was "Europe in the Nineteenth Century," and the newcomer gave papers on "France under the Republic, up to the Present Time" and "Domestic Politics of Russia, Including Reforms of Peter the Great, Alexander I, and Liberalism, Reforms of Alexander II." In the span from 1912 to 1917, which might be described as the Peripatetics' Greek period, Clara presented papers on "The Women of Euripides," "Euripides' Trojan Women," "Philebus," and "Philo and the Philosophy of the Logos." By the 1920s the club would move into a more contemporary mode, with Clara exploring "The Alien World: Despair and Consolation" and "The Problem of the City."[40]

Club members were exemplary and pioneering lifelong learners. It was in large part their experience in study clubs like the Peripatetics that prompted women to envision and support an education equal to that of men for their daughters. There appeared to be no question that the Ueland daughters would go to college, and they did.[41]

Andreas shared Clara's intellectual interests, and they were both determined that their children would grow up stimulated by the knowledge gained from reading great books, from the opportunities to discuss and debate great ideas. As parents they intended to do this by example, making every effort to keep up with the philosophies of past and present. Clara once complained to Andreas, "You cannot read everything in the world." Yet she herself had read Emerson, Carlyle, and Ruskin by the time she reached the age of twenty, and Kant, Dante, Racine, Confucius, and many more by twenty-four. Clara wrote in her journal, "Make yourself intelligent for the sake of your children; read, study, listen, think, that you may bring variety, knowledge and resource into their lives." She took special care to read to her children so that they would learn to love books and ideas. They would in fact do so. In his retirement Sigurd wrote, "This strange urge that I have had to improve myself I think must be my inheritance from my mother." He also acknowledged his father by describing a need "to vindicate my high descent from an indomitable father and a saint-like mother."[42]

The Ueland home was also a center for lively entertainment. Brenda mused about this "curious era in American social life, this nondrinking era, and perhaps there was never any other like it. The main purpose of an evening party was the exchange of friendship and ideas." So it was not surprising that when the well-known actor Richard Mansfield came to Minneapolis in 1906 with the Ibsen play *Peer Gynt,* it attracted not just the Norwegian community but also members of the smart set of that day. In a letter to Anne away at college, Clara began, "Such a Gyntish day as yesterday was!" Giving a talk on the play was Nina Morais Cohen, a woman of intellect whom Clara admired. Cohen was the daughter of a prominent Philadelphia rabbi, as well as a founder and longtime president of the Minneapolis section of the National Council of Jewish Women and an organizer of the Woman's Club of Minneapolis. After her talk and an interval of appropriate music, the gathering of friends went to the theater. Clara was sympathetic with Ibsen's criticisms of society's expectations about the role of women. She would have agreed with the words that he put into the mouth of a woman in his 1886 play *Rosmersholm:* "Live, work, act. Don't sit here and brood and grope among insoluble enigmas."[43]

Clara chose not to brood but to work and act. In the decade after Torvald's birth in 1902, she assumed a number of organizational responsibilities that enabled her to test and refine her leadership abilities. By midlife she had set the course for her own career as a community leader.

3

FROM MOTHERHOOD TO COMMUNITY

I do not approve of meek women.
CLARA UELAND, 1907

In the closing years of the nineteenth century, the United States won a war with Spain and acquired an empire. Bolstered by its victory on sea and land and confident of its strength at home, the nation strutted across the threshold of the new century. The presidential election of 1900 was a repeat of 1896, with the second-time Democratic challenger, William Jennings Bryan, facing off against the Republican incumbent, William McKinley. It proved to be no contest as McKinley's promise of a "full dinner pail" easily garnered voter support over Bryan's allegations of imperialism. Even with the concentration of great wealth in the hands of a few men like John D. Rockefeller and J. P. Morgan— some of whom earned the sobriquet of robber barons—business was booming across the board. Even with the widespread corruption that infected states and cities, government was solvent, and the federal budget enjoyed a surplus of more than $46 million. And although the industrial complex was supported in part by the labor of 1,752,187 children less than sixteen years old, jobs were plentiful.[1]

Nothing—or so it seemed—could diminish the sense of well-being and optimism that permeated the national psyche. Thanks

to James J. Hill, "the Empire Builder," the Twin Cities of Minneapolis and St. Paul were rapidly developing as a railroad hub,
and individuals and communities throughout the country benefited from the more efficient transport of goods and people.
Roads were being improved, and Minnesotans—like Americans
everywhere—began their love affair with the automobile. The
music of the day mirrored the happy times: "Sweet Adeline";
"Shine on Harvest Moon"; "In My Merry Oldsmobile"; and—on
a more patriotic note—"You're a Grand Old Flag." Men, women,
and children were charmed by circuses, educated by Chautau-
quas, diverted by vaudeville, and entertained by stage stars like
the young Maude Adams, whose performances as Peter Pan had
everyone who saw her believing in fairies.

The sense of progress and optimism did not apply, however,
to the rights of women. In one-quarter of the states, wives could
still not own property; one-third of the states would still not recognize a wife's claim to her own earnings; and four-fifths of the
states still denied women an equal share in the guardianship of
their children. Divorce laws were particularly biased against
women. In Minnesota, for example, a woman divorced for adul-
tery had to forfeit any property she had previously owned. Men
ruled the roost—in the home, where they typically exercised
final authority on all matters, in the voting booth, where they
barred women from the polls, and in business enterprises, where
they confined women to machines and piecework.[2]

But a growing band of determined rebels led the march away
from pots and pans and factories. Single women took to the new
typewriting machine with such alacrity that they replaced men
as office secretaries. Their married sisters found that clubs gave
them an opportunity to learn new skills and provided an outlet
for secular good works.

Clara Ueland availed herself of this opportunity with her passage from motherhood to community activism, which began
soon after the birth of Torvald in 1902. Some years later, Brenda
Ueland wrote of her new brother, "He was, unlike the rest of us,
sort of tenderly, gloriously neglected, I mean never admonished,

because he was so nice, so utterly amiable and because he was the youngest. All rules seem to have been suspended." One reason for that tender neglect, a reason that escaped Brenda's notice, may have been her mother's impatience to get on with other things in her life.[3]

Clara Ueland's personal journey, which by 1913 would make her a leader in the state suffrage movement, was not unique among white, middle- and upper-class American women. Her way had been paved by developments that opened doors of opportunity and by changes within the suffrage movement itself that gave the effort to achieve the vote a more pragmatic cast. Clara, and others like her, traveling a road populated with literary societies and women's clubs, acquired a taste for reform and a talent for change. Their experiences in educating themselves and managing organizations provided women with information and know-how. While they could point with some pride to overcoming certain obstacles to women's progress, they realized that their ability to secure other rights and to revoke discriminatory laws depended on suffrage.

Winning the vote became the first priority by the turn of the century because the vote was not only an important symbol of equality but its tangible expression. Suffrage took center stage because women recognized that it was a prerequisite to political power and because, somewhat paradoxically, social progress was beginning to enhance their status in society.

By 1900 women had their own institutions of higher education or could enroll at colleges and universities where co-education was the norm. (Women had been admitted to the University of Minnesota from the time it opened its doors in 1869.) Women could become physicians, lawyers, dentists, and theologians in greater numbers because more training opportunities were available. As a matter of fact, the substantial number of women doctors in the United States in 1900 (7,399) provoked a backlash of protest from male doctors. Across the nation, women were entering the work force in greater numbers and could be found working in almost all the occupations counted in the census. Although still deprived in most states of individual rights within the family unit, some women could now claim the property they brought to a marriage and the children resulting from that marriage. By 1910 a quarter of all women over fourteen were employed—a figure that would remain essentially unchanged until 1940. Minnesota women lagged behind with nearly 22 percent employed in 1910 and nearly 23 percent by 1940.[4]

The new generation of twentieth-century suffragists argued that the ballot was not only a matter of justice—an end in itself—but also the means whereby needed reforms could be achieved in the larger society. Women, they asserted, were uniquely qualified to make those reforms come to pass. This new approach required suffragists to shift their thinking from the idea of equality *with* men to the concept of difference *from* men. Jane Addams, for example, argued that women should be enfranchised because they could benefit society by extending their skills in household management to the larger public arena. Government, as a consequence, would be swept clean of its corrupting influences and measures enhancing the domestic welfare put in place. The rhetoric was a perfect fit for the reform-minded Progressive Era.[5]

That approach made a lot of sense to the growing numbers of women involved in community affairs at the turn of the century, and suffrage began to gain new supporters. More clubs were organized, more members were recruited, and the larger political milieu proved to be conducive to change and reform. Initially leadership in the suffrage movement had come primarily from the ranks of professional women. After 1900, however, the "Ladies of the Club," working as volunteers to bring about particular social and economic reforms, found that suffrage had become an imperative for the achievement of those goals. Women of the middle and upper classes had arrived at a stage in their lives where they no longer averted their eyes from the problems of hunger, housing, sanitation, and education in their own communities. They became increasingly sensitive to the adverse conditions afflicting women and children in the workplace. These new advocates approached the suffrage campaign with greater sophistication and organizational know-how, bringing skills learned from managing volunteer enterprises. As their numbers increased and their effectiveness grew, public attitudes toward suffrage women began to shift from ridicule to a cautious regard and attentiveness. The suffrage movement also benefited from a new politics of reform that was sweeping the nation.[6]

In the late 1800s—initially in southern and western states—a wave of agrarian protest known as Populism demanded a variety of social inventions (the income tax, secret ballot, direct election of U.S. senators, initiative and referendum, rudimentary farm price supports, government ownership of the railroads and utilities) designed to restore the balance of economic power between farmers and "capitalists" who controlled the transport and the markets for their products. The provincial and class-conscious outlook of the new party of Populists was reinforced by Minnesota's own Ignatius Donnelly, who composed the eloquent preamble to the platform of the People's party, which was launched in Omaha, Nebraska, on July 2, 1892. The delegates were meeting, he wrote, "in the midst of a nation brought to the verge of moral, political and material ruin. Corruption dominates the ballot box, the legislatures, the Congress, and touches even the ermine of the bench. . . . The fruits of the toil of millions are boldly stolen to build up colossal fortunes unprecedented in the history of the world. . . . From the same prolific womb of governmental injustice we breed two great classes—paupers and millionaires."[7]

Although the Populists made serious efforts to recruit women candidates and to build ties between black and white farmers in the South, those efforts at coalition building could not offset the otherwise divisive quality of the Populist rhetoric.[8]

When the Populist party declined as a political force in about 1896, a new but related political ideology began to emerge. The Progressives, as they came to be called, exuded a gutsy confidence and took a more benign, less class-conscious view than

Populists did of the ills of society. In some respects John Lind, the Swedish-born governor of Minnesota, personified that transition. Originally a Republican, he lost his first campaign as a fusion candidate of dissident Republicans, Democrats, and Populists. When he won in 1898, he described himself as a "political orphan," but the inauguration of his single term in office marked the beginning of the Progressive Era in the state.[9]

Progressivism urged the correction of abuses associated with the concentration of wealth and economic power, the subversion of idealism to materialism, the seduction of the political process by corrupt machines, and the heedless waste of the nation's natural resources. The movement aimed to restore a type of economic individualism and political democracy thought to have been part of the early American scene and later undermined by giant corporations and the corrupt political machine, but it also represented an effort on the part of middle-class rebels to regain and maintain their power and status. The men who led the Progressive movement had suffered, not from a shrinkage of their wealth, but from a changing pattern in the distribution of deference and power. Newly rich corporate leaders were occupying the status previously enjoyed, as historian Richard Hofstadter said, by "the old gentry, the merchants of long standing, the small manufacturers, the established professional men, the civic leaders of an earlier era."[10]

The first two decades of the twentieth century were distinguished by changes in the structure of government and the electoral process (including many of the reforms proposed by the Populists), the introduction of antitrust and other forms of business regulation, and, finally, by a concern for social justice where women led the way. In Minnesota, under a succession of Republican governors, a number of Progressive reforms were enacted. While Lind did not succeed with his proposal to prohibit railroads from providing free passes for legislators or with some of his other Progressive initiatives, he was able to establish more humane treatment for the insane, to secure arbitration for labor disputes, and to introduce some modest tax reforms. The legislators—and probably the people, too—were unwilling to buy entirely into his proposition that "high civilization and high taxes are inseparable."[11]

Governor Samuel R. Van Sant took effective initiatives against a proposed merger of railroad giants represented by James J. Hill's Great Northern and Northern Pacific. A Minnesota statute prohibited the consolidation of parallel or competing railroads in the state. Ultimately, in a suit brought by the attorney general of the United States under the Sherman Antitrust Act of 1890, the merger was dissolved by a 1904 decision of the U.S. Supreme Court. The Democratic administration of John A. Johnson (1905–09) succeeded in generating bipartisan support to enact legislation initiating tax reform (1906), regulating railroad and insurance companies (1905 and 1907), protecting timber on state lands from undue exploitation (1905), instituting more effective factory inspection (1907), allowing municipalities to own and operate public utilities (1907), and establishing a state department of banking (1909). Johnson's skills earned him a national reputation, but his promising public career was cut short with his death following abdominal surgery. Under Governor Adolph O. Eberhart, a statewide primary law was passed (1912), a program of workmen's compensation initiated (1913), and a commission appointed to determine minimum wages for women and minors (1913). Progressivism crested in Minnesota in 1915, but it left a legacy of decency and independence in government.[12]

The campaign for woman suffrage and the Progressive movement were congenial partners in reform. Much of what Carl H. Chrislock, an eminent Minnesota social historian, has termed "a genuine democratic renaissance" in the era of Progressivism can be attributed to the reforms advanced by women relating to the welfare of the family, children, and the community. The effort by Ueland and her associates to make kindergartens an integral part of the Minneapolis school system was a case in point. Women were also instrumental in obtaining legislation at the state level to grant women co-guardianship of their minor children, to approve the right of married women to hold property, and to acknowledge the legal existence of married women (1905); to establish the Training School for Girls in Sauk Centre (1907); to enact a law for compulsory education and to form women's and children's departments in the state bureau of labor (1909); to pass a mothers' pension act, to prohibit night work for women and children, to limit women to a nine-hour working day, and to appoint a minimum wage commission (1913).[13]

The explosive growth of national women's organizations in the 1890s brought women outside the home—thanks in part to new technologies, fewer children, higher education, and longer lives—to escape domesticity and to engage in activities intended to heal a host of social and economic ills afflicting the body politic. Single-purpose associations, like those for temperance and suffrage, were joined by multipurpose groups, such as the General Federation of Women's Clubs (founded in 1890), the National Council of Jewish Women (1893), the National Association of Colored Women (1896), the Association of Collegiate Alumnae (1881; later the American Association of University Women), and the National Congress of Mothers (1897; later the Parent-Teacher Association), all of them representing a turn outward from self-improvement to public affairs.[14]

The women's club movement was a natural next step after the involvement of women in "culture" clubs like the Peripatetics. As one clubwoman wrote in 1925, "Women had to turn in on themselves and learn to know each other before they dared or knew how to turn outward." Women's clubs became important training grounds for public activity. Members learned how "to speak in public, to prepare and present reports, to raise and manage money." These experiences in what historian Anne Firor Scott has called "miniature republics" enhanced women's political skills and produced a truly impressive array of community institutions, from libraries to health clinics, parks, and playgrounds. Historian Sara M. Evans has emphasized the role played by women in developing "a distinctively American form of public life through voluntary associations that made the vision of active citizenship a sustainable one." American society has been distinguished, as Alexis de Tocqueville observed, not only by the existence of those voluntary associations but by their deeds. Credit for the special contributions of women's clubs and women's organizations to the building of this vital infrastructure has too often gone unnoticed or been misplaced.[15]

The pace of suffrage activity also quickened after 1900. In Minnesota, as in other states, the number of clubs increased, and so did their variety, ranging from one for poor, immigrant women to another for college women. When Eugenia B. Farmer, a proven suffrage leader who had moved from Kentucky to St. Paul, spoke to a mothers club in the fall of 1904 at Neighborhood House in St. Paul (a settlement house on the city's West Side), she inspired these immigrant women to become a suffrage club. Thus in 1904 the Sacajawea Suffrage Club was born, named for the Shoshoni woman who guided the Lewis and Clark expedition. It was an appropriate choice for women who had experienced their own expeditions to a new land. The resident head of Neighborhood House reported that the "Sacajawea club is full of interest and showing a desire to know the wife's & mother's status under our state laws." In 1910 the Sacajawea Club merged with an older St. Paul suffrage club, then suffering from a declining membership. Initially the merged group called itself the St. Paul Sacajawea Club but later chose to be known as the Political Equality Club of St. Paul. Apparently the organization began to take on new life as lawyers and prominent teachers became members.[16]

The organizational mainstay of the suffrage cause in Minnesota remained the Political Equality Club of Minneapolis, the only suffrage association in the state to continue without interruption from the time of its inception in 1868 to ratification of the Nineteenth Amendment in 1920. Originally called the Woman Suffrage Club of Minneapolis, its membership fluctuated from a low of about eighty to a high of seven hundred; its dues were a modest one dollar—sometimes only fifty cents; and it must have established some sort of record, meeting ten of twelve months (with only an occasional miss) for fifty-three consecutive

Leaders of the Political Equality Club of Minneapolis, about 1915

years. Beginning in 1897, physicians who were members main-tained club headquarters in their offices, first in that of Margaret Koch and Cora Smith Eaton, who had been the local chairman for the 1901 national convention, and, from 1906 to the group's disbanding, in the office of Ethel Edgerton Hurd and her daugh-ter Annah Hurd. One of the highlights of the club's history was the visit to the suffrage exhibit at the 1901 Minnesota State Fair by Vice-President Theodore Roosevelt, former Governor David M. Clough, Governor Samuel R. Van Sant, Archbishop John Ireland, and other dignitaries. All registered in favor of women's suffrage. Regrettably, the building housing the exhibit burned and the record of those commitments perished in the fire.[17]

Ethel Hurd, a mainstay of the Political Equality Club of Min-neapolis, was the first woman to graduate from Knox College in Galesburg, Illinois. Following her marriage to a railroad man, she moved to Kansas and other locations. After his death, she

entered the medical school at the University of Minnesota—
again one of the first to do so—receiving her M.D. degree thirty-
two years after her graduation from Knox in 1865. Annah, her
daughter, was also a physician and shared her mother's office,
practice, and interest in suffrage. Ethel served in various capacities at various times in several suffrage groups, some of which she
helped organize, and wrote brief histories of the Political Equality Club of Minneapolis and the state association. She was a pro-
totype of the first suffrage generation—a professional woman
whose commitment to the rights of women and to suffrage
extended from her undergraduate days until the end of her life.[18]

Ethel also served as midwife for the Minnesota Scandinavian
Woman Suffrage Association (swsa), which she organized in
1907. That association's purpose, as stated in its articles of incorporation, was direct and to the point: "Its general business shall
be for the social and economic advancement and to secure for
the women of the State of Minnesota and of the United States
the right of suffrage." Some years later—in 1915—Nanny Jaeger
suggested more colloquially that its aim was "to inject a little suffrage spice into the melting pot." After serving for two years on
the nawsa board, Jaeger became the last swsa president about
1914. The Scandinavian women's group made three important
contributions, first by attracting women of Danish, Finnish,
Norwegian, and Swedish descent as members; second by using all
their powers of persuasion to influence the attitudes and votes of
Scandinavian legislators and congressmen; and, finally, by raising
money for a women's building at the State Fair. Also in 1907, a
College Equal Suffrage Club was formed at the University of
Minnesota to appeal to younger women. Professors Mary Gray
Peck and Frances Squire Potter, both of whom would later work
for suffrage at the national level, took the initiative in this effort.
Clara Ueland's daughter Elsa, then a university student, was the
first president of the new suffrage organization, a fact that proved
to be critical in bringing her mother's commitment to fruition.[19]

Clara Ueland's interest in suffrage had been piqued by the
1901 convention in Minneapolis, and she later joined both the

Political Equality Club of Minneapolis and the Minnesota Scandinavian Woman Suffrage Association. Still, before 1907, the issue was not high on her personal list of priorities. She was not impressed with either the style or the rhetoric of early leaders like Ethel Hurd and Martha Ripley. Clara's discomfort with the older suffrage leaders stemmed from a generational difference. These women, many of them professionals, had made their way in occupations and communities where they were belittled, scorned, and rebuffed. Men ridiculed their aspirations for equal status. No wonder they had to be of sterner stuff if they were to be heard, much less respected. But a change in public perception began to be evident at the 1901 convention in Minneapolis, where reporters found suffragists to be affable, good-humored, eloquent, and even fashionable. In Minnesota, as in other states, well-to-do and well-regarded women volunteers began to join the ranks. Suffrage replaced temperance as the reform priority of the young, educated American woman. Suddenly suffrage was in vogue—it was becoming the thing to do. Good friends like Maud Stockwell, Nanny Jaeger, and Emily H. Bright typified the women who gravitated to the movement and helped to change Clara Ueland's mind about becoming involved.[20]

Although Maud and Clara had known each other since high school days and had both been schoolteachers, their friendship blossomed fully after their marriages—Maud married Sylvanus A. Stockwell, an insurance agent, legislator, and suffrage supporter. Maud Stockwell led the suffrage cause for nearly twenty consecutive years as president of the Minnesota Woman Suffrage Association from 1900 to 1910 and as a director from 1910 to 1919. Unlike the Uelands, the Stockwells remained loyal parishioners of the First Unitarian Society after the death of the Reverend Henry Simmons, and Maud was a member of the board of trustees. Luth and Nanny Jaeger were close to Andreas and Clara Ueland because of both Scandinavian and Unitarian connections. Brenda portrayed Nanny Jaeger as "very stout and rather formidable in the stern scorn of her ideas—piercingly and ironically intelligent—she had a volatile, immediate laugh that made others feel witty." Brenda remembered Emily Bright as "Clara's most dauntless colleague . . . full of an arrogant, saucy, and shocking feminism . . . [with] several children, all original and dashing and pleasantly wild." Bright had served as president of the Political Equality Club of Minneapolis and was Ueland's immediate predecessor as head of the Minnesota Woman Suffrage Association. Her leadership helped to attract women of society to the cause.[21]

Sylvanus Stockwell, Luth Jaeger, and Alfred Bright (Emily's husband and an attorney for the Minneapolis, St. Paul and Sault Ste. Marie Railroad Company from 1891), who were known as "the three steadies," could always be counted on as suffrage supporters, attending rallies and marching in parades. Stockwell voted for suffrage bills during his early terms (1891–93 and 1897–99) as a member of the legislature.[22]

During the 1907 legislative session, Clara Ueland went with Emily Bright, Mary Gray Peck, and Frances Squire Potter to a Senate committee hearing where Potter testified on a pending suffrage bill. Ueland revealed in a letter to her daughter Anne that, while she still did not feel entirely comfortable with some of the participants, she considered it an "interesting experience": "A number of characteristic suffragists were there, so queer, so fond of making speeches, so eloquent on the subject of women's wrongs. So sarcastic as to men's ability to vote. . . . We had lunch together in the café in the Capitol and altogether had quite a jolly time." Despite Clara's disapproval of meek women, she still could not fully accept the aggressive manner displayed by committed suffragists.[23]

The influence of her friends, however, took second place to that of Ueland's daughter, Elsa, who was the first Ueland actively associated with the suffrage movement. Even before she became head of the University of Minnesota's suffrage organization, Elsa was swept up with the idea of women's rights. Tall, blond, and athletic, she rejected the idea of a women's college in favor of the coeducational and more democratic university, where, if she chose to do so, she could study law and engineering in a place that welcomed the poor as well as the rich. When Elsa started attending meetings of a suffrage club at the Unitarian church, she persuaded her mother to participate in the discussions.[24]

Clara felt compelled by Elsa's enthusiasm for the suffrage cause to inform herself through readings, meetings, and travel. On a trip that Clara and Andreas made to Norway in 1909, she wrote to her second daughter, "I am studying the woman suffrage situation here, and interview people whenever I can." Some years later Clara attributed her active work on behalf of suffrage to her daughters, whose college experiences had heightened their awareness of the discriminations facing women. Anne echoed Elsa's concerns about the barriers impeding women's progress, and Brenda became an enthusiastic participant in suffrage parades and other festivities organized by her mother.

In 1911 at the Minneapolis auditorium, Clara Ueland heard Emmeline Pankhurst, the well-known and militant English suffrage leader, for the first time. "Her lecture was rather disappointing to me. Not well arranged and really rambling, but she is earnest and knows what she is talking about," wrote Ueland. Nevertheless Pankhurst apparently succeeded in persuading Ueland that assertiveness had its place: "It strikes me that this gives a different aspect to the militant tactics of women. It may be as justifiable as the Battle of Lexington."

Ueland's growing interest became evident in her journal, which she filled with musings on arguments against suffrage: women would lose their charm as a sex; women should not vote because they do not fight; the undesirable woman would use the vote; suffrage would increase corruption in politics. They took delight in the absurdity of anti-suffrage arguments: "There was severe criticism for Florence Nightingale in the beginning for nursing grown-up men and not staying home taking care of babies she didn't have. . . . A conservative woman said of a girl who had rowed some people around a dangerous coast and saved their lives: 'It is shameful and it would have been much better for her to have stayed home where she belonged.'"[25]

In 1907, the same year that Elsa became president of the University of Minnesota's College Equal Suffrage Club, her mother helped in forming the Woman's Club of Minneapolis. Clara Ueland's leadership in the club broadened the scope of her interests and deepened her understanding of issues. She became involved in campaigns for clean streets, clean water, and clean air. Both she and Josephine Sarles Simpson served as club representatives on the city's Pure Water Commission. In promoting an environment that was not only healthful but beautiful, Ueland found herself supporting the establishment of a city planning commission and encouraging the building of better houses and more attractive schools. Ueland's inherent sense of equality and social justice made her an advocate of decent lodging houses for working women. In short order she expanded that initial commitment, and the club embraced a panoply of protective legislation designed to assure that women and children would be spared abuse and given opportunity and choice in their lives. Efforts on behalf of the "unprotected girl" and reducing the working week to fifty-eight hours for women in "mercantile establishments" represented some of their priorities.[26]

Yet suffrage was not uniformly endorsed by members of the Woman's Club. In the spring of 1912, for instance, the club's nominating committee decided not to ask Josephine Simpson to be a candidate for president because, as Clara wrote Elsa, "she has taken such a *strong stand on the woman suffrage question.* I think I told you the same thing happened to me last year when they were considering the question of a possible president." Ueland was candid, as she usually was, in observing that the three members of the nominating committee were in fact *for* suffrage but fearful of offending those in the club holding opposite views. A "strong stand" was to be expected from a committed and energetic woman like Simpson. She was once described in a newspaper article as "a lady of commanding presence, an easy, graceful, impressive speaker, who frequently and without effort rises to heights of oratory." Like Ueland, she had been a supporter of the movement for free kindergartens and would later

The Ueland family, about 1912. Standing: Kenneth Taylor (Anne's husband), Arnulf, Sigurd, Brenda; seated: Elsa, Andreas, Clara, Anne; on ground: Rolf, Torvald.

serve as a key spokeswoman for the suffrage cause. Ueland was more offended by the nominating committee's rejection of Simpson than she had been by its rejection of herself the previous year, and although she continued with her committee responsibilities, Ueland withdrew from the board later in 1912 and was never again active with the organization.[27]

In August 1912 Ueland gave what may have been the first of her fund-raising suffrage garden parties, complete with speeches, dances, and skits. Brenda recalled the excitement sparked when John Colton, a reporter from the *Minneapolis Daily News*, introduced the party to the turkey trot and the bunny hug, "never seen before in Minnesota."[28]

Ueland's increasing commitments outside the home prompted a modest complaint from Andreas, who confided in a letter to Anne in 1910: "Mother's extensive club work, which I otherwise might take some interest in, becomes, under the circumstances [that is, stresses in his law practice], the cause of additional irritation." Clara Ueland would have objected to any diminution of her overall activities, caught up as she was in a variety of interests congruent with the country's prevailing progressive political mode. Writing to Elsa a few days following her fiftieth birthday on October 10, 1910, she noted that she had been asked "to be toast mistress" later that month at a banquet of the Political Equality Club. "I would like to do a little something for the cause."[29]

4

INTO THE FRAY

*If I can be, in any small way, instrumental in gaining
the franchise for the women of Minnesota, I shall feel
that I have been allowed to be of real use.*

CLARA UELAND, about 1914

 Although Clara Ueland had decided "to do a little
something," she did not make her initial commitment to suffrage leadership until September 17,
1913. On that day, about forty Minneapolis wom-
en, responding to her invitation, came to a meet-
ing in her home to organize a new and different kind of suffrage
club. Ueland presented the case to her friends with some typical
rhetoric and made sure the press was there to report it. She urged
them to join forces in order to increase the influence of women
as mothers, because "the best thing that a nation can do is to
raise a better set of children." She called on them to support suffrage as a means of confronting "the three evils of the day—
liquor, prostitution and war." Ueland also invoked the need to
foster "broader interests and a stronger feeling of sisterhood"
among women. As a way of recruiting women of means and
influence, she touched all bases, appealing to their maternal
instincts, their traditional political concerns, and their desire for
personal growth.[1]

Although Ueland's rhetoric may have been conventional, her plans for the new organization were not. She proposed that the club be open to both men and women: "We want to get rid of the idea that sex antagonism is associated with women suffrage." Less than five months later, an advisory board of nineteen prestigious men and five outstanding women from business, education, and civic leadership circles was in place. She took pains to explain that the proposed organization did not represent dissatisfaction with the Political Equality Club of Minneapolis, which had "reached a great many persons." Rather its intention was to organize Hennepin County by precincts, wards, and legislative districts, so that it would be "thoroughly systematized on political lines." She concluded by reaffirming her belief that it was a great privilege to take part in the movement—"one of the great causes of the world."[2]

The idea was not vaguely conceived. Ueland had planned and presented several committees: a key extension group that would be responsible for developing an organization in every ward and district in the county; a press committee; an education committee; a "junior" committee to recruit young people from schools, factories, and department stores; a membership committee; and a literature committee. The assembly of women at Ueland's home, bound by friendship and the growing acceptability of suffrage as a worthy cause, acceded to her plea, and the Equal Suffrage Association of Minneapolis was formed with Ueland as president.[3]

"You can't have too many clubs," Ueland told the group. "The more clubs there are the more voters we reach."[4]

The statement may have been part of the truth, but not the whole truth. The state suffrage movement had been struggling from the time Maud Stockwell stepped down from her decade-long presidency in 1910. Hampered by a lack of continuity and effective leadership, the Minnesota Woman Suffrage Association made no significant progress except in 1912, when Concheta F. Lutz (its president from 1896 to 1898), with the help of "some of the oldest workers in the state," organized twelve new clubs on

Banners of the Equal Suffrage Association of Minneapolis

behalf of the MWSA in smaller communities, from Austin in southern Minnesota to Grand Rapids in the north. Even then there were only twenty-four clubs in Minnesota, with membership ranging from a high of 186 in the Political Equality Club of Minneapolis to as few as 10 in some of the state's smaller towns.[5]

After the convention in that same year, Lutz and others—still frustrated at the MWSA's failure to reach the voting population as fully as they desired—formed a rival organization, the Minnesota Equal Franchise League. Most of the twelve clubs that had been organized by Lutz in 1912 left the MWSA and joined forces with

the new Equal Franchise League. This transfer of allegiance probably accounted for the bulk of the league's 360 members one
month after incorporation, but the fact that the number of members doubled within two months reveals something about the
ineptitude within the MWSA. For a time, considerable tension
existed between the two. At one point, for example, the MWSA
hired a lawyer to investigate whether Theresa B. Peyton, the
MWSA's former corresponding secretary, had taken some records
and was refusing to return them. He reported that the former corresponding secretary declared that she had no such materials.[6]

In 1913 the MWSA appointed a committee to repair the rupture, but this effort at mediation was initially rebuffed by the
league. Personality conflicts between leaders of the two groups as
well as Peyton's philosophical differences with the MWSA could
have accounted for the Minnesota Equal Franchise League's initial rejection of the attempt to resolve the dispute.[7]

The existence of two suffrage associations bearing the prefix
"Minnesota" also produced organizational confusion. Peyton,
who was serving as the league's president, tried to acquire for her
organization the principal suffrage identity in Minnesota by
claiming as auxiliary members the same suffrage clubs affiliated
with the MWSA. The failure of staff members at NAWSA headquarters to sort this out resulted in Minnesota's having twice the
representation it was entitled to at the 1912 NAWSA convention
in Philadelphia.

During this same period (1913–14), a small group of
women—including Emily G. Noyes of St. Paul and Clara
Ueland—organized a "State Central Committee" to begin a
process of political organization by legislative district. Emily
Bright, who was then president of the MWSA, had wanted to
undertake this task but was unable to raise the money to hire a
field-worker. Continuing squabbles—probably jurisdictional—
between the MWSA and the Central Committee hindered any
progress. In 1914 the MWSA executive board proposed a meeting
with representatives of both the Minnesota Equal Franchise
League and the Congressional Union for Woman Suffrage, a new

national organization led by younger women who had broken away from NAWSA and that was successfully recruiting members in Minnesota. A MWSA suggestion that a single chairman be designated to coordinate the congressional and legislative work of the three state groups was accepted. While the Equal Franchise League maintained its organizational independence, it also paid its dues as an auxiliary member to the MWSA, prompting the executive board to approve a motion extending a cordial welcome to the black sheep returning to the fold. If anything could be said of this period in the suffrage life of Minnesota, it would be that the movement was in organizational disarray.[8]

Although Clara Ueland shared similar frustrations with the critics of the MWSA, she chose not to align herself with the Equal Franchise League. Further, seeing that the State Central Committee, for whatever reasons, seemed not to be working, she stepped forward with her proposal for a new suffrage group to initiate political activity in the state's largest county. With her initiative, the process of political organization on behalf of suffrage got under way. Most important, Ueland made sure that there would be resources to do the job.

Her initial recommendation to set annual dues at five dollars must have produced a gasp of disbelief even from her wealthy friends, who were accustomed to paying dues of one dollar—at the very most—and, more frequently, fifty or twenty-five cents if at all. By the end of 1913, largely through Ueland's efforts, the membership of the Equal Suffrage Association of Minneapolis had increased to nearly one hundred. She evidently succeeded in persuading her friends that dues of that magnitude were essential to fund the work of a different kind of suffrage organization, one that would emphasize political action and outreach to potential new suffrage supporters. By bringing younger women and working women as well as men into the association, Ueland was asserting her belief that the base of the suffrage constituency had to be expanded if the movement was to succeed.[9]

Another priority for Ueland was a businesslike suffrage organization supported by efficient and focused operations and a paid staff. Results mattered most of all. Ueland recognized that a successful outcome required the mobilization of public opinion and the conversion of opposing and ambivalent legislators or their defeat at the polls. In the earlier years, suffragists usually engaged supporters politically by gathering signatures on petitions and traveling extensively to speak before voters and legislators. But the efforts of those campaigns in virtually all the states were lodged more in hope and goodwill than in pragmatic pressure.[10]

Besides Ueland, other women were taking the initiative to revitalize the suffrage effort in Minnesota. In St. Paul, Emily Noyes played a lead role in establishing the Woman's Welfare League in 1912 and served as its first president for four years and as honorary president thereafter. After her experience with Ueland on the short-lived Central Committee, Noyes had committed the Woman's Welfare League to undertake the political organization for suffrage in Ramsey County. Noyes, born Emily Hoffman Gilman in 1854, was the daughter of a businessman who as a young man in Alton, Illinois, had risked his life during riots in 1837 to offer shelter to a radical abolitionist publisher. A good deal of that caring idealism rubbed off on Emily, one of thirteen children. Her marriage to Charles P. Noyes, who, with his older brother, founded a highly successful wholesale drug business in St. Paul, enabled her to spend a considerable amount of time doing good works in the community.[11]

The mission of the Woman's Welfare League was to "protect the interests and promote the welfare of women; to encourage the study of industrial and social conditions affecting women and the family; to enlarge the field of usefulness and activity open to women in the business and professional world[;] to guard them from exploitation and as a necessary means to these ends to strive to procure for women the rights of full citizenship." The Welfare League, which Ueland considered to be the St. Paul counterpart to the Equal Suffrage Association, would prove to be a key suffrage actor in Ramsey County.[12]

In 1914 St. Paul was once again the beneficiary of a new suffrage group when a group of "colored" women, led by Nellie

Griswold Francis, established the Everywoman Suffrage Club. Affiliated with the MWSA, its motto was "Every woman for all women and all women for every woman." Francis belonged to the upper class of black society and was consequently able to forge connections with the predominantly white women's social and political clubs that were then reluctant to include black women. Born in 1874, Nellie Griswold came to St. Paul from Tennessee as a girl and in 1891 was the only black person among the eighty-four graduates from St. Paul High School. Her presentation on "Race Problems" won second prize in an annual oratorical contest and led to a job as a stenographer at the Great Northern Railway Company. In 1893 Nellie Griswold married William Trevanne Francis, who would become the city's leading black attorney. Together they dedicated their lives to the betterment of conditions in the African-American community. Active in church and community affairs, Nellie Francis belonged to the predominantly white Woman's Welfare League and the Schubert Club as well as to the Urban League and the National Association for the Advancement of Colored People (both of which her husband helped organize in St. Paul). After a meeting with the Everywoman Suffrage Club, Ueland noted that the members compared favorably with what she termed "ordinary" club women—"with one or two exceptionally graceful and charming. But the leader of the club is a *star!* Mrs. Frances [sic] is petite and what we call a 'lady,' but her spirit is a flame."[13]

With the two groups that had been formed in the early 1900s—the Minnesota Scandinavian Woman Suffrage Association and the College Equal Suffrage Association—the Woman's Welfare League and the Everywoman Suffrage Club added suffrage support in St. Paul and much-needed diversity in ethnicity, age, and race. There was less diversity in class, even though Professor Frances Potter and the ubiquitous Ethel Hurd had attempted to supply that missing dimension with the organization in 1909 of a Twin Cities–based Workers' Equal Suffrage Club for wage-earning women. Regrettably, the club attracted more professional women, such as teachers and journalists, than it did women working in stores and factories. Nevertheless these later developments were signs of recruitment and organizational progress, which had been lately absent from the movement in Minnesota.[14]

Suffragists' impatience with the organizational status quo was evident on the national scene as well as in Minnesota. As a newcomer to NAWSA's congressional committee, Alice Paul, a young Quaker from a wealthy New Jersey family, introduced the more flamboyant tactics she had experienced as a student abroad in 1909 with the English suffragettes. On March 3, 1913, the eve of Woodrow Wilson's inauguration, she had organized a controversial parade of eight thousand women, which upstaged his arrival in the nation's capital. Early in 1914 the Congressional Union for Woman Suffrage (the reconstituted congressional committee) had separated from NAWSA to pursue suffrage by means of a federal constitutional amendment, ultimately employing the tactics of picketing and partisanship. One of the group's first decisions was to replicate the successful parade in other cities, and NAWSA agreed to join the effort. This rare instance of collaboration between the old and the new suffrage organizations produced the Suffrage Parade Committee in Minnesota.[15]

In the spring of 1914 Clara Ueland agreed to chair the parade committee, which set the parade date for May 2, a Saturday. Dismissing those who argued that it was "un-ladylike" to march, Ueland reminded the skeptics that once it had also been considered un-ladylike to eat hearty food, to be healthy, and to go to school and to college. Nevertheless this represented a new kind of suffrage undertaking designed to galvanize the community's attention and generate support for the cause.[16]

The great suffrage parade in Minneapolis drew 1,972 marchers—including men, women, young women from the University of Minnesota, high school students, and small children—and was led by general marshal Josephine Schain, an attorney and suffrage activist. They followed a route from

A humorous and supportive explanation of reasons behind the parade, published in the *Minneapolis Sunday Tribune*, April 12, 1914. "Mrs. Bright" leads the charge; "Mrs. Ueland" is third from left, holding a scroll.

Second Avenue to Fourth Street and back on Nicollet Avenue to the city auditorium. Clara's daughter Brenda, one of forty women on horseback, charged back and forth to make sure the divisions were "properly aligned." Julie Plant, Ueland's future daughter-in-law, portrayed Joan of Arc; her son Arnulf and his university friends were among Joan of Arc's "men-at-arms." Ueland herself marched with the Minnesota Scandinavian Woman Suffrage Association contingent.[17]

Helen Jones, a senior at Minneapolis's Central High School and president of the Junior Mobile Suffrage Squad, recorded her feelings about her participation: "It's been a great day! I feel as if I have been a part in creating history." She continued:

The Scandinavian Woman Suffrage Association unit of the suffrage parade,
Minneapolis, May 2, 1914

We bore the American flag and marched at the head of the students
section. . . . We were told to keep our heads up, eyes in front of us,
and to walk in dignity and silence. . . . I never felt so serious in my
life and didn't look at the crowd at all. . . . Some horrid men threw
money on our flag and did and said other rather insulting things. It
really seemed absurd that the red-faced, course [sic], sneering men
whom we passed could vote, and the noble, fine women in the
parade could not.[18]

The *Minneapolis Tribune* pronounced the final gathering at
the auditorium "a fine mass meeting in the cause of suffrage" and,
in a comment that must have been especially pleasing to the participants, noted that the parade constituted "a revelation and a
bump" to those whose ideas of suffragists came from cartoonists
and humorists. These women, the paper said, were "not a bevy of
hopeless spinsters, unhappily married women and persons who
have nothing else to do." Ole O. Sageng, state senator from
Dalton in Otter Tail County and a stalwart supporter of suffrage,
wrote Ueland to congratulate her and her coworkers on their
splendid success—"the best people of Minneapolis were in the
parade. . . . For the cause of suffrage it was one of the best things
that has happened in the state." The greatly admired educator

Maria Sanford (both she and Sageng had been among the speakers at the auditorium) commented in a letter to Ueland, "I have
not a great passion for spectacular affairs, and I have not felt
great enthusiasm for the parades, but I was quite corrected. The
whole affair was dignified and impressive. . . . With congratulations for the fine management."[19]

Meeting on May 6 to indulge in a few postmortems, committee members were elated by their own success and by the fact
that more than a thousand towns and cities in thirty-five other
states had held parades or some other kind of suffrage demonstration. Ueland and her fellow organizers were amused that three
women who had offered cars for the event had to withdraw their
offers because their husbands objected. They were gratified that
one older woman said that having her whole family march for
such a cause was the happiest day of her life. They were proud
that they had demonstrated the ability of women to work as a
team for a common purpose and to march in good order. They
laughed because Clara Ueland was taken for Emmeline Pankhurst, the famed English suffrage leader. The whole process had
been so much fun that they voted not to disband, and at their
next meeting they agreed to send the surplus from the parade's
receipts to North Dakota and South Dakota—to help in their
referendum campaigns—and to the Congressional Union.[20]

In August, deciding to embark on another special fund-
raising effort, suffragists began melting down old jewelry.
Ueland contributed a silver baby mug that had belonged to her
daughter Anne.[21]

Ueland was next recruited by the MWSA to plan activities for
the State Fair. The July 1914 minutes of the executive board
reported that she had submitted "elaborate and comprehensive"
plans. The fair gave suffragists the opportunity to entice recruits
with refreshments, to have a few sing-alongs, to peddle their
tracts, and to make a case for suffrage with a larger and more
diverse audience. Despite a deficit from the motion-picture show
Your Girl and Mine—a suffrage melodrama—the MWSA board
deemed the effort a success.[22]

Given Ueland's increasing activity and visibility, no one was surprised when she was asked to head the state organization. Five years earlier Ethel E. Hurd had written to the national president, Anna Howard Shaw, recommending Ueland as a possible member of the state association's executive committee. Hurd's recommendation was not acted on, however, probably because the state president at the time, Ueland's good friend Maud Stockwell, felt that Ueland's commitment was still not firmly formed. Stockwell was probably correct in assuming that such an invitation would have been premature.[23]

The timing, however, was right in 1914, and Ueland graciously accepted the invitation: "Of all the honors which have been offered me . . . none appeals to me as does this one. . . . At the present time, in a state of unenfranchised women, there is no work so important as this work for the ballot." Any previous hesitations she may have had about suffrage were now forgotten. In one year's time, Clara had organized and served as president of a fast-growing suffrage organization in Hennepin County; she had orchestrated a major parade, an event that gave suffrage needed visibility; and she had developed plans for the State Fair and helped raise money for suffrage amendment campaigns in North and South Dakota. Her commitment had matured, and she was now poised to accept the responsibility of suffrage leadership in Minnesota.[24]

On October 17, 1914, Clara Ueland became the thirteenth—and last—president of the Minnesota Woman Suffrage Association. When she took office, the association had had four presidents in the preceding four years. At her first meeting with the executive board as president, Ueland made her priorities clear: to hire an efficient organizer, to raise money to support that person, to organize by political districts in order to magnify the association's political clout, and to assign specific responsibilities to each board member. She also urged the board members of the Equal Suffrage Association of Minneapolis to take public-speaking classes at the University of Minnesota. Ueland was determined to improve the operations of the association and to transform suffrage organizations throughout the state, as well as the urban-based clubs, into a highly sophisticated mechanism of persuasion and pressure.[25]

In the first month of her presidency, Ueland attended the NAWSA convention from November 12 to 17 in Nashville, Tennessee, where she hired Maria McMahon, a native of Newport News, Virginia, who was an experienced suffrage organizer. McMahon began working the southern counties of Minnesota early in 1915. In January Ueland engaged a Miss Mathews of Ohio and Gertrude Hunter of Minneapolis for three months to do organizational work outside Ramsey and Hennepin counties. She also recruited Harriet Grimm and Maud McCreery of Wisconsin as summer workers in Minnesota.[26]

An organizing stalwart in the person of Rene E. Hamilton Stevens came on board in January 1916. Her salary of seventy-five dollars a month plus expenses was paid for by the "kindness of some of our men friends." Stevens's commitment to suffrage had been shaped by the antislavery heritage of her mother, a woman—like the Grimké sisters—whose experience growing up on her father's Kentucky plantation had turned her into an ardent abolitionist. Stevens's parents, radicals both, had been pioneering Nebraska farmers. Given her background, it was not surprising that Stevens left her position as a school administrator in Omaha to join forces with the movement. Many of the women who became suffrage organizers followed similar career paths.[27]

The high priority given organization came from the new president's awareness that success in mobilizing public opinion was a crucial first step if decision makers were to be persuaded to endorse suffrage. In one of her frequent "Dear Suffragist" letters—initiated by Ueland to communicate more personally in regular mailings with suffrage leaders around the state—she spoke to the importance of organization, of recruiting local women from precincts and townships to take responsibility for each unit within a legislative district. They in turn would organize, promote, and proselytize to make local communities come

"alive to the question," electing to the legislature men sympathetic to suffrage. This method, she believed, could best assure
ratification of the federal amendment.[28]

Organizational work required resources, and Clara Ueland,
recognizing this, continued the series of fund-raising garden parties that she had initiated in 1912. She put fun foremost at these
events. On a warm August day in 1915, for instance, the activities that went on from noon to late at night at the Ueland family
home included tennis, a "burlesque" girls track meet in which
the contestants, including Brenda Ueland, interspersed their
broad jumps and pole vaults with arguments for the vote; folk
dancing; fortune-telling; a theatrical production, "How the Vote
Was Won," by the Linden Hills Players; a picnic supper; a dish-
pan band; a white elephant booth; and a country store, where
suffragists sold apples and vegetables, doughnuts, jellies, pickles,
and spring chickens. Of special interest was a game imported
from Newport, Rhode Island, called the Hoppetaria, where players hopped from one suffrage state to another, skipping nonsuffrage states and landing with only one foot on partial-suffrage
states like Minnesota. Everyone was welcome at the festivities,
and five hundred guests attended. General admission was twenty-five cents, but "voters" (men) had to pay fifty cents.[29]

Buttressed by the efforts of paid workers in the field, Ueland
copied the model of New York in organizing Minnesota by legislative district. In 1915 Carrie Chapman Catt, as chairman of
the Empire State Campaign Committee, had introduced into the
New York referendum campaign the idea of matching the suffrage organization with the existing political organization in
order to magnify the impact of suffrage supporters on their voting
representatives. Although that first effort failed, suffragists
around the country saw in it the seeds of future success. In
December of that year they chose Catt as the president of
NAWSA, succeeding the popular Anna Howard Shaw. Fifteen
years earlier, Catt—then forty-one—had inherited the mantle of
leadership of NAWSA from Susan B. Anthony, but she had been
forced by her husband's illness to resign in 1904. She had been

succeeded by Shaw, a remarkable woman who was both an ordained minister and a medical doctor but whose leadership skills were more rhetorical than organizational.[30]

The election of Catt to the presidency brought to that office an exceptional—and sorely needed—talent for organization. When she took office, only twelve states had suffrage, eleven resulting from state constitutional amendments (except Wyoming, which had enacted suffrage in its territorial days) and the twelfth (Illinois) from legislative enactment, which permitted women to vote only in presidential elections. Prior to the NAWSA convention that met in Atlantic City from September 4 to 10, 1916, Catt unveiled to presidents of thirty-six state associations a plan to place the highest priority on the passage of a federal suffrage amendment and to obtain ratification from thirty-six state legislatures. While the details of the plan remained secret, the framework for its implementation was built at the convention that followed: concentration on the federal amendment and assignment of specific tasks to every state. Catt succeeded in providing NAWSA with the blueprint for the plan that finally established the necessary political muscle to turn the tide in favor of woman suffrage.[31]

Carrie Chapman Catt

Catt's "Winning Plan" embraced four levels of activities. The first was to press legislatures in the existing full-suffrage states and in the presidential suffrage state of Illinois to enact resolutions asking Congress to submit an equal suffrage amendment to the states. The second was to campaign for constitutional amendments in certain states, such as New York, where the prospects of passing state constitutional amendments were not so difficult as in Minnesota. The third was directed toward the southern one-party states, where work for the passage of suffrage in the primaries would guarantee success in the general election. In the remaining states (Minnesota among them), activists would try to obtain the right to vote for presidential electors, which could be accomplished by an act of the legislature rather than an amendment to the state's constitution. Suffragists believed that by increasing the number of women who could vote for president, their political power would be enhanced. Under Catt's plan, the persistent debate about which was superior—a state or a federal approach—was subsumed in a comprehensive effort to achieve by one means or another more suffrage states and, consequently, more votes in Congress for a federal suffrage amendment.[32]

In some respects the new national president and the Minnesota state president were mirror images of each other. They were contemporaries—Ueland the younger by less than two years. Both had been schoolteachers, though Catt was a college graduate and Ueland was not. They were midwesterners by birth and by adoption—Carrie Lane born in Wisconsin and raised in Iowa, Clara Hampson born in Ohio and raised in Minnesota. Both married well—Ueland to a lawyer, Catt to an engineer in her second marriage (she was widowed soon after her first marriage)—which allowed them time to devote themselves to the cause. George Catt enthusiastically supported suffrage, while Andreas Ueland's endorsement seemed more restrained. The restraint reflected less his ambivalence about suffrage than his annoyance with Clara's time-consuming suffrage activities and his worry that she might be bearing a burden that would damage her health.

Both women had commanding personalities, were well organized, and were tenacious and civil in the pursuit of suffrage. Although Carrie Chapman Catt had reservations about assuming the responsibilities of national suffrage leadership, she was heartened by signs that the organization had become impatient with the futile effort to obtain suffrage solely through the state-amendment route and was now willing to concentrate on winning suffrage with a federal amendment. Further, she was encouraged by the power to choose her own board and by a generous bequest from Mrs. Frank Leslie, wife of a New York publisher, that gave her the resources to do the job. "Her greatest gift," wrote one historian, "outranking even her excellence as an organizer, was the statesmanlike vision which enabled her to conceive a plan of action. . . . She could also assure its implementation, because she had developed a corps of lieutenants who could carry every last detail into execution." Clara herself said of Catt, "There has been perfect confidence in her ability and wisdom, and joy in her benignity and her sense of humor. She has been a great instrument sent to accomplish a great task." Friends would have said that it was an apt description of Clara as well.[33]

Even though Catt and Ueland and women of similar organizational and political skills were now at the helm of the suffrage ship and had positioned themselves on a speedy tack, they had rough seas ahead. They had to contend with the prejudice that infected their own movement and with the passionate intensity of some of their own gender who opposed suffrage.

5

OPPOSING FORCES AND OTHER AGITATIONS

*Our problem lies . . . with unlimited immigration
and dangerously diverse franchise laws.*

LAVINIA COPPOCK GILFILLAN, DECEMBER 1914

Late in 1914 two of Clara Ueland's fellow members
of the Peripatetics stood before an audience at the
University of Minnesota to express opposition to
woman suffrage. One was described by Brenda
Ueland as the "beauteous" Lavinia Coppock Gil-
fillan; the other was the "formidably intellectual" Florence Welles
Carpenter. Except for their difference of opinion on this important issue, the Minnesota women who opposed suffrage and those
who championed it were cast in the same mold: They were socially prominent, intelligent, and influential. And although Gilfillan
urged women on each side to avoid ill feelings and to maintain
"the kindliest courtesy in our antagonism," strains in previously
cordial relationships emerged as friends took one side or another.[1]

Representatives of the "suffs" and the "antis," as they came to
be called, had gathered for this great debate in the university's
library. This event was just one of a series of in-person and in-
print debates between many of the same protagonists in the years
directly preceding the ratification of the Nineteenth Amend-

Mrs. William Davis and Lavinia Coppock Gilfillan, who testified against suffrage on February 16, 1917

ment. Speaking for the "advantages" of suffrage were Clara Ueland and Josephine Schain, identified in the proceedings as a "Special Writer for the Minneapolis Tribune"—though she was also an attorney, a prominent clubwoman, and an MWSA director in 1912–13. Speaking for the "disadvantages" were Carpenter and Gilfillan.[2]

In Minnesota three antisuffragist organizations represented the opposition: a statewide group and one each in Minneapolis and St. Paul. Lavinia Gilfillan was president of the Minnesota Association Opposed to Woman Suffrage. Ella Lawler Pennington, whom Brenda Ueland described as "a charming and imposing person whose husband was a great railroad magnate," was president of the Minneapolis Association Opposed to the Future Extension of Suffrage to Women. Isabel Seymour Stringer, who had served for twenty years as secretary of the Woman's Missionary Society of the Presbytery of St. Paul, headed the Association Opposed to Woman Suffrage in that city. Gilfillan was considered the opposition's principal leader, but some observers thought Pennington was more lucid in her arguments.[3]

Hannah Lavinia Coppock had been a teacher in Washington, D.C., before marrying John B. Gilfillan, a prominent Minneapolis politician, banker, and judge, who was about twenty-five years her senior. An activist who was committed to good works, as this class of women all seemed to be (irrespective of their views on suffrage), Lavinia Gilfillan was fully engaged as a volunteer for worthy causes. Probably because of her husband's service as a regent, she was instrumental in helping to establish the first cafeteria for women students at the University of Minnesota.[4]

Florence Carpenter had a firmly established reputation for her fine intellect and eloquence. When Anne Ueland inquired about the university debate in a letter to her mother, she expressed a sense of intimidation that was probably not unusual for those contending with Florence Carpenter: "I shouldn't mind Mrs. Gilfillan but Mrs. Carpenter is a fluent creature." Carpenter devoted most of her time to educational and intellectual pursuits, although she shared the musical interests of her husband, Elbert L. Carpenter, a founder, president, and benefactor of the Minneapolis Symphony Orchestra and vice-president of Shevlin, Carpenter and Clarke Company, one of Minnesota's principal lumber companies. She was admired and respected by Clara Ueland. In fact, knowing that Carpenter was a graduate and a trustee of Wells College in Aurora, New York, helped Ueland decide to send her eldest daughter, Anne, to that college.[5]

Florence Welles Carpenter

Josephine Schain, Ueland's colleague in the debate, represented the younger generation of college-educated suffrage supporters. She was an experienced hand, however, having been active in the movement for seven years. After receiving a master's degree in law from the University of Minnesota in 1908, she had worked as the legal aid attorney for Associated Charities of Minneapolis and had served on the executive board of the Hennepin County Juvenile Protection Association. In 1915 she would become active at the national level, moving to New York to work on the referendum campaign under the leadership of Carrie Chapman Catt and beginning an association that lasted into the 1940s.[6]

In their presentations, Gilfillan and Carpenter moved beyond the earlier theological and biological arguments against suffrage. These two sophisticated and educated women resisted suggesting that the division of labor between man and woman had been ordained by the Creator, although this argument was still invoked by suffrage opponents. Neither did they put any stock in the proposition that women lacked the ability to reason or that they were not equipped physically to withstand the strain of political life. Rather they rested their case on the argument of separate spheres, specifically the centrality of the home and family. Carpenter declared, "The home is the core of it all, as it is the core of civilization. The woman works for the home inside: the man works for the home outside. It is all one. Why, then, have a new alignment of tasks and responsibilities, especially since the proposed arrangement is not an equalizing of burdens between the sexes, since men cannot assume women's functions?"[7]

They argued that political responsibilities would impose additional and inappropriate burdens on women. Carpenter took pains to point out that a woman was exempt from voting, from serving on a jury, and from fighting wars "because she serves the state in other capacities." Those other capacities were bearing and rearing children, homemaking ("a field in which men seem utterly at a loss"), and "bearing more than half the burden of the

churches and of philanthropies." Gilfillan also expressed appre-
hension about voting rights for blacks and immigrants:

> Of our adult female population, 1 in 5 are foreign born. Of our adult
> male population, almost 1 in 4 are foreign born. 14 per cent of the
> women and 12 per cent of the men are illiterate. Woman's fran-
> chise would double the negro vote. One of the great dangers to our
> Republic since the adoption of the 15th amendment has been the
> unintelligent franchise. Some of the most deplorable features of our
> public life, both North and South, have grown out of it. . . . In the
> homogeneous immigration which we had until about 1850, there is
> a minimum of danger. Since then there has been *no* homogeneity.

Carpenter reinforced these fears, referring to "masses of foreign
born women, even more illiterate than their men; masses of
ignorant black women of the South; masses of indifferent and
corrupt women in our cities."[8]

Gilfillan did not accept the allegation that states already possessing the franchise had better laws, and she took some time to
document the shortcomings of woman suffrage states and the
enlightened legislation of man suffrage states. Wyoming and
Utah, for example, still did not have compulsory school attendance. Nonsuffrage states such as Ohio, Kentucky, and Minnesota
had the most enlightened child-labor laws. The reforms and protective legislation advocated by both suffrage advocates and suffrage opponents, Carpenter and Gilfillan insisted, could best be
achieved through the shaping of public opinion, "the real power
behind stable improvement in ethical conditions."[9]

In her presentation, Josephine Schain spoke as a professional
woman who had experienced years of struggle to correct injustices and to enlarge opportunities for women in all walks of life.
Taking issue with Florence Carpenter, who advanced the case for
indirect influence, Schain held out for the vote as "the guarantee
of personal sovereignty that men have fought for through all the
ages." She also invoked the contemporary suffrage argument for
reform, calling the ballot "a tool for bringing about social betterment." It was not enough "to prepare the children for the world";

women also had to "have a hand in preparing the world for the children." Suffrage, she asserted, was "not a panacea but a system under which society can work to best advantage." She dealt with Gilfillan's worries about the immigrant vote by noting that "most of us can trace our ancestry back to those who fled to this country . . . seeking liberty and opportunity." Her experience of living at the Pillsbury Settlement House in Minneapolis for two years had shown her that "often the most valuable voter is the one who knows most about social misery." Schain concluded by saying, "This is not a battle of women against men. . . . The best home is the home where the father and mother work and council [sic] together for the welfare of the family. So we believe the best community will be the place where the men and the women work together in the solution of the problems of government."[10]

In what was probably Clara Ueland's most personalized and comprehensive statement on behalf of equal suffrage, she, too, made the case on the basis of both justice and the special contribution that women could make to polity. She began by saying:

> One of the most impressive chapters in the development of the Anglo Saxon man is his emergence from a state of bondage and serfdom to a position of freedom, and, little by little, to the attainment of self government.
>
> Not less impressive is the emergence . . . of woman from a state of ignorance and a position of dependence to the modern woman, who is just now taking the last step in her development—the demand for political independence.[11]

She observed that the "hardest lesson in this one thousand years—and one not completely learned yet—is that it is not safe to leave government in the hands of one man or a group of men, and that one class can not judge wisely or decide fairly for the whole." Her argument also rested on the assertion that vital human resources were being wasted: "No one can tell what the world has lost because of the idea that girls were inferior beings to their brothers. How many aspiring girls have been disheartened and discouraged by the public sentiment that they were not good enough or fine enough to do the things their immortal souls craved to do."[12]

Clara tied the enfranchisement of women to progressive themes, arguing that suffrage would make elected officials more attentive to housing, pure-food laws, clean streets and the disposal of garbage, hours of labor for working women, and sanitary conditions in the workplace. As mothers, women were concerned with the care of their children, most particularly with better food, safer shelter, more education, beauty, opportunity— all of which provided a more abundant life: "This intensive concern for home should be expressed in government." The interests of men, whose primary preoccupation was with business, should be balanced by the interests of women in the home and family. Fairness, justice, compassion—these were the virtues that Clara Ueland attached to the idea of equal suffrage.[13]

Suffrage was thus not an end in itself (though it could be justified that way) but was rather a means to wield influence on a wide range of social, economic, and political issues. Women, caring as they did about the primacy of life, would—with the ballot—be able to bring their influence to bear more effectively on behalf of a disarmed and peaceful world. Striking a new note of sisterhood, Ueland also noted how, through their efforts to secure the ballot, women had come to a new understanding of one another and were expressing a new loyalty to womankind. In a single, short sentence Ueland articulated both strands of the suffrage rationale: "The mainspring of this movement is not selfishness but a love of justice and a desire to serve."[14]

This Minnesota debate was a microcosm of the arguments being advanced by the two sides in a rhetorical confrontation taking place throughout the country. Arguments against suffrage— "remonstrances," as they were termed—had been formally presented since 1876, when the first society of women opposed to suffrage emerged in Washington, D.C. Throughout the 1890s, the antis organized similar societies in other states, responding to the increasing number of suffrage referendum campaigns. By the time opposition to suffrage peaked, from 1911 to 1916, the national membership totaled only 360,000 and societies opposed to suffrage could be found in just twenty states. (By contrast NAWSA claimed two million members in its final years.) This small but determined network of opposing forces proved to be formidable contestants in the battle for the votes of men and became responsible, as historian Anne Firor Scott notes, for the "failure of every state suffrage referendum between 1896 and 1910. They had, of course, the advantage of defending the status quo." Despite their successes in defeating state referenda, the organization in 1911 in New York City of a National Association Opposed to Woman Suffrage could be interpreted as a compliment to the gathering storm of suffrage forces.[15]

According to the antis, the franchise was not a privilege but a burden. Men and women occupied separate spheres: Politics was man's sphere, and good works was the province of women. Minnesota's Ella Pennington saw great danger in lowering the barrier between these spheres. Although many suffragists were "self-sacrificing, earnest, philanthropic" women, she said, "we also see that the emotional nature of woman has carried many [of them] to the disgraceful conduct of the Militant, and the repelling doctrine of the Feminist. Where would emotionalism carry these women in the Political Arena? Would the Militant accept the will of the majority? Would the Feminist not destroy the ideals that have grown with the triumphs of civilization and Christianity?" Pennington blamed the introduction of coeducation fifty years previously for "leading women into alarming extremes of thought."[16]

Ueland attacked this narrow view on the role of women. Writing in 1915, she saw suffrage as "primarily a question of right and justice. Under republican form of government every one should have a right to a voice in the laws they are forced to obey, irrespective of whether they desire to exercise that right or not." She believed that "the effort of women, both for and against suffrage, conclusively proves how vitally interested they are in public affairs and in itself is proof of their fitness to use the franchise." In contrast to the high-powered rhetoric that usually

An MWSA tableau: Colonial Dame Belle M. Purdy, who could not vote, poses with young men and immigrants, who could.

characterized the suffrage debate, Clara Ueland's claims tended to be more modest and realistic: Although suffrage could not "correct all evils," women voters would in the long run be an influence "on the side of good."[17]

Opponents of suffrage were not the only contenders who used arguments based on racism and nativism. One of the dark pages in the history of the suffrage movement is the abandonment of its equalitarian heritage. Even though the movement had originated as first cousin to the drive to abolish slavery, the passing years had dimmed the closeness of that kinship. White women who sought the vote resented their constitutional status as political inferiors to black men. Moreover, the suffrage movement in the South was based on the premise that woman suffrage would maintain white supremacy. Progressives in the South were uneasy with the claims of black Americans to equality. Even this more liberal segment of the white population tended to accept the segregationist racial doctrines of the early twentieth century.

The apparent inconsistency of the progressive philosophy and this retreat from principle (and even rhetoric) was a commonplace of the time. The era was distinguished for its mistreatment of black Americans. Never before had so many black men been so systematically disenfranchised, never before had segregation been so legally pervasive. Racial terrorism was at an all-time high: there were eleven hundred lynchings of blacks from 1889 to 1898. Racism was not only in place, but respectably so. The persistent shame of American racism reached its post–Civil War peak in the three decades of the Progressive Era—from about 1890 to the 1920s. Given this environment of bigotry, it is not surprising that suffragists, in the interest of pragmatism (to put the matter in the best possible light), had dissolved the abolitionist alliance of the early and mid-1800s, an alliance in which they had been major participants along with white men and black men.[18]

A visible sign of that dissolution was the National Association's ill-fated and short-lived support of a constitutional substitute for the Susan B. Anthony amendment. The Anthony amendment clearly stated the suffragists' goal: "The right of citizens of the United States to vote shall not be denied or abridged by the United States or by any State on account of sex." But in order to garner the votes of southern Congressmen, Ruth McCormick, chairman of the Congressional Committee, succeeded in persuading the NAWSA board of directors to endorse the Shafroth-Palmer amendment, which was touted as a means of easing the state amending process. (John Shafroth was a senator from Colorado; A. Mitchell Palmer, a representative from Pennsylvania. They were both Democrats and suffrage supporters.) The measure, introduced in Congress on March 2, 1914, would have permitted the electorate to decide the issue in states where more than 8 percent of voters signed a petition requesting such a referendum. If a majority of voters approved the question, women of that state would be enfranchised, regardless of any contrary constitutional provisions.[19]

The 1914 convention acquiesced but not without opposition from suffragists who were not convinced of the proposal's merit. The very thought of mounting separate initiative and referendum campaigns in the thirty-nine nonsuffrage states seemed to many a fruitless and time-consuming exercise. The idea of an initiative petition was very much in the progressive mode, however, and to others seemed to offer a reasonable way of dealing with the Democrats' continuing insistence that suffrage was the responsibility of the states. This reasoning was reinforced by the decision of the Democratic caucus not to endorse the establishment of a House woman-suffrage committee, making the Shafroth-Palmer amendment appear to be a viable alternative to congressional intransigence on this issue.[20]

Directors of the MWSA remained unconvinced of the merits of this tactic and unanimously protested the national organization's support of Shafroth-Palmer. (One NAWSA reply indicated that support had been "a matter of immediate practical politics" in the previous year.) Responding to the tirade of complaints, the national leadership—to the great relief of many suffragists, Minnesotans among them—rejected that tactic in December 1915. The issue of states' rights, however, remained a stumbling block in the way of suffrage success. While Carrie Chapman Catt, as president of NAWSA, soft-pedaled racist rhetoric, she and other suffrage leaders made no frontal attack on white supremacy.[21]

Southern suffragists, fearing the Negro vote, made common cause with those northern suffragists who feared the votes of the foreign born. With the influx of immigrants to the United States in the latter part of the nineteenth century, the case against suffrage was bolstered by "anti" rhetoric inveighing against the idea of "ignorant, indifferent, and corrupt" women, as Carpenter put it, going to the polls. Suffragists and their opposites were both concerned, but for different reasons: The antis were alarmed that enfranchisement would bring uninformed immigrant women into the electorate; the suffs worried that their case for the ballot might be imperiled by these same immigrants, often uneducated and of another class. Many new-comers arrived from countries where men expected women to be subservient and women complied.[22]

In 1894 Elizabeth Cady Stanton had proposed that literacy and ability to use the English language be imposed as qualifica-tions for voting. While Stanton believed that education was a social equalizer and that the working classes would profit from the expansion of educational opportunities, she also, writes historian Elisabeth Griffin, "held paternalist views about blacks, immi-grants, workers, and Cubans." During the 1901 suffrage conven-tion in Minneapolis, even Susan B. Anthony expressed appre-hension about "the introduction of vast numbers of irresponsible citizens." Although increasing numbers of suffrage women aligned themselves with the notion of an educational requirement, many, like Stanton, viewed this in a positive way and supported programs designed to improve literacy and impart civic educa-tional skills. Given these and other ambiguities that permeated the suffrage movement, allegations about racism and nativism deserve careful analysis within the context of time and place.[23]

If the turning of the suffrage movement toward racism was induced by pragmatic considerations, similar considerations impelled its turning away from nativism. Practical politics pre-vailed over prejudice as suffrage leaders recognized that if the vote was to be won in big-city states like New York, foreign-born male voters could not be ignored, and immigrant women would therefore need to be brought into the suffrage fold. Progres-sivism, the prevailing political mood of the country, was domi-nated by a middle class that was generally sympathetic to the aspirations of wage earners, recent immigrants, and nonwhite minorities. That sympathy, however, took the form of a paternal-istic humanitarianism tempered by apprehension over the alliance between the urban poor and the political bosses who bought support by providing jobs and rudimentary social ser-vices. Disrupting that dependency was the new generation of educated women who were associated with settlement houses and with the burgeoning profession of social work (such as Jane Addams, Florence Kelley, and Sophonisba P. Breckinridge).[24]

The settlement houses that had emerged in the 1890s proved to be places where young women like Elsa Ueland, searching for nontraditional ways to do good works, could live, work, and "agitate for change." When her parents expressed reservation about Elsa's going to New York City to work in the Richmond Hill settlement house after her graduation from the University of Minnesota in 1909, she responded with a youthful outburst: "I suppose I have the wild 'get away' feeling. If you knew the wild longings and dreams of the Phillipines [sic] and Turkey and Alaska, you would realize how mild is the Richmond Hill House."[25]

Not only did Elsa and her colleagues agitate for a litany of improvements for children, for women workers, for the poor, and for more responsive government in general; they also became champions of newly arrived immigrants. Women staffing the settlement houses sought both to ameliorate the condition of the underclass and to "Americanize" the foreign born. The settlement-house movement enjoyed some measurable success in these endeavors, thereby diminishing the argument (much to the distress of the opposition and to the relief of the suffragists) that immigrant women could not be expected to fulfill the responsibilities of citizenship.[26]

Their efforts were reinforced by the sympathetic public response to the shirtwaist makers' strike of 1909 in New York City and by the devastating 1911 Triangle Fire—also in New York—which took the lives of 146 women garment workers. The strike also struck a responsive chord with women of wealth, bringing them to the suffrage fore and energizing the national Women's Trade Union League (WTUL), which employed Frances Squire Potter of the University of Minnesota in 1910 as a lecturer to broadcast the news that the day of the working woman had arrived. For one brief moment during the Progressive period, the conventional wisdom that women of different classes could not share common concerns seemed to dissipate.[27]

The principal agent of this change was the WTUL, which had a branch in Minnesota. Although the American Federation of Labor generally supported suffrage and women's rights, organized labor was not free from sexism within its own ranks. Consequently, women had to look elsewhere for training as labor leaders and for help with their roles in existing unions and in forming new unions. The WTUL served that purpose, among others. The participation of working women in the suffrage movement, whether through the WTUL or other groups, clearly advanced the cause of enfranchisement. The horrible working conditions endured by women provided a powerful argument for the ballot; their involvement diluted the traditional opposition of working-class men; and these women could reach sectors over which mainline suffragists had no particular influence. However different their reasons for wanting the vote might have been, women of diverse classes came together for a common cause.[28]

Minnesota suffragists were not, as a rule, offended that male immigrants, Negroes, and American Indians (if they were found "competent"—they did not become full voting citizens until 1924) had the right to vote while women did not. If they were, they held their peace. When Ojibway women on a reservation near Bemidji were given the right to vote in tribal council in 1917, an MWSA news bulletin cheered: "It is no longer 'Lo, the poor Indian' but 'Lo, the free Indian.' . . . How about it, White Men of Minnesota?"[29]

One reason for nativistic restraint was the fact that, according to the 1905 state census, more than two-thirds of Minnesota's inhabitants had at least one foreign-born parent. Because there were so many immigrants, Minnesotans were generally sympathetic to them and respectful of their power. As for minorities, they were scarcely noticed in the political milieu of Minnesota. There were few blacks in the state (only 0.4 percent of the population), and the 8,761 Indians were not regarded as a political force. The issue for Minnesota women who were suffragists was not with the haves but with their own status as have-nots.[30]

Other circumstances in Minnesota tended to mitigate against expressions of nativism and racism. By 1915 women in all of the Scandinavian countries except Sweden had won the vote, as the Minnesota Scandinavian Woman Suffrage Association was quick to point out to legislators and congressmen from that region. Nanny Jaeger noted how proud they were "of the suffrage record" of their brothers in the old countries, and they did not "expect to be disappointed in their American kinsmen." Given the reality of women voters in the old countries and the fact that Clara Ueland was married to a Norwegian immigrant, she could correctly observe that objections to women voting did not sound good in Minnesota. Also, many of the suffrage supporters in the Minnesota legislature represented districts with large foreign-born populations. Those groups tending to favor suffrage were the Norwegians and, to a lesser extent, the Swedes. The Germans, by contrast, who usually opposed any anti-liquor proposals and progressive measures in general, tended to resist suffrage. Like the liquor interests, they feared that the addition of women voters would result in legislative restrictions on alcohol.[31]

Contrary to the rhetoric employed by some suffragists in other states, Ueland had made a point of saying on January 26, 1915, in testimony before the Committee on Elections in the Minnesota Senate, "We have no fear of the foreign-born voter as have the 'antis.'" On another occasion she remarked that while this democratic experiment that is the United States invited "people of all colors, religions, and nations to become citizens. . . . The only ones they are afraid of are the women." Suffragists in Minnesota made an effort to include women of different religions, ethnic groups, and classes in their meetings. An MWSA organizer urged a woman in Ironton to generate petition activity among the Finns in her community, particularly because women in Finland had won the vote in 1906. Ueland wrote to a woman in Mankato urging her to make a special effort—as suffragists were doing in Winona—to involve Polish, German, and Catholic women. The last generation of Minnesota suffragists began to count among their leaders immigrant women such as Fanny Fligelman Brin of

Romania and Eleanore H. Bresky of Russia and trade unionists such as Myrtle A. Cain.[32]

Still, there was an occasional lapse in the Minnesota suffragists' tolerant views. In her speech before the 1916 MWSA convention, Ueland lamented that suffragists were forced to seek votes from every man of every race and color and with every degree of intelligence. In a communication from Ueland and others urging delegates to the national party conventions to "give the women a man's chance" and include a suffrage plank in their platforms, they asserted that it was difficult for women to get what is "so freely given to all of our sons, our foreign-born citizens and the Indians." However, these were rare and relatively mild invectives.[33]

Even though political reality dictated that the broader the representation, the more effective the advocacy, the Minnesota suffragists' attempt to reach rural women was less ardent and less successful. Women in greater Minnesota had been energized less by suffrage organizations than by the Nonpartisan League (NPL), although the lack of commitment to suffrage from rural constituencies may have had much to do with the practical hurdles of farm chores and distance from towns. Organized in 1915 by angry farmers of North Dakota who blamed their economic ills on the domination of the St. Paul–Minneapolis troika of banking, milling, and railroads, the NPL soon branched out into Minnesota and other states. Its basic message included calls for a better marketing system, better prices for farm products, and more representation in government. A few women became important leaders in the organization, but most functioned at the local level, doing the traditional scut work of arranging the rallies, picnics, and meetings essential to the organization's maintenance.[34]

Officers of the Women's NPL Club at Princeton, Minnesota

At its first postwar convention in St. Paul in December 1918, the NPL adopted a statement calling for "the complete enfranchisement of women, equal opportunities with men, and equal pay for equal services." But like many such resolutions, this one was more rhetorical than real. The league's newspaper, the *Nonpartisan Leader*, did provide women with a new means of communication through its "Farm Woman's Page," and in March 1919 women were encouraged to organize women's Nonpartisan clubs. Articles and letters from readers, however, suggested that all was not equal on the home front or, for that matter, within the league. Suffrage never received any particular notice from the *Leader* until after the fact, when farm wives were exhorted to vote for candidates endorsed by the league. Even then the league was not keen to see the arrival of suffrage for fear that while women in cities and towns would vote, country women would be too busy or would find other excuses not to go to the polls.[35]

The *Farmer's Wife*, a commercial venture of the Webb Publishing Company in St. Paul, also paid little heed to suffrage until July 1919, after the U.S. Senate had finally passed the Susan B. Anthony amendment: "After all its ups and downs, *equal suffrage is here* and will make its own way. . . . Most women and some men believe that it will prove a friend indeed. Let us watch and wait."[36]

The Minnesota suffragists' concern for a broad spectrum of representation extended to what was then commonly perceived as radical ideologies. When the Socialist Woman's Suffrage Club applied for admission as an auxiliary organization in April 1914, the MWSA board welcomed it with great enthusiasm. In an earlier meeting that same month (before Ueland became president), the executive board passed a resolution opposing certain clauses of the pending Burnett immigration bill, which would have permitted secret hearings and denied admission to the U.S. to those purportedly advocating the destruction of property. The resolution said in part that the bill was "contrary to American traditions and precedent and subversive of liberty and freedom of speech."[37]

Debates over means and goals plagued and prolonged the suffrage movement throughout the United States. Although the movement backed away from its abolitionist origins, it welcomed working-class women. In Minnesota, where minorities were few, the retreat was less profound. Upper- and middle-class suffragists probably found it easier to cross class lines to approach and involve foreign-born or first-generation working women because many immigrants (except for newer arrivals on the Iron Range) had similar northern European ancestries. Altogether, tensions relating to the various constituencies were relatively rare in Minnesota's suffrage movement. Most troublesome to suffragists in Minnesota was the opposition of otherwise like-minded women, the persistent antagonism of the liquor interests, and sometimes even disagreements among the suffragists themselves.

Ueland, as leader of the Minnesota movement, liked the opportunity to engage in a "quiet battle based on intelligence and discussion" with those of opposing views. The "battle," while generally intelligent, was not always quiet, but—whatever the decibels—her engagement made a difference. She was as respectful a listener as she was an effective speaker and an efficient field commander. Clara's decision in the first month of her presidency in 1914 to become MWSA's chief lobbyist proved to be a wise one. It enabled her to employ all her considerable diplomatic skills at a time when the debate over suffrage intensified and the votes became cliff-hangers. As her friends recognized and her foes grudgingly acknowledged, Ueland's unparalleled abilities in the legislative halls were severely tested, beginning with the 1915 session of the Minnesota legislature.[38]

6

THE FRUSTRATIONS OF LEADERSHIP

*It is not self respecting for women to submit to
discrimination without a protest.*
CLARA UELAND, MARCH 1916

 After 1900 Minnesota's male voters never had an
opportunity to register their opinions on votes for
women because one suffrage amendment after
another failed to pass the legislative screen. Indeed,
between 1898 and 1907, no suffrage bills emerged
from legislative committees in either the House or the Senate.[1]

In later years, however, moments of hope began to arise on
the suffrage horizon. A proposed suffrage amendment to the state
constitution was defeated in the Senate by only two votes in
1911. It was defeated again by only three votes in 1913, a particularly keen disappointment since the House had approved an
amendment for the first time by the requisite two-thirds majority.
"A shrill scream of triumph from the gallery, followed by subdued
cheers and the clapping of a thousand pairs of hands" greeted
that affirmation, reported the *Minneapolis Journal*. But the opposition remained persistent. Representative Ellis J. Westlake of
Minneapolis wanted to know whether women wanted to be
policemen, members of the legislature, speaker of the house, or
governor; "he for one did not want to see women compelled to

stand in line at the polls and be contaminated by contact with politics."[2]

Clara Ueland's debut as leader of the suffrage forces in the 1915 legislative session proved to be a baptism by fire. As a result of a law passed two years before, this was Minnesota's first nonpartisan legislature. Governor Winfield S. Hammond, the only Democrat to serve between 1909 and 1931, proposed a number of reforms in his inaugural address, but legislators, intent on the issue of regulating liquor sales through county option, gave other matters slight attention. They were, however, attentive to suffrage—the suffragists made sure of that, and so did their opponents.[3]

Early in the session, on January 26, the Senate Elections Committee held a hearing on Ole Sageng's bill to submit the question of woman suffrage to the male voters of Minnesota. The suffragists and the antis were identified by their botanical badges: yellow jonquils for the supporters and red roses for the opponents. The hearing had to be held in the Senate chamber, where the galleries overflowed with spectators. Lieutenant Governor Joseph A. A. Burnquist gave up his chair to a fashionably gowned suffragist, who shared it with a diminutive page. People who could not find space in the chamber milled about the corridors. Sixteen speakers, fourteen of them women, waged a rhetorical war. The principals for the proponents included Clara Ueland, Mary Gray Peck, Bessie L. Scovell of the Minnesota Women's Christian Temperance Union, and Emily Noyes. David F. Swenson of the University of Minnesota and Julius F. Emme, a socialist leader, took major responsibility for rebutting the arguments of the opponents, who were led by Lavinia Gilfillan. Other antis included Minnie Bronson, secretary of the National Association Opposed to Woman Suffrage, Kittie E. Sullivan (whose husband, George H. Sullivan, was a prominent state senator from Stillwater), Florence Carpenter, and Isabel Stringer, head of the St. Paul Association Opposed to Woman Suffrage.

In its front-page report on the following day, the *St. Paul Pioneer Press* quoted Ueland's remarks refuting the argument that women have more influence because they are not enfranchised: "It is utter nonsense; it is foolish. What greater influence can any body of persons have than the possession of the right to vote? In all the Scandinavian countries, from whence we derive such a large proportion of our immigrants, the women have equal rights with the men."

Isabel Stringer protested that the vote was a franchise that women did not need and that "the majority do not want," insisting that "the wage earning woman does not want to vote; the woman who does is she of the idle hands." Gilfillan noted that while the antis were opposed to women in politics, they were *not* against women in public life. Politics was the province of men, good works the province of women.[4]

The debate had an important result: The testimony convinced listeners that women were able to articulate their convictions and hold their own in a debate. As a consequence, the men of the legislature acquired a new respect for the intellectual abilities of women on both sides of the question.

On Thursday, March 4, 1915, the Sageng suffrage bill was scheduled for a vote by the full Senate. Hundreds of women crowded the galleries and corridors of the state Capitol to hear the three-hour debate. Senatorial protagonists were identified by yellow jonquils or red roses supplied by the women who watched and waited. Bouquets from both sides decorated the desk of Lieutenant Governor Burnquist, who presided. Clara Ueland was flanked by Emily Bright, Maud Stockwell, and Ethel Hurd; Lavinia Gilfillan by Ella Pennington and Florence Carpenter. Despite the strong feelings on both sides, the suffs and the antis were attentive and not disruptive. Enjoying the attention, legislators spoke their minds.[5]

Francis A. Duxbury from Caledonia in Houston County was showered with roses by the opposition, who regarded him as one of their best speakers. They were not disappointed. In the words of one newspaper account, he "turned a crashing battery upon invaders who'd break up the home." The same report said of George Sullivan that "The Big Fellow of the Senate, volleyed and thundered before the threatened fireside." He invoked the familiar bromide that the ballot was not a privilege, and said that no one would want Minnesota to suffer the consequences that had befallen Mormon Utah, implying that the ballot had either been cause or consequence (it was not entirely clear) of polygamy. Republican Senator Frank E. Putnam of Blue Earth in Faribault County led the supporters, asserting that suffrage for women was inevitable, a cause that would not die down: "I believe the cause a just one, one which should appeal to all fair men." It was one of the best speeches of his career. Others speaking on behalf of suffrage included John W. Andrews of Mankato, William S. Dwinnell of Minneapolis, and Richard Jones, the twenty-eight-year-old "boy" senator from Duluth. Ole Sageng, seeking to shorten the debate, chose not to speak.[6]

When the debate was at last finished, Lieutenant Governor Burnquist called for the vote. Several weary senators who had absented themselves had to be rounded up. As one after another returned to the tense chamber, the vote inched up to thirty-three to thirty-three. Only one senator still had not voted. On the fifth call of his name and not knowing that his "no" vote would be a tiebreaker, Alexander S. Campbell of Austin in Mower County returned to the Senate chamber and cast the decisive vote against suffrage. Once more suffrage had gone down to defeat in the Senate, but the margin had been reduced to one vote. The next day, a disappointed but undaunted Clara Ueland announced plans for a vigorous two-year campaign to win legislative approval in 1917.[7]

On March 23, near the end of the session, Adolph S. Larson of Sandstone in Pine County introduced a bill in the House to give women the right to vote in presidential elections. Because it came so late, legislative procedure required a two-thirds vote to place the bill on special orders for consideration. On April 6—the date set for consideration—Albert F. Pratt of Anoka moved to table the measure, and the motion prevailed. Eight days later Knud Wefald of Hawley in Clay County moved that the rule be suspended, and while that motion fell short of the required two-thirds, it did poll an encouraging and substantial majority of seventy-five to forty-eight.[8]

That belated stratagem to achieve presidential suffrage would become the main emphasis of the MWSA in future sessions. Carrie Chapman Catt's master plan stipulated that states like Minnesota, whose constitutions were difficult to amend, should try the presidential-electoral route. The MWSA validated Catt's strategy at its 1916 state convention by focusing on the right to vote for presidential electors, but the effort to get something more comprehensive than the existing school and library suffrage legislation remained stalemated in Minnesota until 1919. "The Minnesota electorate," wrote historian William Watts Folwell, "restrained by immemorial tradition and by the surviving conviction that Sacred Scripture excluded women from independent public activities, was slow to welcome the innovation."[9]

Another piece of legislative business eventually turned organized labor from its long-held position of suffrage support to opposition. In February 1915 the legislature passed a county-option law, and by July male voters in forty-three counties had chosen to ban the saloon; only eight counties voted to the contrary. The liquor interests, fearing that suffrage would make matters even worse, renewed their campaign of opposition. It was probably no coincidence that when a routine resolution on behalf of suffrage was introduced on the floor of the convention of the Minnesota Federation of Labor in Winona in that same month, it surprisingly failed to pass. Mary D. McFadden, who, speaking on behalf of the MWSA, had earlier thanked the convention for its progressive stand on the citizenship of women, must have been embarrassed to learn later of its reversal.[10]

The federation's withdrawal of support for suffrage represented a dramatic turnabout. In an attempt to explain the federation's action, the *Labor Review* of Minneapolis published a long editorial expressing surprise that suffragists had supported the move to make Hennepin County dry and had thereby thrown "thousands of toilers out of employment." "Men who see the poorhouse staring them in the face," the editorial asserted, "can hardly be expected to express friendship for those who show favor to the people who are hastening them into poverty." It concluded by expressing the hope that organized labor and the working girl in the suffrage movement (if not the "professional and well-to-do women") would recognize that organized labor is "the best friend" the suffragists ever had.[11]

An unsigned article in the *New Republic* of March 11, 1916, commenting on this development in Minnesota, laid the blame squarely on the liquor interests, which were "attempting to induce trade unionism to repudiate a principle for which it has fought and bled during the last twenty-five years." A few months later at a labor union convention in Hibbing, suffrage was the burning topic of debate. Frank Hoffman, a Minneapolis delegate from the bartenders union, rose to his feet to say, "I am not going to say that I deny to the women of this country the right to vote. But I do deny their right to vote the men of the beverage industry out of employment. It is a well known fact that where women vote, the states go dry." Although his statement was greeted with applause by some delegates, others took issue with him. "You want liberty for yourselves and political slavery for the women. . . . I am always against the dry movement, and always for woman suffrage," said a Minneapolis carpenter. A St. Paul machinist observed, "You men who fear the loss of your jobs through suffrage are so badly mistaken[,] I am sorry for you." The motion to table the suffrage resolution carried by a vote of 127 to 87. Obviously, a majority of delegates continued to be alarmed by the victories of the drys in county-option votes, attributing those wins, if not to the votes of women, then to their influence.[12]

Actually, there is no mention of any county-option action on the part of the Equal Suffrage Association of Minneapolis (the predecessor of the Hennepin County Woman Suffrage Association) except a decision made on October 2, 1915, not to join in the county-option parade as a body, although individuals could participate if they wished. That decision was shaped by the response of the association's advisory board, which probably included wets as well as drys. A few days later, the 1915 MWSA state convention passed two resolutions, one recommending that every effort be made to rid communities of the saloon ("this intolerable burden") and another deploring the Federation of Labor's action in repudiating suffrage, "the principle of democracy." It seems fair to conclude, however, that while there may have been strong professions of support for the county option, suffragists were not exactly in the front lines of the battle over that issue.[13]

The *Minneapolis Labor Review* carried no news of any discussion of suffrage at its 1917 convention in Faribault, but the suffrage drama resumed the next year in Virginia on the Iron Range. Once again a resolution favoring woman suffrage was reported favorably by the resolutions committee. "A hush fell over the convention" and once more Frank Hoffman of the Minneapolis bartenders union rose to speak. On this occasion, however, impressed by the work of women in the early months of the world war, he retracted his earlier opposition, moving the adoption of the resolution "by a unanimous rising vote." The convention recovered from its surprise and, with only three opposed, restored the Minnesota Federation of Labor's support for suffrage.[14]

Despite the repercussions on suffrage from the liquor-legislation battles, Clara Ueland and her colleagues turned their attention to organizing for legislative success in 1917. Where the first generation of suffragists had relied on informal networks of supporters and personal appeals to legislators, the second generation's system of organizing by political district introduced a different and persuasive dimension. Legislators had been able to excuse their negative votes by claiming that their districts were against suffrage. After 1915, however, the new system of working within political districts made it easier for suffragists to mobilize opinion and to communicate voter opinion to senators and representatives. Legislators were sometimes surprised to discover that constituents were singing a different tune.[15]

The goal of the MWSA's new system was to have a committee in each urban precinct or rural township that reported upward, through the political chain of command, to ward or county committees and then through legislative district committees to state and national committees. This whole process was implemented by experienced national organizers, by the Minnesota women whom they trained, and by the MWSA office, which alerted districts when legislators needed to be pressured. The work went on throughout the year, with the state office constantly calling on local suffrage units for petitions, letters, and visits to their elected officials serving in both the Minnesota legislature and the U.S. Congress. Clara Ueland monitored the entire process, and her persuasive pleas for cooperation and action had positive results.[16]

National organizers seldom stayed for extended periods in one place; they moved from one critical campaign to another. In a letter approving the loan of Rene Stevens to South Dakota for a state referendum campaign, Ueland wrote, "I feel that well directed efforts in South Dakota are not lost even though we are sure that the vote will go against us. All educational work is to the good, especially when it is in territory next [to] our own." On another occasion Maria McMahon left Minnesota for four months in 1916 to help with the Iowa campaign. Ueland, by way of reinforcing her belief that success in neighboring states could have a spillover effect, lent her presence as well, making a speech in Dubuque on behalf of the referendum. She sent another "Dear Suffragist" bulletin, asking, "What Can You Do to Help Iowa?" and urging her readers to write to male voters they knew and ask for their support, to go to Iowa and work, and to send money. "To help Iowa now means to help ourselves." She added, "Within three months the women of the great provinces to the north of us, Manitoba, Alberta, and Saskatchewan, have become enfranchised. Let us do our best to help Iowa to step into line in this splendid march of freedom." She was reluctant, however, to let Stevens return that same year to faraway New York for another state referendum campaign, writing, "It comes to me as a good deal of a blow that New York wants to take you away from us." Finally persuaded by Catt's confidence that there was a good chance for success, Ueland acquiesced. The training of local women to take on more responsibility became a critical component of the job of these experienced organizers, compensating in part for their occasional absences.[17]

The women who worked as professional organizers in Minnesota were genuinely fond of Clara Ueland. When Stevens's proposed move to New York was being considered, she wrote Ueland that there were no "finer, fairer, more sympathetically understanding or generous [people] than those directing and financing the suffrage cause in Minnesota" and that Minnesota had first claim on her allegiance. Following an MWSA automobile journey by Ueland and some of her associates in the summer of 1916 to Pipestone—they stopped at eleven other communities along the way—Stevens, who had stayed behind to solidify the enthusiasm into organization, wrote to Ethel D. Briggs, the office secretary: "Tell Mrs. Ueland that many have tried to convey to me their sense of her sweet wisdom or wise sweetness or that intangible something which makes her her and affects so satisfyingly those upon whom her presence is shed." The following exchange between Ueland and Bertha C. Moller, one of several Minnesota women who had been trained by national organizers, demonstrated both wit and affection. From Ueland, asking Moller to come on the state board: "I have a fine idea. I only hope it will seem as brilliant to you as it does to me." Moller's reply: "The more I think of it the less brilliant I think your idea is. . . . If you're not sorry you asked me, I'm yours for the job—heart, soul and gizzard." Moller continued as an organizer and took on the responsibilities of MWSA's work with the Minnesota congressional delegation—a stepping-stone to a distinguished career with the National Woman's Party.[18]

The organizers spent long, often lonely, and frustrating hours during their travels around the state. Bertha Moller's letters in the summer of 1917 suggested the range of emotions she experienced. "I rather despair in Wadena, not a live suffragist in the place." She was more encouraged by the response in Park Rapids, and one Sunday earned $2.60 in contributions and $8.50 in pledges from the citizens of Wilton. Moller felt that she had struck gold the previous October in Crookston, where there "may be a suffrage organization completed here this week. . . . Hip! Hip! Hurrah!! . . . I'm going to a Sunday evening vaude-ville for a change." In a February 1917 letter to Maria McMahon, who had trained her, Moller wrote: "Please rejoice with me. I organized a Wilkin County Suffrage Organization this evening with 16 charter members! Thurs. I go to Campbell & Friday to Fergus Falls. Mon. I will be ready to go to Elbow Lake."[19]

Ueland was also active on the organizational trail. In January 1916, for example, her visit to Albert Lea prompted a local newspaper article praising her "splendid plea for suffrage." In May she undertook the major responsibility of organizing and presiding at a Mississippi Valley Conference of suffragists in Minneapolis, a conference that, in one observer's view, rivaled a national convention in numbers and activity. From 1912 to 1917 the Mississippi Valley Conference, formed by a group of Chicago women, provided suffragists from the Middle West the same benefit of coming together that eastern women enjoyed at national conventions in Washington, D.C. On the night of the banquet in Minneapolis, Josephine Simpson, the toastmistress, introduced Ueland as the "Moses who is leading Minnesota to the promised land." Six hundred guests endured fifteen speakers, including George Edgar Vincent, president of the University of Minnesota, Carrie Chapman Catt, Alice Ames Winter, and Nellie McClung, a Canadian suffrage leader and close friend of Ueland. They and others finished speaking their respective pieces well past midnight, a clear sign that suffragists possessed both verve and stamina.[20]

The other important work for suffragists in 1916 was the effort to persuade delegates to the forthcoming national conven-tions of the Republican and Democratic parties to add suffrage planks to their platforms. During this period of women's struggle for recognition the United States was enjoying a surface afflu-ence even while working men and women protested their condi-tions of work with 2,093 strikes and lockouts. Suffragists and labor unions were joined by other causes making their voices heard: birth control, advancement for African Americans, progressive education, Prohibition, and socialism. War in Europe seemed far away, and President Woodrow Wilson, who had kept the nation out of war, would be reelected with the expectation that he would continue to do so.[21]

In preparing for the political party conventions, Ueland wrote to MWSA members throughout the state asking for their help. One young woman became a personal favorite of Ueland's over the years. Anna Dickie Olesen of Cloquet, who was active in the Federation of Women's Clubs, had been appointed in 1914 by Governor Adolph Eberhart as a delegate to the International Child Welfare Congress in Washington, D.C. Ueland would say of Olesen, who had been one of the speakers at the Mississippi Valley Conference, that she was "a remarkably good little orator . . . a real spell binder." With some prescience, Ueland predicted: "Mrs. Olesen is one of our finest young women. She herself is an orator and has really considerable gifts as a speaker and promises to fill a very important place in the development of Minnesota." On May 20 Ueland asked Olesen to talk with both Republican and Democratic delegates from communities in the eighth congressional district (except Duluth) and press for their support of the suffrage plank. She wrote similar letters to numbers of prominent men—not being one to discriminate—asking for their help also in this endeavor. She received numerous promises of help from Republicans and Democrats alike.[22]

As Ueland prepared to go to Chicago for the Republican National Convention, she wrote to her daughter, Anne, on June 4, 1916, "Just today I have a feeling that suffrage will be defeated in Iowa tomorrow, that the Republicans will not adopt the Suffrage Plank. . . . But then, I always have an interesting family to fall back on." She was right on all counts. Iowa voted against the amendment, and Chicago was a traumatic experience. On June 7 the winds came up and the rains came down, but thousands of suffragists were determined to march, and march they did. The *Chicago Tribune* applauded their courage: "What a disgrace that ten thousand women, among them the best in the country, should be compelled to expose themselves . . . in order to prove to their own sons and brothers that they are entitled to justice and political freedom!"[23]

For a moment it looked as if their determination had yielded results. The Republicans seemed to be about to adopt a suffrage plank. Listening to Senator Henry Cabot Lodge of Massachusetts read the plank, the women broke into cheers. They stopped when they heard the last deflating phrase, which gave to each state the authority to settle this question. The plank was a hoax, a joke. Clara wrote to Andreas, "I have been uncertain about going to St. Louis but Mrs. Catt thinks I should go, as the Democrats are likely to do the same thing."[24]

The Democrats convened in St. Louis on June 14. At Davenport, Iowa, Clara climbed aboard the steamboat carrying the contingent of Minnesota suffragists down the Mississippi River from the Twin Cities to the convention. In St. Louis the tactics were different. Rather than marching, the suffragists formed a silent twelve-block "Golden Lane" of five thousand women through which the delegates had to pass to get from their hotels to the convention hall. (The one potential silence breaker who "may not be able to restrain his emotions," noted the *Minneapolis Morning Tribune*, was "Suffrage plank," the donkey.) The gold was provided by the yellow hats and sashes that the women wore and the umbrellas they carried (as protection from the sun, not the rain). The climax at the end of the lane was a tableau of Liberty posed on a pedestal with eighteen figures, standing tall, who represented the suffrage states. The figures depicting the other states were garbed in black, bowed and beaten.[25]

Ueland and Josephine Simpson impressed crowds of delegates with their arguments for suffrage as they talked from autos and an improvised bandstand in front of the headquarters hotel. Despite their efforts, the outcome was no different: The Democrats, like the Republicans, favored leaving suffrage decisions up to the states. Since the party had traditionally stood for states' rights, however, the decision was more expected and seemed less heartbreaking than that of the Republicans.[26]

At the end of Clara Ueland's second year as MWSA president, Sophie G. Kenyon, the first vice-president, commented that "with a competent president like Mrs. Ueland, always well and ready to preside, the president's work does not fall on the vice-president's shoulders." But Ueland's presidency was not spared occasional criticisms. Eugenia Farmer assumed the prerogatives of an elder suffragist and complained in two letters to Ueland and in one to Maud Stockwell about the dues structure and about insufficient notice for a meeting. She also charged that the board—which had spent most of the previous year at war with NAWSA over the Shafroth-Palmer amendment—was not adequately reflecting NAWSA policies and positions. In response to these allegations, Ethel Hurd, once again coming to Ueland's defense, pointed out that Ueland's friends were providing the most significant financial support for the organization and that, in many respects, she was the ideal president, "able, generous, untiring, devoted, able to give almost unlimited time to our cause." Hurd wrote Farmer that her three letters "make me sick at heart and discouraged" and said of Ueland that "she is doing a work for Minnesota never before equalled or found possible. This being *true*, I ask are we going to make her way unpleasant and trying, by unjust criticism?"[27]

In her report to the MWSA annual convention on December 4, 1916, Clara Ueland gave her own sense of the highs and lows of her second year in office: "In these days our emotions swing . . . from exasperation and resentment at the immobility of those who stand for things as they are, at the opposition of incorporated selfishness, to splendid enthusiasm, as in high moments we sense the romance of being a part of a mighty world movement that is rapidly culminating." The achievements of 1916 had been made possible by the increasing numbers of women "who have given devoted service to our cause. . . . In all of these activities," Ueland concluded, "we are learning team work—a valuable lesson. . . . Our work is growing enormously—with this growth comes greater confusion, greater complexity, but we cannot stop to perfect details—we must go on undertaking greater tasks."[28]

One of those greater tasks arose during the 1917 legislative session. Although the MWSA and the Minnesota Equal Franchise League had settled their earlier differences three years before, the league for some unexplainable reason played the role of spoiler—again acting independently—and requested the introduction of a state-amendment bill that, if passed, would refer the question to voters and require for passage a majority of all voting in the election—not just of those voting on the amendment. A. M. Peterson of Coleraine in Itasca County did so in the House on January 12, 1917. By this time, because the temper of the legislature had changed, few representatives wanted to go on record as being *against* suffrage—with the House tending to be more sympathetic than the Senate. In an atmosphere of confusion, members of both houses began to respond to the accumulation of suffrage endorsements solicited by the MWSA. As these expressions of support came pouring in from an improbable assortment of organizations, including dairymen, letter carriers, spiritualists, laundry owners, educators, editors, Universalists, as well as those supporting good roads and local option, legislators were prepared to vote for any form of suffrage legislation.[29]

But between 1900 (after the constitutional-amending process had been made more difficult) and 1916, thirty-four amendments had been rejected by voters and only ten approved. That reality, coupled with Carrie Catt's proposal that Minnesota be one of the states seeking presidential suffrage, underlay the MWSA's opposition to the amendment route. Suffrage leaders in the organization also feared that rejection by male voters at the polls would jeopardize any probability of subsequent success by legislative action. Given the difficulty of passing controversial constitutional amendments, the antis gleefully pounced on the proposed amendment as a means of forestalling suffrage—to the dismay of the MWSA but not of the Equal Franchise League, whose leaders may have felt that the temper of the times would have resulted in a favorable vote on the amendment at the polls.[30]

In any event, even though the Minnesota association announced that it would support the amendment if it passed,
Ueland and her associates regarded its introduction as a mis-
guided effort that had to be averted. The House easily passed the
bill on February 21 by the sizable majority of eighty-five to forty-
one. Meanwhile, the Senate was considering the MWSA-supported
bill (introduced on January 17, just five days after the league's bill,
by senators Ole Sageng and Frank Putnam) enabling women to
vote in presidential elections. That bill, falling victim to still-
pervasive platitudes (a vote in the hands of women would destroy
the home; suffrage would lead to governmental takeovers by
women and the nation would be forever ruined; only unattractive
and unmarried women wanted the vote), went down to defeat on
March 29 by thirty-five to thirty-one votes.[31]

Given the House passage of the state-amendment proposal
and the Senate defeat of the presidential-election measure, the
MWSA found itself in the paradoxical position of attempting to
persuade the Senate to defeat the House bill. It was not an easy
position to explain. There were letters to be written, petitions to
be circulated, and literature to be distributed. Yellow jonquils
and red roses were to be seen everywhere as the controversy
heated up and the suffs and the antis paraded the legislative
halls. Jeannette Rankin of Montana, the nation's recently elected first congresswoman, stopped in Minnesota on her way to
Washington, D.C., and was invited to address both houses of the
legislature. Although Rankin spoke for suffrage, she diplomati-
cally avoided the subject of the pending state-amendment bill.
But the irreconcilables remained unreconciled. Senator George
Sullivan predictably inquired, "Does anybody think that the dear
little woman who came here this morning . . . is any better off
than if she had a couple of children and a husband to manage?"
Senator Frank H. Peterson of Moorhead moaned, "The home is
not what it used to be."[32]

In the state Capitol the efforts of the MWSA finally paid off.
The Senate Elections Committee recommended that the equal
suffrage amendment passed by the House be indefinitely post-

poned, and the Senate—overriding the objection of league president Theresa Peyton—obliged with a vote of forty-nine to fourteen. Ueland and her supporters could savor a tactical victory,
but no more. Because the Senate had defeated the presidential-
electors bill, there was no point in advancing the similar bill that
had been introduced in the House on January 19.[33]

The MWSA succeeded in defeating the amendment bill in
part because of the struggle still being waged over Prohibition,
which was the next goal of the antisaloon forces after the passage of county option. The prospect of a Prohibition amendment and a suffrage amendment appearing on the ballot in the
same year could put both in jeopardy. Although supporters of
Prohibition in the legislature tended to be prosuffrage as well,
they feared that a suffrage amendment would endanger the
Prohibition amendment, turning out more voters who would
vote against both. Their strategy was to get Prohibition enacted
and then pursue suffrage. Legislators who opposed Prohibition,
fearing that women voters would support it, were against suffrage in any form at any time. The failure of a state-suffrage
amendment could also work against eventual ratification of a

Women demonstrating for Prohibition, Madison, Minnesota, about 1917

federal amendment on the theory that legislators—to be consistent—would feel compelled to vote against a federal amendment if their constituents had rejected the state one.

The suffragists' most enduring friend among the legislators in those years was Ole Sageng, a farmer from the small community of Dalton in western Minnesota. First elected as a representative in 1900, he was subsequently elected to the Senate in 1906 and served there until his first

Senator Ole Sageng

retirement in 1922; he was elected again in 1950 at the age of seventy-eight, serving for another term. According to legend, this dirt farmer—the legislature's only avowed Populist—was converted in 1909 from "placid approval" of woman suffrage to active interest by the comment of a fellow senator that "if the men of Minnesota continued to take that complacent view . . . we would wake up some day and find the Turkish women voting before the Minnesotans." This statement startled Sageng out of his lethargy, and, according to an MWSA report, "he consented to espouse our cause, with most vigorous earnestness, and has done so ever since."[34]

Sageng was the chief author of a succession of Senate suffrage bills and often lent his rhetoric from public platforms. Speaking in the Minneapolis auditorium after the great parade of May 1914, he revealed his views on the similar obligations of men and women to home and family:

It is true, a woman's highest duty is to her home but that is just as true of man. . . . But what an absolutely crazy and absurd proposition would it not be to argue that he would be a better father and a more loyal husband if we take away from him the right to vote. Why[,] American manhood would resent as an insult any serious mention of such a theory. And, friends, it is just as much an insult to American womanhood to say that giving her the full right of citizenship will interfere with a mother's devotion to her children and her home.

Moreover, women deserved the right to vote because they shared with men the accountabilities and obligations in the public sphere. They had "a common accountability to the civil and criminal laws of society; a common obligation to give of their substance for the support of the government; a common duty to suffer and sacrifice in times of war. . . . In a word, women should vote because theirs with men is a common humanity and a common human destiny."[35]

The suffragists understandably adored him, and others respected him for his integrity and abilities, if not always for his political ideals. Disagreements over tactics and strategies occasionally diluted but never diminished the suffragists' affection for the senator from Dalton. In the aftermath of a discussion with Sageng, Ueland was accused by a friend of looking tired. "Well, perhaps I am a little," she admitted. And then—probably with a wry smile—she confessed, "It is not easy to work with a Norwegian at both ends of the journey."[36]

Just eight days after the defeat of the MWSA's presidential-electors bill, Americans faced the sober reality of their nation's entry into war. World War I provided women with an opportunity to display their loyalty and versatility, and their participation brought growing sympathy and support to the suffrage cause. But before war came to the nation, another kind of war confronted the suffrage movement.

7

THE SUFFRAGE
HOUSE DIVIDED

I am being imprisoned . . . not because I
obstructed traffic, but because I pointed out to
President Wilson . . . that he is obstructing the
progress of justice and democracy.

ALICE PAUL, OCTOBER 1917

 In 1913, the same year that Clara Ueland organized
the Equal Suffrage Association of Minneapolis,
momentous events were occurring on the national
front. A new generation of young women, eager to
redirect and energize the suffrage movement,
stepped forward to take responsibility for the somnolent congressional campaign of the National American Woman Suffrage
Association. The two leaders of this revival met in a London police station, where they had been taken after their arrest for
demonstrating with the English suffragettes. Alice Paul had gone
to England for graduate studies in 1907 and—though never
before politically active—was soon swept up in the British suffrage movement. Lucy Burns had been in Germany for three
years doing graduate work in foreign languages. When she went
to Oxford in 1909 to begin work on her doctorate, she was capti-
vated by the radical wing of the suffrage movement. Shifting
gears, she moved from scholarship to activism and worked for

three years as an organizer for the Women's Social and Political Union.[1]

The movement in England was divided between two factions. The moderate "constitutionalists" (brought together as the National Union of Women's Suffrage Societies in 1897) used orthodox political behavior to advance their interests. The militant "suffragettes" (organized in 1903 as the Women's Social and Political Union) waged guerrilla warfare through arson, sabotage, hunger strikes, the mutilation of artworks, and physical assaults on cabinet ministers. In 1909 Alice Paul and a friend, Amelia Brown, had entered London's Guild Hall disguised as charwomen and disrupted a banquet at which Prime Minister Herbert Asquith was to speak. Brown broke an undecorated pane in a stained-glass window in a banquet room wall, and she and Paul shouted, "Votes for women!" through the broken pane. Because they refused to pay the fines that the court imposed at their trial, they were imprisoned for one month with hard labor and were forcibly fed. Their bold action typified the movement, and so did the punishment imposed by the authorities, whose penalties often exceeded the seriousness of the crime.[2]

Led by Emmeline Pankhurst, a lifelong social activist, and her two talented daughters, Christabel and E. Sylvia, more than a thousand members of this militant vanguard were imprisoned, many experienced the agonies of forced feeding, and some even died. Despite these grim consequences, many American women were inspired by the vitality of the Pankhurst wing of the British suffrage movement. Harriot Stanton Blatch (Elizabeth Cady Stanton's daughter) had lived in England for twenty years, and five years after she returned to the United States in 1902, she formed the Equality League of Self-Supporting Women (later called the Women's Political Union) to "introduce new methods of propaganda and to guide the suffrage ship into political channels." While Blatch and other American suffragists—impatient with the lack of progress—were receptive to alternative strategies, the existing suffrage establishment led by Anna Howard

Shaw seemed content to do things the old-fashioned way, relying primarily on the arsenals of persuasion and perseverance.[3]

As a youthful veteran of this radical movement, Alice Paul returned to the United States in 1909 convinced that the tactics of the militant suffragettes gave verve and visibility to the movement. She was determined to bring that same activism to the American suffrage scene. In 1912 Paul and Brown went to the NAWSA convention in Philadelphia with a proposal for more militant tactics, but it was rejected out of hand by Shaw and most other NAWSA leaders. Jane Addams, however, had listened sympathetically to the unorthodox plan of these two enthusiastic young volunteers and advised them to revise their ideas to make them more acceptable. With a more moderate proposal in hand, Addams then successfully championed their cause. When Anna Howard Shaw subsequently gave Paul the responsibility for directing the moribund Congressional Committee, she could not possibly have known that this appointment would lead to a schism in the women's movement that would last for years to come.[4]

Alice Paul recruited to the committee a coterie of mostly young women who were equally impatient with traditional forms of political advocacy. She added Crystal Eastman (a New Yorker then living in Wisconsin), an attorney and the wife of Wallace Benedict, who later became Brenda Ueland's first husband; Mary Ritter Beard of New York, a scholar and soldier for the cause; and Dora Kelley Lewis of Philadelphia, who possessed both enthusiasm and money. In less than two months' time these women orchestrated a major suffrage parade that captured the nation's attention and overshadowed the inauguration of Woodrow Wilson on March 4, 1913. On the eve of his big day, the newly elected president arrived in Washington, D.C., only to be greeted at the station by a sparse group of supporters. When Wilson asked where the people were, he was told, "Over on the Avenue watching the Suffrage Parade." The oddity of women marching in the streets drew enormous crowds. More than half a million people lined the streets of Pennsylvania

Avenue and watched some eight thousand marchers, twenty-six floats, and ten bands. Not all of the bystanders were suffrage supporters, however, and when hecklers began to close in on the participants, the police stood idly by (and the superintendent of police lost his job as a result). More than two hundred persons were treated for minor injuries at local hospitals, and a cavalry unit of the U.S. Army, poised on the parade's periphery, had to be activated to contain the conflict.[5]

Just a month later—on the opening day of the new Congress—delegates appeared on the doorsteps of the Capitol bringing petitions from men and women in their districts in support of the Susan B. Anthony amendment. In that same month Paul formed the Congressional Union for Woman Suffrage and—with the assent of Anna Howard Shaw—proposed that it be regarded as a distinct entity with the authority to raise money and recruit volunteers. The Congressional Union described itself as "a group of women in all parts of the country who have joined together to secure the passage of an Amendment to the United States Constitution enfranchising women." Although the union had Anna Howard Shaw's blessing, this tactic was not entirely congruent with NAWSA's strategy, which included pursuing the vote through the adoption of state suffrage amendments as well. There were three elements in the Congressional Union's strategic plan: to pin responsibility on the party in power for the failure of Congress to act favorably on the Anthony amendment; to generate publicity; and to make protest the vehicle for influencing public opinion.[6]

Paul's new group, believing that collaboration was essential, had no reason to go its own way and petitioned to become a NAWSA auxiliary. But Laura Clay of Kentucky, chairman of NAWSA's membership committee, defined the group as a national organization (it was in fact forming state branches) and, therefore, ineligible to be an auxiliary. The issue proved to be irreconcilable, and in February 1914 the two suffrage organizations—agreeing to disagree—parted company.[7]

What was left of this increasingly fragile relationship was shattered later that year when the union decided to campaign against Democratic candidates—regardless of their position on suffrage—in the congressional elections of the twelve states where women were enfranchised. Because Democrats (the southern Democrats being the most intransigent) had controlled the Congress for four years, the Congressional Union held them responsible for impeding the progress of the Anthony amendment. In NAWSA's view, such a strategy overlooked the political reality that a two-thirds favorable vote in both houses required the support of both Democrats and Republicans and, ultimately, the approval of representatives of both parties in three-fourths of the states. It also jeopardized the movement's long-standing policy of nonpartisanship.[8]

Alice Paul and her close cohort Lucy Burns were undeterred and sent organizers to campaign against Democratic candidates in the nine western states where women were enfranchised. By 1915 the union was seeking organizational support in every state as a means of increasing constituent pressure on congressional delegations. At this point the leadership of the Minnesota suffrage association saw no reason not to cooperate fully with Paul's efforts. Given the difficulty of amending Minnesota's constitution, it was not surprising to find Clara Ueland's name first on a list of women calling a meeting in Minneapolis on June 28 to organize the Minnesota branch of the Congressional Union—a group dedicated to the passage of a federal amendment.[9]

Jane Bliss Potter, who chaired the MWSA's congressional committee, was elected to serve as head of the new branch. Other officers were Emily Bright, former MWSA president; Gertrude Hunter, founder of the Wage Earner's League of Minneapolis; and Anna E. R. ("Anita") Furness, granddaughter of former Governor Alexander Ramsey and a St. Paul activist. Directors included such well-known suffrage supporters as Sarah Colvin of St. Paul, who was appointed chairman of the state finance committee, and Sophie Kenyon, also of St. Paul, who took charge of promoting subscriptions to *The Suffragist*, the union's official publication. Elsa Ueland, elected organizer in charge of arranging deputations to Minnesota congressmen (as lobbying visits were called), was described in *The Suffragist* as a "graduate of the University of Minnesota and ... well known throughout the state."[10]

In a matter of weeks Clara Ueland declared that the "campaign of the Congressional Union ... is receiving more publicity and apparently making a deeper impression than anything that has been done in the state." The deputations were much more elaborate than their predecessors and were embellished by public meetings. On July 23 the deputation scheduled to call on Representative Carl C. Van Dyke of the fourth congressional district convened in St. Paul's Rice Park. A procession to Van Dyke's office was organized by Elsa Ueland and Josephine Schain, accompanied by a band, and led by Potter and Clara Ueland. After gaining Van Dyke's promise to give suffrage serious attention, the participants returned to the park and made stump speeches on behalf of the cause to anyone within hearing distance.[11]

In the third congressional district, Elsa Ueland organized a street meeting the night before their visit with Representative Charles R. Davis in St. Peter. On the morning of the next day— July 30—a distinguished delegation marched to the congressman's office. It included a professor from Gustavus Adolphus College, a woman member of the school board, and a well-known teacher. Ueland presented the delegation, all of whom urged Davis to vote for the federal amendment. He expressed his appreciation for their interest and said that he would make his decision, not on the basis of numbers—"Whole nations have gone wrong on majorities"—but on what would be in the best interest of the country. That night Elsa Ueland, Josephine Schain, and Gertrude Hunter held a large street meeting in Le Sueur and, at a Saturday afternoon meeting in a Le Sueur home, recruited union members. Schain then went on to Fairmont, and Ueland and Hunter headed for Shakopee, where they organized another street meeting. The energy and enthusiasm generated by these young organizers was, as Clara Ueland observed, producing results.[12]

By the end of October, Minnesota's Congressional Union could report to the national headquarters that organizers—with the full cooperation of the MWSA—had recruited significant numbers of women to call on their congressmen, urging their support for the federal amendment. Most of the state's ten representatives promised to vote for the amendment. Sydney Anderson of the first district did so because the increasing number of women in the workplace indicated to him that there was no longer a "special 'sphere'" for women. Charles A. Lindbergh, Sr., from the sixth district said he regarded the ballot as a fundamental right for both men and women. Two of the three uncommitted representatives promised to give the matter friendly consideration, and the third had not yet been seen because he was away.[13]

The NAWSA convened a special conference of suffrage leaders in Chicago in June 1915 to discuss congressional strategies and to placate those among them who were entirely opposed to the competing Shafroth-Palmer amendment. This amendment, introduced by prosuffrage Democrats as a means of defusing the objections of their southern colleagues, was viewed by many suffragists as an entirely meaningless and futile gesture. Yet NAWSA's only strategy in evidence in Chicago seemed to be an attack on the Congressional Union and a defense of Shafroth-Palmer.

Delegates from Minnesota, and other states as well, were incensed that substantive sessions were set aside and replaced by vitriol and negativism. Rebelling against these diatribes by national leaders against the Congressional Union, Jane Potter of St. Paul moved a resolution to drop the Shafroth-Palmer amendment in favor of the Susan B. Anthony amendment, but it was defeated fifty-seven to twenty-one. Another resolution supporting the Anthony amendment was passed unanimously, but the NAWSA position supporting two federal amendments remained difficult to explain and to implement. MWSA vicepresident Sophie Kenyon wrote home to the association's exec-

utive board, "Your president [Ueland] made the finest and most
fundamental speech against the Shafroth amendment of any
that was made. . . . Minnesota can be proud of her president."
Emily Bright's detailed and critical report to the October MWSA
convention in St. Paul on the Chicago conference highlighted
the dissatisfaction of the Minnesota contingent with both the
conference process and the outcome. In response, the convention adopted a motion expressing its support for the Anthony
amendment and no other.[14]

Gratified by the union's performance in Minnesota, Clara
Ueland testified on its behalf at a congressional hearing for the
federal amendment on December 16, 1915, before the House
Judiciary Committee. Her testimony spoke to the difficulty of
achieving suffrage via the state-amendment route, documenting
that assertion by pointing out that only one of eleven proposed
amendments had passed in the previous Minnesota election, and
it had been unopposed.[15]

In the midst of this controversy over strategy, Clara elaborat-
ed on her views about the union in a letter to Nellie Sawyer
Clark, president of the Michigan Equal Suffrage Association.
After explaining that Jane Potter was serving in the dual capaci-
ty of MWSA congressional chairman and state chairman of the
Congressional Union, she commented:

> With their usual vigor, the Congressional Union has sent some
> young women into the state into places where there has never been
> a suffrage meeting. (Minnesota is an untouched field compara-
> tively.) They have got up labor meetings and street meetings in ten
> counties and over fifteen towns, and they have arranged deputa-
> tions to three of our Congressmen—all in about two weeks. . . .
> They are Minnesota girls—one of them is my own daughter—and
> their work has certainly reinforced our own. . . . I see no reason
> why we should not work together in this way indefinitely.

Ueland confessed to some concern that the Congressional
Union might once again embark on an anti-Democratic campaign in the 1916 elections. She was not, however, apprehen-

sive—as some apparently were—about any confusion resulting from two suffrage organizations working the same territory: "We think it is better to have some confusion, and active work going on, than to have everything perfectly simple and clear and *nothing being done*." Ueland also expressed her disenchantment with NAWSA's support of the Shafroth-Palmer amendment and characterized the Chicago conference, which was "apparently called for the purpose of discussing and condemning the Congressional Union," as "a sad waste of energy and enthusiasm." She did not regard the union as militant: "It is not militant to send delegations to Congressmen and the President. Those are entirely legitimate methods." She believed that the union had successfully "advanced the sentiment for the Federal Amendment" and saw no reason not to continue the fruitful collaboration between the two suffrage organizations in Minnesota.[16]

The letter illustrates Ueland's view that there was no virtue in quarrels that dissipated or misdirected energy that might otherwise be put to good use. It also revealed her pragmatic approach. While she appreciated the need to be well organized, she also did not want process to stand in the way of purpose. She once urged a group of Minneapolis Young Women's Christian Association domestic-science graduates not to be too systematic, "for this can dry out beauty, freedom, affection, sudden fine new ideas." So, in Minnesota, the relationships between the two suffrage groups remained cordial and harmonious, with many of the same women sharing leadership responsibilities in both organizations.[17]

The MWSA's own organizational work was stimulated by the Union's organizers and by Ueland's enthusiasm for their efforts. On July 13, 1916, Clara wrote to Rene Stevens in Pipestone, "We have to meet a very marked attitude of criticism of our organization work from the Congressional Union members on our Board and outside of it, so we want to put up the best showing possible." The "triumphant [auto] tour" from the Twin Cities to Pipestone was probably a product of that request for "the best showing." Ueland was determined to take a leaf from the union's notebook and adopt the same more visible tactics (street meet-

ings and parades) "to attract attention and gain supporters."
More important, the Congressional Union had provided a single
focus (the federal suffrage amendment) and a format (deputations to members of Congress) that showed more promise for
success than had NAWSA's earlier more diffused efforts. This approach energized suffrage supporters and gave them a sense of
practical accomplishment. Minnesota suffragists derived satisfaction from their ventures into the political minefields of pressure
and persuasion at the national level, and, although they were
relieved of the responsibility to work for a state constitutional
amendment, the push of the MWSA for the right to vote in presidential elections also required action at the state legislature.[18]

The strategy put in place by Carrie Chapman Catt in
September 1916 differed from that of her predecessors and also
from Alice Paul's. Catt's plan was based on the premise that an
increase in the number of suffrage states—by whatever means,
including state amendments and bills to enfranchise women in
presidential elections—was essential to compel senators and
representatives to support the effort on behalf of the federal
amendment. That proved to be the case. Despite their tactical
differences, Catt also attempted—without success—to make
common cause with the union and to persuade Paul to drop the
strategy of opposing all Democratic candidates. Success in Congress would be achieved only with the votes of both Democrats
and Republicans, Catt reasoned.[19]

In June 1916, just three months before Catt unveiled her
"Winning Plan," the Congressional Union established the National Woman's Party (NWP) to represent women of the eleven
full-suffrage states and Illinois (where women could vote for
presidential electors) and to campaign against President Wilson and the Democratic congressional candidates. While
Wilson narrowly won the election, he carried all but Oregon
and Illinois out of the twelve states, and the Democratic party
retained its strength in Congress. In January 1917, frustrated by
its lack of success in the November elections and the continuing
recalcitrance of the president, the NWP began picketing the

White House. By this time the strategies of the two suffrage organizations could not have been more different: The NWP intended to influence Wilson by militant behavior, NAWSA by persuasive argument.[20]

Woodrow Wilson's evolution from opposition to support of woman suffrage would prove to be agonizingly deliberate. Initially he pleaded ignorance: It was a matter to which he said he had given no thought and on which he had no opinion. (In fact, as a young southerner of nineteen years, he had declared that universal suffrage lay "at the foundation of every evil in this country.") In 1914 he begged off using the political argument of states' rights. In 1915 he voted for suffrage in his adopted home state of New Jersey but refused to go any farther. He permitted the principle of suffrage to be included in the Democratic party platform of 1916 and addressed NAWSA's convention of that year, but he remained uncommitted to the Anthony amendment and made no move to persuade Congress. The emerging role of women in World War I, the NWP pickets, pressures from his own daughters, and Catt's rhetoric about democracy beginning at home began to break down Wilson's resistance. It would be another year, however, before he would capitulate and actively work on behalf of the passage of the federal amendment in Congress.[21]

In January 1917 Alice Paul, who had remained head of the Congressional Union, invited state leaders of the union and the NWP to meet to determine their course of action in the event of war. The decision was an easy one—to continue the work to secure political liberty for women. (Unlike Catt, Paul made no appeal for NWP members to participate in the war effort.) The real purpose, however, was to accomplish a merger of the two organizations, and that was easily achieved. Paul took over the reins of leadership from Anne Martin, who had served as chair of the party. Martin, who had also been an American participant in the English suffragette crusade, became vice-chairman and legislative chairman. (In 1918 she would become the first woman to run for the U.S. Senate.)[22]

With the amalgamation, the NWP took on the aura of a single-issue organization with political muscle. While the purpose—passage of the Anthony amendment—remained unchanged, picketing became the major focus. In April, when the special war session of Congress convened, the pickets extended their watch from the White House to the nation's Capitol. The picketing at a time of national war hysteria brought to an end any efforts to maintain at least the surface cordiality that had once existed between the suffrage association and the former Congressional Union. Though some women in the suffrage movement were attracted to the flamboyance and symbolism of the picketing, others felt that it was counterproductive. Clara Ueland was one of the latter, and so was Carrie Catt, who privately and publicly appealed to Alice Paul to withdraw the pickets. In Catt's view, they constituted an insult to the president and an annoyance to the Congress. Some congressmen had threatened never to vote for suffrage as long as there were pickets. But Catt's plea to Paul fell on deaf ears, and the NWP continued the practice.[23]

One incident in particular stirred emotions on both sides. Members of a delegation from the Provisional Government of Russia were greeted at the White House gates on June 20, 1916, by an NWP picket banner reading in part: "We women of America tell you that America is not a democracy. Twenty million women are denied the right to vote. President Wilson is the chief opponent of their national enfranchisement." A crowd gathered, and one man tore down the banner. Undeterred, the pickets continued their protest until two days later, when Burns and a colleague were the first of 168 NWP members to be arrested and imprisoned.[24]

As a consequence of disagreements and confrontational incidents, suffragists began to choose up sides, and leaders made no further attempts to mediate these strategic differences. In the summer of 1917, when pickets engaged in hunger strikes by way of protesting their arrest and imprisonment, they were forcibly fed. Former Congressman Charles A. Lindbergh, Sr., of Minnesota charged Wilson with responsibility for denying the pickets' constitutional right to petition the government. He argued that a word from the president would ensure their safety and fair treatment under the law: "Yet you did not speak the word, you did not exercise the authority, and you withheld the nod." Lindbergh's letter, which appeared in newspapers across the country, fueled public controversy over the practice of picketing and the treatment of the picketers.[25]

Clara Ueland learned that other influential Minnesotans disapproved of picketing when she solicited their help in a petition campaign directed at U.S. Senator Frank B. Kellogg, whose position on the federal suffrage amendment remained undefined. She became convinced that growing resentment of the picketing and the partisan tactics of the NWP was endangering prospects for success. In a formal break with the policies of that organization, Ueland and other MWSA activists issued a statement in late June 1917 regretting "that a body of suffragists should employ a policy tending to embarrass and discredit our government in the present difficult situation" (referring to U.S. entry into the war that April). As might be expected, Minnesota suffragists were not of one mind, and the issue of picketing provoked dissension during the November 1917 state convention. MWSA members favoring the tactics of the NWP recruited a dark-horse presidential candidate from the state board—Genevieve I. Schwarg of Dodge Center—who agreed to represent picketing supporters. The convention experienced an especially contentious moment when Angie V. Kingsley of the Minnesota Scandinavian Woman Suffrage Association took the floor to denounce "the kaiserism of the state association leaders." The audience hissed. Clara Ueland retorted, "I shall have to ask you to stop speaking" and banged her gavel. Most of the Scandinavian association's delegation left the floor. After the close of the convention, former MWSA fieldworker and board member Bertha Moller (whose relatives were prominent political figures in Sweden) announced her intention to join the NWP and to volunteer as a picketer, and she did. The impressive accomplishments of the MWSA under Ueland's leadership, however, overwhelmed the relatively mild rebellion, with the convention casting 181 votes for Ueland and 53 votes for Schwarg.[26]

After surviving that challenge to her presidency, Ueland summed up the conflict in letters to several correspondents: "We made it quite clear, although having some rather disagreeable experiences, that we do not stand for the picketing." More positively she had stated on an earlier occasion: "We believe that the enfranchisement of women should be brought about by orderly and constructive methods and we are united in the endeavor to bring about, by such methods, the early political liberation of the women of America." Nevertheless, a few defections and the announced opposition of the MWSA to picketing tactics did not diminish the effectiveness of the NWP, the loyalty of most of its members, or the presence of many Minnesota women in leadership positions. Bertha Moller became Minnesota's representative on the NWP board of directors and one of the faithful picketers. She was arrested eleven times and jailed twice. Clara Ueland's good friend Emily Bright was a member of the party's national advisory council, and Jane Potter, who had been succeeded by Sarah Colvin of St. Paul as president of the Minnesota branch, served as a vice-chairman of the council. Minnesota's suffragists, who once supported both organizations, now came to a parting of the ways as their differences made further collaboration impossible.[27]

Like other states, Minnesota found itself with a divided suffrage house. Yet the disagreements over tactics and strategies worked to the advantage of the cause. The pragmatic forces of two million members led nationally by Carrie Catt produced a steady increase in the number of states in which women could vote, with a consequent impact on congressional attitudes. The flamboyant protests of the much smaller but more disciplined group of sixty thousand supporters led by Alice Paul riveted the nation's attention and began to influence public opinion. No matter that the reactions to picketing were often negative—the tactic heightened awareness and transformed it into a groundswell of favorable opinion. President Wilson's earlier indifference had been converted into support by the protests of the NWP, careful political nourishing by NAWSA, and a growing sense that there ought to be some sort of reward and recognition for the significant work of women during World War I.[28]

8

THE RELUCTANT WARRIORS

We are in a world transformed. . . . Nothing
is more certain than that the women
of America should at this time give of their best
to the common danger.

CLARA UELAND, NOVEMBER 1917

 In November 1916 Woodrow Wilson won a second term as president in an election so close that his opponent, Charles Evans Hughes, reportedly went to bed that night in the belief that he had been the winner. Wilson's promise to keep the nation out of war gave him the slim margin of victory, a margin that may have been established by the support of women voters in suffrage states. The choice had not been an easy one for women, who were torn between Hughes's advocacy of suffrage and Wilson's stated aversion to war, coupled with his conversion to the principal tenets of progressivism.[1]

After the 1916 elections, Clara Ueland, having taken charge of the effort to win over the members of Minnesota's congressional delegation, prepared a frank analysis of eleven of the twelve men representing the North Star State with the convening of the Sixty-fourth Congress in 1917. Her descriptions, intended for internal use, were pithy and candid:

- Senator Frank B. Kellogg, . . . St. Paul, Republican. New member. Able lawyer; said by people who do not like him to be bound up by "the interests." His wife is a suffragist and he seems to be open minded and friendly. Asks for literature. *I* believe he will favor suffrage but needs education on the subject of the Federal amendment.
- *1st District.* Sidney [Sydney] Anderson, Lanesboro, . . . Republican. Re-elected. Has always been for suffrage but has not answered recent letters.
- *2nd District.* Franklin F. Ellsworth, Mankato. Republican. Re-elected. Last reports are that he is friendly and will vote for the amendment. His district is not strong for suffrage and we do not feel very sure of him.
- *3rd District.* Charles R. Davis, St. Peter. Republican. Re-elected. Non-committal. I believe he is not unfriendly, but his district is largely German and anti-suffrage.
- *4th District.* Charles [Carl] C. VanDyke [*sic*], St. Paul. Democrat. Re-elected. He makes no public statement but we believe he is friendly. Is a labor man and the Minnesota Federation has gone against suffrage the last two annual meetings.
- *5th District.* Ernest Lundeen, . . . Minneapolis. Republican. New member. Out-spoken for suffrage on all occasions. Not considered a man of weight, but thoroughly committed for suffrage and the Federal amendment.
- *6th District.* Harold Knutson. St. Cloud, Republican. New member. Refuses to discuss suffrage. Unwilling to be interviewed. Formerly as editor of a newspaper, he printed articles in favor. His district is unfavorable as a whole.
- *7th District.* Andrew Volstead, Granite Falls. Republican. Re-elected. For suffrage and the Federal amendment.
- *8th District.* Clarence Miller, Duluth, Republican. Re-elected. Claims he is a suffragist but non-committal or opposed to Federal amendment.
- *9th District.* Halvor Steenerson, Crookston. Republican. Re-elected. For suffrage and the Federal amendment.

- *10th District.* Thomas D. Schall, . . . Minneapolis. Progressive. Re-elected. Claims to be a suffragist. Non-committal on Federal amendment. Poor material. He is blind and was elected over a first class man by the emotional appeal of oratorical ability of himself and wife in connection with his infirmity. We have no idea he will ever do anything besides look out for his own interests. (*Nov. 25th:* A delegation called upon Mr. Schall yesterday and he assured the women again and again that he will support the Federal amendment, altho he does not believe we will ever get it ratified because of the southern states.)[2]

There was no need for her to describe Senator Knute Nelson's position, which was firmly and enduringly prosuffrage. "He had been so long our friend," noted NAWSA's chief lobbyist, "that he was always greatly vexed when anyone spoke or wrote to him as if he needed to be converted or stirred to activity. . . . But I could not keep the Woman's Party quiet, and once, when some of them had been especially annoying, he got into such a peppery temper that he threatened to line up with our opponents if he weren't left alone." Although it was not clear how the twelve men would actually vote in the Congress—given the temper of their districts and the contrary opinions of some of their constituents—most appeared to support suffrage.[3]

Two months after Ueland wrote her assessment, the war in Europe loomed even larger on the American horizon. Woodrow Wilson's promise that the United States would not intervene faded when the Germans decided on February 1, 1917, to resume unrestricted submarine warfare in the Atlantic Ocean. They sank four armed American merchant ships in March. On April 2, 1917, the first day of the first session of the Sixty-fifth Congress, Wilson delivered a memorable message declaring—in response to what he called the German war against mankind and against all nations—that "the world must be made safe for democracy." He maintained that while "it is a fearful thing to lead this great peaceful people into war . . . the right is more precious than the peace." The Senate passed the war resolution by a vote of 82 to 6 on April 4; the next day the House voted for the declaration of war by a margin of 373 to 50.[4]

Many newspaper accounts had Jeannette Rankin of Montana, the nation's first congresswoman, breaking down and sobbing in the aftermath of her vote against going to war, but NAWSA lobbyist Maud Wood Park, who was in the gallery that day, saw no evidence of tears. "I was entirely out of sympathy with Miss Rankin's point of view, and I feared that she was lessening the chances of the suffrage amendment; but I knew that her vote was heroic." Like Rankin and Park, many suffrage leaders were divided over the war issue. Catt, who had collaborated with Jane Addams in founding the Woman's Peace Party in January 1915, was also a reluctant warrior; she believed, however, that winning votes in Congress and in state legislatures for the suffrage amendment would be largely determined by women's efforts in support of the war. Rejecting the British model of putting the issue on hold for the duration, Catt viewed the extension of suffrage to women as totally compatible with those efforts. Her reasoning would prove to be correct.[5]

Many Minnesotans, both men and women, expressed their reluctance about going to war. As late as March 31, three thousand people attended a mass rally in the St. Paul Auditorium and applauded the speakers who opposed the war. The *St. Paul Daily News* called the meeting "a patriotic protest." Minnesotans were not of one mind, however, and others began to move from endorsing neutrality to supporting intervention. Business elites and the Twin Cities newspapers shifted gears and approved the president's decision to go to war. The dominant German and Scandinavian populations continued to express reservations— the Germans not wanting to engage in conflict with people from their homeland, and the Scandinavians (in particular the Swedes) hesitant about abandoning their tradition of neutrality. Old-time Populists and their successors in the Nonpartisan League expressed a radical bias that also gave voice to anti-British and pro-German sentiments. Former Congressman Charles Lindbergh's conviction that "lords of special privilege" had conspired

Members of the Minnesota Commission of Public Safety, about 1918

to push America into war for profit was a point of view that res-
onated with Minnesota radicals. Concerned about this antiwar
sentiment, Minnesota's power elite took steps to dampen dissent
and inspire loyalty.[6]

The most nefarious of these steps was the establishment on
April 16 of the Minnesota Commission of Public Safety, a state
agency whose pursuit of patriotism resulted in the persecution—
and in some cases the prosecution—not only of German
Americans and their institutions but also of other ethnic groups
and of any activity that smacked of economic radicalism. More
benign but no less intense were efforts to bolster the patriotism of
young people and the expansion of programs to "Americanize"
recent immigrants by teaching them English, the history and
traditions of the United States, and citizenship.[7]

On the national scene, NAWSA reviewed its policies in light of
the country's entry into the war and decided to press forward on
two fronts: to continue the campaign for suffrage and to demonstrate the patriotism of the suffragists by involving them in a

variety of activities supporting the war. As early as February 1917, Carrie Chapman Catt had asked the state associations for their views as to the appropriate course of action in case the nation went to war. The Minnesota response was consistent with the position later adopted by the national association—maintain the organization and render patriotic assistance.[8]

Clara Ueland had worried about the prospect of war. She viewed the boys involved in drills on the Minneapolis parade grounds as victims of spurious excitement—like children playing with fire. Referring to the incident that had provoked another American intervention in Mexico (Pancho Villa, the Mexican bandit and revolutionary, and his band had killed eighteen American engineers), Clara wrote in her journal in 1916, "I am afraid our Mexican relations have been muddled and bungled and that perhaps our country is to blame, and anyway back of it all, our commercial interests are eager for intervening, a military foot in the door." With the decision to go to war against Germany, Andreas found himself a reluctant supporter and Clara confessed to suffering from irresolution. She was opposed in principle to war and applauded Rankin's vote against the war resolution in the House, noting that she, "like every other member of Congress, voted according to her conscience." Suffrage opponent Florence Carpenter voiced a contrary view on the congresswoman's vote: "Why take a man's place unless one is willing to stand up and be counted like a man? Why take a man's place, anyway?"[9]

Opinions in the Ueland family produced a great correspondence debate. Anne Ueland Taylor, then overseas with her husband, Kenneth Taylor, wrote that she was against war in every way but did not think she believed in absolute nonresistance. She and Kenneth had been bound for Germany, where he had planned to pursue postgraduate studies in medicine, but they lingered in England when the war broke out. Kenneth soon joined the staff of the American Hospital in Paris and then served with the American forces when the United States entered the war. As the war continued, Anne became enraged at the killing and the folly and the phony rhetoric. "Perhaps I am all wrong. But my melancholy is very deep," she wrote to her family in August 1917. "I wish I were home. I wish I were twenty, and making wet tracks on the hall floor after a swim!"[10]

From her post as president of Carson College for Orphan Girls in Flourtown, Pennsylvania, Elsa wrote a long letter to family members in which she asserted that arguments advanced on behalf of war to make the world "safe for democracy" were both hypocritical and illogical; she was unambiguously against the decision to go to war. From Harvard Law School Sigurd replied, "I don't approve of trying to crush Germany but I think we should show her that even her own . . . desperation does not warrant any interference with our decent and fundamental rights as neutrals, that is, with the *lives* of American citizens." Brenda, living in Philadelphia and New York and in the first year of marriage, reflected on the wide gamut of feelings she saw among Americans. She was horrified that people caught up in an anti-German fever would support the burning of books by German authors and the banning of music by German composers. She was equally appalled by the "simpering debutantes" who pinned white feathers for cowardice on the lapels of young men who had not yet enlisted. Other people (the senior Uelands among them) were "searching in despair for an answer to the nightmare." With "agonizing conscientiousness," Andreas and Clara had studied and sifted the facts about the war. Brenda believed that despite her parents' reservations, "they came to the conclusion, with the greatest sorrow, that it had to be; it was the only course; the President could not do otherwise."[11]

Sigurd, who had earlier been rejected as being too young for officer's training, began to have second thoughts. Writing to his father in April 1917, he explained that he did not feel "the slightest obligation to volunteer," because he was "out of sympathy with the Administration's war aims and peace views." Later, in another letter to Andreas, he acknowledged, "If I am at fault for not being in the military service it is a mental, not a moral weakness. One thing I have learned from you, Father, is to have the highest contempt for the opinion of the multitude, and of the orthodox, when that opinion is contrary to my own." He went on to express his appreciation for his parents' willingness to let him make his own decisions: "We have not been in perfect agreement about the best method of ending the war, nor the best method of carrying it on, but you both have wanted me to act for myself. . . . I hope to have an opportunity to demonstrate to Mr. and Mrs. Ueland, how tremendously I appreciate them, but I probably won't have, and they will have to take it on faith."[12]

Arnulf, who was graduated from the University of Minnesota in 1917, was commissioned a first lieutenant in the artillery in 1918. Soon after his marriage to Louise Nippert of St. Paul, Arnulf went to France, where he was assigned to a large-gun unit for the few remaining months of the war. The two youngest Ueland sons were less affected by the war. As a freshman at the University of Minnesota in 1917, Rolf was making a name for himself as a track star with the coach proclaiming him the "find" of the season. Torvald, who was still in high school, often accompanied Andreas on vacation trips when Clara was too busy to go along.[13]

Despite their misgivings about the war, Minnesota's suffrage activists moved quickly to keep their vow to aid the war effort. They made front-page news with their offers to replace men in industry, to increase food production through intensive gardening, to help the American Red Cross, and to plan educational programs for foreign-born women of the state. Governor J. A. A. Burnquist appointed Clara Ueland to the Food Production and Conservation Committee of the Minnesota Commission of Public Safety, a group charged with the responsibility of educating Minnesotans about means of helping maintain the nation's food supply during the war. Clara was the only woman serving on the labor subcommittee, which was expected to determine the demands of summer farmwork and to recruit young women and girls to meet those needs. In addition, she, Lavinia Gilfillan, and other women were assigned to the home-economics committee, which

Red Cross canteen workers, St. Paul, 1917–18: Mrs. W. Coons, Florence Davenport, Dorothy Thompson, Alice Warren, Eleanor Kinkead, Evelyn F. Lightner.

Mrs. S. D. Flagg operating a bandage roller and Miss Mary Morrissey at a knitting machine, Navy League headquarters, St. Paul, 1917. The poster at right says, "Gee!! I wish I were a man / I'd join the Navy."

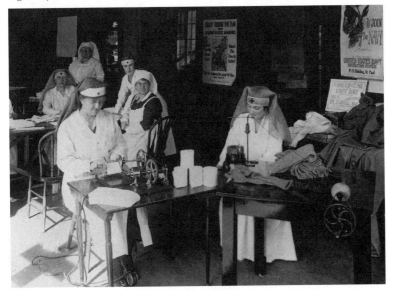

would provide information to homemakers about food conservation and substitute ingredients.[14]

Several suffrage clubs in Minnesota opened Red Cross headquarters, which turned out thousands of finished articles of clothing for the armed forces. The state association raised nearly three thousand dollars to support the first of the Women's Oversea Hospitals in France. This fifty-bed hospital near the front, staffed entirely by women—from plumbers and chauffeurs to doctors and nurses—was NAWSA's "War Baby" and had been accepted by the French government after the United States declined the offer because women were not eligible to serve in its medical reserve corps. Before war's end, NAWSA had raised funds to support two additional hospitals, one tending to the medical needs of three thousand refugees in southern France and the other for the exclusive treatment of gas victims.[15]

Meanwhile, the suffrage work went on. Dr. Effie McCollum Jones, a Universalist minister from Iowa and an exceptionally able suffrage organizer, worked in Minnesota in May 1917. During her stay she spoke to approximately 10,000 women and men in twenty-six towns (only four had been previously organized), recruited 670 new members, and raised $480. Jones's visit to Hastings, where the MWSA had been founded thirty-six years before, turned out to be a disaster. Clara M. Heckrich, the association's office secretary, wrote Bertha Moller an account of the meeting, describing it as "very poor. The lady who introduced her to the small gathering of 30 would get up and object to her calling for enrollments or pledges. (Wouldn't that frost you?)" Jones collected only $2.25 from nine women, but her experience in Red Wing, which she viewed as new territory, turned out to be more satisfactory. She reached nearly five hundred people, speaking six times in two days. Nonetheless, the financial contributions from seven women and one man totaled only $9. After leaving Minnesota, Effie Jones wrote to Heckrich, saying, "There never was a nicer group to work with than the Minnesota women. . . . Mrs. Ueland, Mrs. Moller and you were all three a source of joy and satisfaction to me."[16]

That same spring the national association expressed its concern to state workers about the suffrage positions of two representatives from Minnesota—Clarence Miller of the eighth district and Davis of the third district. Three organizers—Bertha Moller, Anna Dickie Olesen, and Maria McMahon—were put to work in the eighth district in northern Minnesota almost immediately. Following an April MWSA conference in Duluth, Ueland and organizer Florence Monahan followed their path across the eighth district, going to Eveleth and to Virginia, where they each had successful meetings. Monahan was sent again into the eighth district, Bertha Moller to the sixth, and then both would converge on the third district "if that seemed wise." By August the organizers had formed suffrage committees in all the Iron Range towns, where they worked with a ethnic mix of unknown suffrage views—not only among the Finns, whose homeland was the first European nation to enfranchise women, but among the Slavs and southern Europeans who also populated those communities. They boldly started a petition campaign to collect citizen signatures, which was scheduled to be completed in September. Although the association had launched an intensive campaign to win the vote of Miller, who was a Republican in the progressive mode, the effort was tempered with the usual Ueland tact and diplomacy. She cautioned Monahan on July 23 not to antagonize Miller's friends or to appear in any way unpatriotic: "There never was a time in which we have to be to such an extent 'as wise as serpents and as harmless as doves.' I am sure a word to the wise is sufficient."[17]

Ueland's correspondence with fellow workers and with local suffrage groups was never-ending. In one of her "Dear Suffragist" letters in June, she wrote, "Since we have been drawn into a war in order 'to make the world safe for democracy' it behooves us to do what we can for the cause which will make our Country a democracy in fact as well as in name." She kept in touch with key suffrage leaders throughout the state, imploring them to step up their efforts for the current petition campaign, to obtain resolutions of support from conferences (such as farmers' institutes) and from meetings of temperance societies and other organizations, to persuade newspaper editors to write favorable editorials, and to present their representatives with those petitions, resolutions, and editorials. Occasionally Ueland's efforts met with success. Bertha Moller wrote of the reaction of Lavinia A. Gemmell of Brainerd, chairman of a district committee of the Minnesota Commission of Public Safety, who commented that while she had been slightly opposed to suffrage, Ueland's talk and personality "showed her what a natural thing it would be for women to vote," and she was now convinced of the "real need of the ballot for women."[18]

Under Clara Ueland's leadership the MWSA was gaining momentum in the drive to generate support for woman suffrage at both the state and national levels. Corresponding secretary Maud Stockwell documented the organization's progress in her report covering the thirteen-month period ending in October 1917: The executive board had met fourteen times; the office mail was counted at more than fourteen thousand letters; and as many as six organizers, working periodically, had gone to congressional districts where representatives were doubtful, enlisting both men and women to sign petitions of support. Meanwhile "our indefatigable president" had been responsible for directing efforts at the state legislature in 1917, where (as previously noted) a presidential suffrage bill, supported by the MWSA, lost by a scant four votes in the Senate, and a state suffrage amendment bill passed by the House—but opposed by the MWSA—was finally defeated in the Senate. (In April the executive board, with a standing ovation, had approved a motion extending a vote of thanks to the president for her "sacrificial devotion to the cause as chairman of the Legislative Committee.") Even though the MWSA-supported presidential suffrage bill failed, Ueland had successfully orchestrated a legislative strategy of the greatest complexity.[19]

"Civilization is in a state of flux," Ueland said in her address to the two hundred delegates at the 1917 MWSA convention in the St. Paul Hotel. "The path of suffrage partakes of the uncertainty of the time. . . . We must do double duty." She prepared a persuasive statement refuting the arguments of those who thought a vote on suffrage should be deferred until war's end. Every woman, it said, should engage in activities to help "her country in its time of trouble" by giving time to Red Cross work and to food conservation. But "great causes" like education and social work "must not be allowed to languish." Referring to suffrage progress in countries like Canada (where Ontario joined the western provinces in enfranchising women in February 1917) and in England (where in March 1917 the House of Commons, by a ratio of seven to one, had approved "full emancipation") Ueland wrote, "Like these women, American suffragists can stand by their country and at the same time give allegiance to the cause of suffrage." The statement was reproduced in NAWSA's publication the *Woman Citizen*.[20]

Ueland's own work for the cause in the preceding year had been unstinting. She had given about a dozen speeches in the state, most of them outside the Twin Cities. She attended the National Council meeting in Washington, D.C., and had presided at the Mississippi Valley Conference in Columbus, Ohio, in May. In keeping with her role on the Food Production and Conservation Committee, her annual garden party on August 15 (which raised eight hundred dollars) had featured foods raised and cooked by suffragists, a University of Minnesota School of Agriculture demonstration of canning and drying of foods, as well as samples of "war bread" containing substitutes for wheat. There were other attractions as well: a patriotic speech by Minnesota's famed educator and orator Maria Sanford; ethnic dances; music; palm reading; a tennis round robin; a chamber of horrors; a corn roast on the beach; and a Hoover supper to dramatize the need for food conservation. (U.S. food administrator Herbert Hoover had inaugurated wheatless Mondays and Wednesdays, meatless Tuesdays, and porkless Thursdays and Saturdays. The whole spartan process was called Hooverizing.)[21]

Capping this eventful year, the Minnesota Scandinavian Woman Suffrage Association—with appropriate pomp and ceremony—presented to Ueland as MWSA president the new

Mrs. F. W. Miller and Mrs. William Thwing, barkers for the menagerie at the Uelands' annual garden party, August 15, 1917, which raised funds for suffrage and the Red Cross work of Minneapolis suffragists.

Woman Citizen Building (built at a cost of $2,350) on the State Fair grounds. The fair was an important outreach site, and propaganda was served along with food—in 1911 the suffragists had offered "Susan B. Anthony pie" and "legislative pudding." To raise the visibility of the cause in a more dignified setting, the SWSA had decided to construct a women's building. After years of fund-raising events (chain parties—beginning with one party of four at fifty cents each and extending the chain to a total of eight parties—teas, bazaars, and plays), the Woman Citizen Building became a reality. Dedicated on September 3, 1917, it was blessed by Maria Sanford and presented by Nanny Jaeger to Clara Ueland as a memorial to suffrage pioneers and as a prophecy of the success still to come.[22]

Except for the trauma and additional duties associated with the war, 1917 was a typical suffrage year filled with energy, effort, and enthusiasm. Across the nation there were significant gains, with four states enacting presidential suffrage and Arkansas granting white primary suffrage in one form or another. The year's highlight was the victory of the New York referendum, which granted full voting rights to the state's women in early November. Undaunted by the referendum's defeat two years before, the women of New York succeeded in getting a second referendum bill passed by the legislature. They raised more than $525,000, announcing (as a result of a canvassing campaign) that 1,030,800 New York women were asking for "yes" votes on November 6. They circulated eighteen million pieces of literature and sent speakers to every nook and cranny throughout the state. Both President Wilson and Republican Governor Charles Seymour Whitman endorsed the referendum. Most important, however, were the appointment of thirty-four women as members of the governing council of Tammany Hall, New York City's powerful Democratic machine, and its subsequent decision to remain neutral (renouncing its earlier opposition) and let every voter express his personal opinion on suffrage at the polls. Carrie Chapman Catt proclaimed that the stunning victory was not New York's alone but the nation's.[23]

The outlook in Congress, however, was still not bright. There had been—beginning in 1878 and before 1917—eleven reports on the Susan B. Anthony amendment from the Senate Woman-Suffrage Committee, eight of them favorable. Only twice in those thirty-nine years had the full Senate voted on the proposed amendment, in 1887 (16 yeas, 34 nays, 26 absentees) and in 1914 (35 yeas, 34 nays, and 26 not voting). Even this one favorable Senate vote had fallen far short of the necessary two-thirds required for the passage of a constitutional amendment. On the House side, there had been seven committee reports (two in favor, three in opposition, and two without recommendation); the first House vote in 1915 (the judiciary committee reported out a bill without recommendation) had produced 174 yeas and 204 nays.[24]

The single hopeful action taken by the House in 1917 was a vote to establish a suffrage committee similar to the Senate standing committee. Although the House vote was favorable by 181 to 107 (142 not voting), it was also far from the two-thirds necessary for approval of an amendment. Nonetheless, both houses of Congress now had standing committees to which suffrage bills could be referred, another measure of the increasing clout of suffragists and their national organizations. The vote of the Minnesota delegation in the House was mixed: voting yea were Charles Davis, Franklin Ellsworth, Harold Knutson, Ernest Lundeen (all Republicans); voting nay was Andrew Volstead (Republican); not voting were Sydney Anderson, Clarence Miller, Halvor Steenerson (Republicans), Thomas Schall (Progressive), Carl Van Dyke (Democrat). The vote was not a true test of sentiment on the issue but rather an organizational matter, which may explain why Volstead, who was a supporter of suffrage, voted nay and why some chose not to vote at all.[25]

An analysis of the earlier, more substantive Senate and House votes in 1914 and 1915 revealed that the yes votes tended to come from states in which women could vote by virtue of full or presidential enfranchisement. This was the reasoning behind Carrie Chapman Catt's emphasis on continuing efforts to secure state amendments or legislation establishing the right of women to vote for presidential electors. Strange to say, the final outcome was influenced not only by the growing political strength of the suffrage forces but also by the continuing conflict between NAWSA and the NWP over the most effective means of achieving their common aim of political equality. Each organization in its own way had given the suffrage movement reason for hope. They both had paved the way for a breakthrough.[26]

9

THE BREAKTHROUGH

We believe that we are on the last stretch
of the road to the attainment of
political freedom for women.
CLARA UELAND, AUGUST 30, 1918

 The new year of 1918 dawned with a significant suffrage victory in the Congress as the House of Representatives gave the necessary two-thirds approval to the suffrage amendment by the margin of · a single vote. Four prosuffrage members left their sickbeds to participate in the voting, one having been carried in on a stretcher. Frederick C. Hicks (Republican, New York) left the deathbed of his wife—an ardent suffragist—and returned after the vote to attend her funeral. All ten members of the Minnesota delegation voted yea.[1]

The reason for the House members' change of heart was more practical than theoretical. The number of presidential electors voted for in part by eligible women voters had increased in less than eight months from 91 to 172 out of the total of 531 electors (the New York referendum victory accounting for nearly one-quarter of the increase). From the time of the previous House vote on the amendment in January 1915, as many as 56 representatives changed their votes from nay to yea. The New York delegation, with its constitutents' mandate fresh in mind, approved the amendment by a vote of 35 to 4. With the probability of those numbers continuing to rise, momentum was clearly on the suffrage side.[2]

The favorable vote by the Minnesota delegation precipitated understandable joy and celebration, but with barely a pause the work went on. A woman from St. Cloud in Harold Knutson's district wrote to Ueland expressing her gratitude for the outcome and for Ueland's efforts: "You have worked wonders." Ueland, who had targeted Knutson (giving herself the task of being "responsible for his upbringing") with all her persuasive powers, replied to the praise by saying, "Of course, we don't take it all to ourselves but being human we do enjoy a little enthusiastic appreciation."[3]

The nation then turned to the Senate for its decision. Senators—those from the South in particular—were more resistant to the idea of a suffrage amendment. Suffrage supporters, whose analysis indicated that they were ten votes short of sixty-four (the required two-thirds), assumed a conservative and pragmatic posture and refrained from pressing for a vote as long as the outcome seemed uncertain. They counted Frank B. Kellogg, the junior senator from Minnesota, as among six doubtful votes. Bit by bit, inch by inch, suffragists gained three votes, but that gain was offset by the astonishingly high Senate death rate during the term of the Sixty-fifth Congress. Of the ten who died, seven had been on the suffrage side. As time went on, some senators changed their positions, and those who switched their positions—together with some of the replacement senators—brought the magic number of additional affirmative votes needed for the amendment down to two.[4]

On May 10—the day set for a vote—a conference of Democratic suffrage senators decided not to take up the amendment because the votes were not in hand. A second attempt to bring the matter to a vote on June 27 found the Senate still lacking those two votes, prompting another strategic withdrawal.[5]

All the while, the pressure to pass a suffrage amendment was building. Various political groups and associations, as different as the General Federation of Women's Clubs and the American Federation of Labor, expressed their support. Ueland had written to both Minnesota senators in May with news that Lutheran ministers were now signing up for suffrage: "While many Scandinavians have been for the cause, we have considered the Lutheran clergymen, as a class, a bulwark on the side of the opposition."[6]

The suffrage amendment finally emerged on the Senate floor on September 30. President Woodrow Wilson made a personal appeal in favor of the amendment, reminding the senators of the significant contributions of women to the war effort: "We have made partners of the women in this war; shall we admit them only to a partnership of sacrifice and suffering and toil and not to a partnership of privilege and of right?" His words were to no avail. Senators rose in opposition. The debate dragged on, and the vote was taken the next day, on October 1. The amendment lost by two votes. Senators Knute Nelson and Frank Kellogg of Minnesota both voted on the suffrage side.[7]

Hoping that the Senate would follow the House lead and vote to pass the amendment, Minnesota suffragists had made plans in the late summer of 1918 for celebrations and a ratification campaign. They had sent letters to all legislative candidates seeking their opinions on ratification and had invited distinguished citizens to serve on a ratification committee. Following the two-vote loss, however, the celebrations had to be canceled and the ratification effort put on hold. Still, Ueland was as resolute as ever. She sent encouraging letters to suffragists, acknowledging their discouragement yet assuring them that "it is only a question of a short time [before the amendment] will come up again, and we hope with a different result."[8]

Before the fall elections, Ueland considered having the MWSA contribute money directly to prosuffrage incumbents and candidates. The organization shied away from this then-novel strategy, however, preferring to help by sending organizers into certain districts and urging women there to provide such financial support. Both practical and political considerations governed the decision. The association simply did not have money to spare, and it seemed prudent—at least in certain races—to maintain a low profile. Clara suggested to Representative Hilding A. Swanson, who was seeking a Senate seat, that it "probably would not be wise or good politics" for women in his area (Brainerd) "to work for you *as suffragists*, as this might alienate those who might otherwise vote for you, but might they not have a quiet campaign, without publicity of any kind, on your behalf?"[9]

The MWSA also urged workers to continue collecting signatures on petitions of support for a federal suffrage amendment: "These petitions will be used sometime, if not immediately, and furthermore this is the best suffrage propaganda we have done in Minnesota for some time." By early November more than 350 towns had petition committees, and the small town of Clitherall (population 187) registered the support of every woman but one. Every male voter signed up in one Minneapolis precinct, and in the eighth ward in Minneapolis, eight thousand signatures of women were secured. In one of her final communications of the year, Ueland noted with pride that the national organization had more than two million members, more than thirty thousand of them in 450 towns and cities throughout Minnesota. An example of growing sentiment in favor of suffrage came in a letter from Charles E. Purdy, a Minneapolis attorney who said he had been converted by the "temperate and judicial manner in which the school suffrage has been exercised." He believed that the MWSA's success was "due in a large measure to the . . . sane and even tempered women who are directing it."[10]

Tragedy interrupted this progress when the worldwide influenza epidemic reached the state that fall and when devastating forest fires ignited on October 12 in northeastern Minnesota. The epidemic, which killed an estimated twenty-one million people around the world, took more than ten thousand lives in Minnesota. To combat its spread, state health authorities prohibited assemblies of all kinds, thus forcing the cancellation of the MWSA's state convention. The fires that swept through an area stretching from Cloquet to Moose Lake to the outskirts of Duluth displaced more than 52,000 people, killed 453, and destroyed 1,500 square miles of an 8,400-square-mile region. It was the autumn that also saw the end of war in Europe, with the signing of the Armistice on November 11.[11]

As 1919 began, Clara and her cohorts readied themselves for a new legislative session and a new Congress. On January 2 she wrote to state legislators requesting support of a resolution urging the U.S. Senate to pass the federal suffrage amendment. On January 6 she asked Governor Burnquist to speak in favor of woman suffrage in his forthcoming address to the legislature, and two days later he sent her a copy of his message, in which he recommended the adoption of a resolution requesting Congress to submit the suffrage amendment to the states, and its ratification by the legislature. Before the month was out, the legislature acquiesced in the governor's request and passed a resolution asking that the U.S. Senate join with the House of Representatives in proposing a suffrage amendment to the federal Constitution.[12]

Although the resolution was a positive expression of support, the MWSA's major legislative focus was to secure passage of a bill giving Minnesota women the right to vote in presidential elections. That effort was disrupted by a group calling itself the Minnesota Equal Suffrage Constitutional Amendment League, which persuaded legislators to introduce a state suffrage amendment. MWSA board member Marguerite Wells wrote Representative Le Roy E. Brophey that the association could not discover the reason for the league's preference for an amendment, which would require a majority of all votes cast in the election. Its president, Wells and Ueland both pointed out, refused to name any members (other than the four or five women who made up the group and two recently defeated legislators) or any plans to raise funds for the organization. The president was Mary A. Cunningham of St. Paul, but the "real head" was Angie V. Kingsley, listed as secretary. (This was the same Kingsley who had accused Ueland and her MWSA associates of "kaiserism" tactics during the 1917 state convention.) Wells referred Brophey to a number of other senators and representatives for more information on Kingsley. When rumors of this activity reached Clara Ueland, she called it "almost the worst thing that could happen to us," coming as it did at a time when increasing numbers of legislators were prepared to pass "almost any kind of a suffrage measure."[13]

And that they were. Immediately after the Minnesota House passed the resolution calling on the U.S. Senate to take action in support of a federal amendment, it passed a state-amendment bill. Ueland's hunch about the legislature's new enthusiasm for suffrage held true. But Ueland thought the state-amendment bill was "a near catastrophe" for Minnesota suffragists. Legislators defended themselves by saying they would have been perceived to be inconsistent had they voted for a federal suffrage amendment and against a state suffrage amendment. And there was truth in that contention. An MWSA staff member described the legislators' puzzlement:

> The poor dear men are in quite a confused state of mind, because three distinct and separte [sic] groups of women are besieging them in the interests of suffrage—Mrs. Bertha Moller for the National Party working for a resolution, Mrs. Angie Kingsley the female arch-fiend who persists in bringing up the State amendment and always gets some fool men to stand behind her, and our group working for the National Association's policy—I do not wonder that the poor old dears look confused and bored when all or sundry of us appear.[14]

The opposition happily exploited this confusion, and while those few women supporting the state amendment irritated Ueland, the antis exasperated her even more: "We marvel at the stupidity of these people," she declared. When the antis brought in a Miss Roe ("we think that is the name") from the national organization to plead their case against the presidential-electors bill before the Senate Elections Committee on March 6, Ueland commented, "She was dreadful!" (Ueland wrote to Catt that Miss Roe was "particularly obnoxious.") The male opponents also had their final say, voicing old fears for "'the safety and sanc-tity of womanhood'" and propping up the "'pedestal'" argument with "the straining timbers of sentiment and biology."[15]

Once more the troops had to be rallied. The MWSA urged suf-frage leaders throughout the state to write their senators to vote against the state amendment as "unwise and inexpedient." Every day Ueland and her colleagues made their views known in the legislative halls. During that period she wrote to a colleague, "I can say briefly that I am one of the busiest women in the state as President of the Suffrage Association." On February 28 the state Senate did indeed vote down a motion to pass the state-amendment bill; the Senate then immediately decided to post-pone the bill indefinitely, an action that had been recommend-ed by the Elections Committee. With that impediment out of the way, the Minnesota legislature acknowledged at long last the right of women to vote for presidential electors, with House members voting 103 to 24 and Senate members 49 to 11. The St. Paul Dispatch reported that suffragists, who were "joyous over victory," expressed their delight at this "good beginning."[16]

The vote was a testimony to the deft strategies of the MWSA. Four MWSA workers had organized every legislative district and had increased the number of working committees in cities and towns outside Minneapolis, St. Paul, and Duluth from 450 to 480. A poll of both houses had been carefully planned and exe-cuted by Ueland before the vote. Because there were many new faces and new names, it was no easy task and required Ueland's infinite tact and diplomacy. Governor Burnquist, surrounded by suffragists, signed the bill on March 24 "with his native grace, great decision and stout stub pen."[17]

The St. Paul Daily News editorialized after the bill's signing: "We are glad Minnesota women are to vote for the next president—or against him! Particularly we congratulate the thousands of devoted workers in this cause, under the leadership of Mrs. Andreas Ueland. They deserve the grateful remembrance of all their sisters." Hattie S. Bordewich, the cashier of the Olivia State Bank, wrote to Ueland that month, "It has been a source of great satisfaction to a business woman to see the sort of campaign you have conducted. . . . It has been dignified and intelligent and has not resulted in the antagonism to the movement that the so-called 'militant' campaign has caused."[18]

Action at the national level had rested with the lame duck Sixty-fifth Congress, in session until March 4, 1919, and then with the special session of the new Congress convened by the president in May. NAWSA had hoped that the congressional Democrats, who had lost to the Republicans in the 1918 elections but who still controlled the lame duck session, would decide to bring the suffrage amendment to a vote and take credit for its passage. But on February 10, 1919, the Senate again defeated the amendment, this time by a margin of only one vote.[19]

Still, the prosuffrage tide was rolling in. The number of suffrage supporters had increased in the House, and three states—Michigan, Oklahoma, and South Dakota—had passed their own amendments enfranchising women. By the time of the 1918 elections, women had been enfranchised in fifteen states, and—along with women of two other states who could vote in primary elections—they helped to elect 34 senators and 130 representatives. Women could also vote for presidential electors in fourteen additional states. These figures on women voters provided the dynamics for the Sixty-sixth Congress, in which Republicans held the majority in the House and took control of the Senate.[20]

Woodrow Wilson called the new Congress into special session in May to attend to matters relating to postwar settlements and the proposed League of Nations. In Europe earlier in the spring of 1919 to attend the Paris Peace Conference, Wilson had cabled from France that "every consideration of justice and of public advantage calls for the immediate adoption" of the suffrage amendment. In the House, Republican James R. Mann of Illinois used his authority as chairman of the Republican Committee on Committees to make himself chairman of the House Woman-Suffrage Committee. Making it appear all the while that opposition to suffrage resided exclusively with the Democrats (and the solid Democratic South gave this allegation some validity), Mann waived hearings and brought House Resolution 1—the federal suffrage amendment—to the floor.[21]

On May 21, two days after convening, the House passed the measure by a vote of 304 to 89 (58 of the 70 nay votes by Democrats came from representatives of southern states; only 6 of 110 new members voted no). More than 92 percent of the members from suffrage states voted for the amendment, as compared with 53 percent from nonsuffrage states. The discrepancy demonstrated once more the efficacy of the Catt strategy in attacking the issue on several fronts: for state amendments where the process was relatively easy; for primary suffrage in southern states; and for presidential suffrage in states like Minnesota where state constitutions were difficult to amend.

Once again the Senate took up the amendment, and this time the outcome was never in doubt. In addition to two new prosuffrage senators from Massachusetts and Delaware, Senator William J. Harris of Georgia had promised Wilson that he would support the amendment, and Senator Frederick Hale of Maine had been "converted" by the achievement of presidential suffrage in his state. There were a few anxious moments, however, as four amendments were introduced—two proposing to make the ratification process more difficult by resting that authority in state conventions rather than in legislatures, one to limit the extension of suffrage to white women, and one to give states the primary right of enforcement. They were all defeated, and the suffrage amendment—the proposed Nineteenth Amendment to the U.S. Constitution—was passed by a vote of 56 to 25, a somewhat comfortable margin of 69 percent.[22]

Assessing this victory, Maud Wood Park minimized the effects of World War I, of Woodrow Wilson's conversion, and even of NAWSA's effective lobby, which she directed. While all these things were useful in some measure, Park credited Carrie Chapman Catt's 1916 master plan and "the execution of her plans by our state suffrage organizations" as the principal reasons for the success. Before the final vote, Catt's strategies had brought about these impressive results:

- Fourteen state legislatures in 1917 and twenty-six in 1919 passed resolutions asking Congress to submit a federal amendment for woman suffrage. (Minnesota was one of the twenty-six in 1919.)
- After 1916, four states adopted state constitutional amendments for woman suffrage.
- Eleven state legislatures granted presidential suffrage to women. (Minnesota did so in 1919.)
- Two more states gave women the right to vote in primary elections, and the total number of presidential electors for whom women were eligible to vote rose from 91 to 339 of a total of 531 electors.[23]

As more and more women gained the right to vote, the potential of grassroots woman-power became a political reality that senators and representatives could no longer ignore. William Watts Folwell, a contemporary historian, credited the experience of war, identifying "a sudden outburst of hospitality for reform" as women demonstrated the diverse capacities in which they could serve their country. Clara Ueland also believed women's greater participation in the world of work during the war had changed the environment for women.[24]

The unanimous affirmative vote of the Minnesota delegation in both the Sixty-fifth and Sixty-sixth Congresses cheered those Minnesota suffragists who had worked so energetically to generate support from their representatives and senators. One more step remained: Before the amendment could become the law of the land, three-fourths of the state legislatures had to vote to ratify it. Nevertheless, supporters took time out to plan a victory celebration for the evening of June 9 on the steps of the state Capitol. Clara Ueland asked special friends and supporters to speak. She urged Ole Sageng, Marion L. Burton, president of the University of Minnesota, Maria Sanford, Governor Burnquist, and Anna Dickie Olesen to participate. They all came, and not even the torrents of rain that moved the celebration inside to the rotunda dampened the enthusiasm of the evening. There were some 250 automobiles festooned in yellow bunting in the two

parades—one coming from Minneapolis and the other wending
its way through downtown St. Paul. The *Minneapolis Morning
Tribune* described the assemblage of several thousand suffragists
and their friends as including "snowy-haired veterans, . . . girls
from the university, nurses in uniform, teachers, club women,
members of the National Women's [*sic*] party, officials of the
state and county Woman Suffrage associations." Burton greeted
the "fellow voters," noting that "every person who believes in
democracy must believe in woman suffrage." Anna Dickie Olesen described the "millions of American women forgetting differences in social conditions, . . . religion, . . . nationality—we
stand united . . . while all over America there glows a brighter
light, and liberty is born anew in the land we love."[25]

Although Ueland did not speak, she came forward to receive
an ovation from the crowd. In a subsequent report describing the
event, the always-ebullient press chairman, Vivian Stanley Thorp,
concluded: "Had we not possessed a leader, Mrs. Andreas Ueland,
who really puts Job in the discard in the matter of patience, we
should probably have thrown up our hands in despair; but anyone who knows Minnesota's president knows that once em-
barked on a career we go through to the end—bitter or sweet."[26]

The celebration was a prelude to one last effort—persuading
the governor to call a special session to ratify the amendment.
Carrie Chapman Catt had sent four women, two Democrats and
two Republicans, to eleven states to get pledges from governors to
call sessions for that purpose. The Republican team—Christine
Bradley South of Kentucky and Marjorie Shuler of New York—
came to Minnesota in August, stopping first for a visit with MWSA
leaders at the Ueland home. Ueland told them that she had
received assurances from Governor Burnquist that, if other governors would do the same, he was willing to call a special session in
the early months of 1920. Early in June he sent telegrams to governors in at least thirty-five other states with that proposal.
Burnquist, who was probably vacationing in northern Minnesota,
rode four miles on horseback and thirty-six miles in a car to meet
Shuler and South at a small town; he promised to call a special

session. Ueland also reported that he had probably consented to let them use his name when they talked with other Republican governors.[27]

As states around the nation began to ratify the Nineteenth Amendment, Clara Ueland wrote letters of congratulations. To Theodora Winton Youmans, president of the Wisconsin Suffrage Association, on June 26, 1919: "How wonderful that Wisconsin could be among the first to ratify. I rejoice with you and envy you both at the same time." Following ratification by Massachusetts, she wrote to Alice Stone Blackwell on July 12, 1919, "We are particularly happy on your account. To think that your share of the long struggle is about over, and that you see your own splendid effort, as well as that of your father and mother, crowned with victory. With love and congratulations."[28]

She permitted a bit of pique to show through, complaining in an August 25 letter to Democratic party activist Jessie E. Scott about the NWP taking credit for the success of suffrage: "I wonder they can keep their faces straight while they are trying to humbug those who do not know the real situation." Ueland's momentary irritation over what she perceived to be an unfounded exaggeration of reality, however, was quickly subordinated to the achievement itself. "But after all," she continued, "the main thing, and really the only thing is, that the work is nearly finished." It was a characteristic Ueland response.[29]

Historian Eleanor Flexner, too, took issue with the NWP's claim: "To say that the Woman's Party was the sole cause of the breakthrough which finally occurred is to ignore history." Among the forces at work, she affirmed, were appreciation for the work of women in the war and the "mounting crescendo of suffrage work under the leadership of the National Suffrage Association." Another historian, writing about the NWP, observed that while the party "took full credit for the suffrage victory," scholars have differed in their assessments. Alice Paul is rightly credited with renewing the suffragist commitment to a federal amendment, but the suffrage victory was "a triumph for the strategy of compromise," with Carrie Chapman Catt as the mastermind of that strategy. In no way does that reality diminish the spirited leadership that Paul, at a particular moment in suffrage history, brought to the cause.[30]

In mid-August Governor Burnquist issued a call for the special session to be convened on September 8, 1919. "The proposed Woman Suffrage Amendment," he declared, " . . . involves the electoral rights of five hundred thousand persons within our commonwealth and millions of the citizens of our country." MWSA board members were invited to sit on the Senate floor on the day that the legislature convened. The House vote for ratification was 120 to 6, followed by the Senate vote of 60 to 5. The whole process was completed in thirty minutes. "Lawmakers Surrender Under Fire of Smiles, Cheers and Blossoms," proclaimed the headline in the St. Paul Pioneer Press. Among those who had surrendered was former foe Senator George H. Sullivan, who had written Ueland that he favored the special session and would vote for the federal suffrage amendment. Vivian Thorp described the scene that followed:

> The moment the Senate vote was polled the corridors, floors and galleries of both houses were in an uproar, hundreds of women cheered and laughed and waved the suffrage colors while in the rotunda a band swung into the strains of the Battle Hymn of the Republic. . . . Mrs. Andreas Ueland, radiant and beautiful as usual, was the center of congratulating men and women. . . . "It is my happiest day," she said.[31]

A thank-you luncheon was prepared and served by suffrage workers, not all of whom were accustomed to such domestic tasks. Ueland's colleague Josephine Simpson told the press on ratification day, "I feel today as one who has come into a great inheritance after being a political pauper; I have such a feeling of comfort and power and dignity." Capping the day was a celebratory dinner for suffrage supporters at the St. Paul Hotel, where Ueland expressed her fear that the remarks of the spokeswomen for the Republican and Democratic parties might elevate their rivalry to a "rift in the lute." However, the evening went off without a hitch. In recognition of her leadership, Ueland's colleagues presented her with a platinum-and-diamond pin.[32]

Governor Burnquist signed the ratification certificate on September 11 and presented the pen to Clara. An editorial published that day in the *Minneapolis Journal* linked the success of the suffrage movement to its "Sanity of Leadership": "Mrs. Andreas Ueland . . . knows how to temper enthusiasm with moderation, and to unite zeal with courtesy and good taste. . . . This wise leadership has secured for the women the respect of those who doubted the wisdom of equal suffrage, and has disarmed all opposition, because it is an earnest of calm and sane use of the ballot."[33]

The *St. Paul Daily News* praised the long years of work "by small groups of devoted women, with the support of all who believe in fundamental democracy. At times the fight was up hill and disheartening, but it went on unceasingly until general indifference turned to general indorsement [sic]. Five years from now we will look back and wonder why anyone ever opposed woman suffrage!"[34]

Across the nation suffragists continued their campaign to win ratification in thirty-six of the forty-eight states—the three-fourths required by the Constitution for adoption of amendments. Within a month of the U.S. Senate vote on June 4, 1919, eleven states had ratified the amendment. By the end of September that number had increased to seventeen states, including Minnesota. Then came an inexplicable pause, prompting Carrie Catt to embark on a personal "Wake up America" tour that succeeded in registering five more states in the ratification column by year's end. Although there was no time limit for ratification, suffragists had established their own deadline: They wanted to be able to vote in the 1920 presidential elections. There were good gains early that year, and by June thirty-five states had ratified the amendment and eight had defeated it (Delaware being the only state north of the Mason-Dixon Line to do so). Of the five remaining states, Florida and North Carolina were expected to oppose ratification, and the antisuffrage governors of Vermont and Connecticut refused to call special sessions.[35]

There was one last hope before the 1920 presidential election
—the state of Tennessee. Although Governor Albert H. Roberts
was sympathetic to suffrage, a provision in the state's constitution that prohibited ratification of a federal amendment until
after the next election seemed to be an insuperable bar to calling
the Tennessee assembly into special session. In a related case,
however, the U.S. Supreme Court ruled that the federal constitution, not state constitutions, controlled the method whereby
the U.S. Constitution could be amended. That ruling allowed
the U.S. Department of Justice to declare that a state constitution could not impose any barrier to the ratification of federal
amendments.[36]

President Wilson, who had sought this opinion at the
NAWSA's request, wired Governor Roberts on June 23, urging him
to call the assembly into special session as "a real service to the
party and to the nation." After a delay to allow time for a supportive decision by the state's attorney general, the governor
scheduled the session to begin on August 9. Suffragists began to
deploy their forces, as did the Southern Women's League for the
Rejection of the Susan B. Anthony Amendment. Carrie
Chapman Catt, who had sent her press aide, Marjorie Shuler, to
scout the situation in Tennessee, received an urgent call to help.
With twelve hours' notice and a handbag, Catt left for Tennessee
on June 15, expecting to stay less than a week. She returned to
her New York home more than two months later.[37]

Four days after the session began, the Tennessee Senate
approved the amendment by a vote of twenty-five to four, but
that comfortable margin was not a harbinger of easy going in the
House. After several delays caused by the machinations of suffrage opponents, the House finally voted favorably on August 18
by the narrow margin of fifty to forty-six. Even after its passage—
thanks in part to a young member's response to his mother's
plea—a motion for reconsideration had to be defeated and an
injunction dissolved before the certificate of ratification could
make its way to the nation's capital, where it was received and
reviewed at 4:00 A.M. on August 26 by the solicitor general. Sec-

retary of State Bainbridge Colby signed the certificate later that morning and, in response to Catt's phone call, invited her to see the proclamation before it was released. She was accompanied by NAWSA vice-president Harriet Taylor Upton, a prominent Ohio suffrage worker, and Maud Wood Park, who recalled, "We almost had to stick pins in ourselves to realize that the simple document at which we were looking was . . . the long sought charter of liberty for the women of this country." The Nineteenth Amendment to the U.S. Constitution had become the law of the land.[38]

The next morning—August 27, 1920—photographers and reporters from the Twin Cities newspapers, three national news services, and a California film studio gathered in South St. Paul, Minnesota. They were there to report on a special waterworks bond election that would bring women voters to the polls for the first time under the entitlement of the amendment. The headline in the home edition of the *South St. Paul Daily Reporter* read: "National History Made in South St. Paul Today When Women Vote Under New Law." Front-page pictures—"Local Women Try Out Their New Franchise"—featured three women voters. Eighty-seven women from South St. Paul voted that day, and even though their ballots were segregated (just in case), those first voters brought their town momentary fame.[39]

That fame was the product of a seventy-two-year-long struggle eloquently described by Carrie Catt and Nettie Rogers Shuler, who wrote:

> Millions of dollars were raised, mainly in small sums, and expended with economic care. Hundreds of women gave the accumulated possibilities of an entire lifetime, thousands gave years of their lives, hundreds of thousands gave constant interest and such aid as they could. It was a continuous, seemingly endless, chain of activity. Young suffragists who helped forge the last links of that chain were not born when it began. Old suffragists who forged the first links were dead when it ended.[40]

Women who had worked so diligently for suffrage were thrilled at the opportunity to participate in the political process.

A newspaper reports the first women voting under the Nineteenth Amendment.

Now, because they possessed the power of the vote, they could put muscle behind their demands for economic and social reforms and on behalf of their work for world peace. And many did. But it was a new world—not necessarily brave—that greeted the American woman voter. There were new freedoms of sexuality and behavior. There were new organizations. The millions who had joined forces under NAWSA's banner drifted into different interest groups or simply drifted away from public affairs. Nothing replaced the single-minded cause of suffrage. As a consequence, the coherence of the women's movement became replaced by diversity and—once more—by division.

10

POSTSCRIPT TO VICTORY

*Today is the commencement rather
than the end of our work.*

CLARA UELAND, SEPTEMBER 1919

 A few days before the Minnesota legislature ratified
the Nineteenth Amendment in September 1919,
Clara Ueland wrote to her MWSA associates that
they would be "leaving the old struggle for suffrage
behind" and turning their faces "to the new order
in which women will be full and equal citizens." She was speaking not only to equality in the abstract but also to the different
roles that women would assume so that they could bring about
that new order. It is unlikely that she could have predicted the
liberating attitudinal and behavioral changes soon to be mani-
fested by younger women in their dress, manners, and morals,
and she would have been disappointed at the numbers who
chose to drop out of public life. Rather, Ueland's statement
reflected her preference for the public-spirited women who gravitated to the political parties and especially for those who made
the transition to the MWSA's successor organization—the National League of Women Voters.[1]

On March 24, 1919, just three days after the Minnesota
House gave its approval to presidential suffrage for Minnesota
women, NAWSA convened its Jubilee Convention in St. Louis.

Carrie Chapman Catt used the occasion to propose a new organization of women citizens as "the most natural, the most appropriate and the most patriotic" memorial to suffrage leaders of the past. She envisaged that women banded together in a new nonpartisan, nonsectarian association would secure the final enfranchisement of American women, would remove remaining legal discriminations, and would help liberate women around the world. Essential for the achievement of these goals was the "political restoration" of democratic institutions. Catt believed that women in such a nonpartisan organization free from racial and religious bias could help reverse the prevailing contempt for the electoral process. "Lift this incubus from our public life," she said, by changing "custom, laws and education." The convention responded to her vision with enthusiasm.[2]

There was much ado about the name that the new organization was to take. Most suggestions derived from the name of the existing body: the National Alliance of Women Citizens; the American Women's Alliance of the United States; the National Woman Citizens Alliance; and the National Alliance of American Women. When Catt, who wanted "a name that will leap out at one . . . a name that everyone could pronounce and remember," asked members of the press corps covering the convention for their preference, they gave their unanimous vote to the League of Women Voters. A motion by Maud Nathan of New York City endorsing this last suggestion was ratified by the convention, which then agreed to proceed with the establishment of leagues in suffrage states.[3]

Not everyone welcomed the prospect of a new organization emerging out of the suffrage movement. Political parties feared that the league would be a new competitor in the public arena. Some men worried about the development of a women's bloc. Partisan women—especially Republicans who were also NAWSA leaders—opposed the league because it might drain off a major potential source of GOP support, energy, and commitment. The language of dissent was vivid as protesters such as the Women's Republican Club of New York castigated the infant league as a

"menace to our national life." Catt and others tried to be reas-
suring, saying again and again that the league was not radical
but interested in advancing the general welfare, not political but
nonpartisan, and by no means threatening to but supportive of
democratic institutions.[4]

Ueland, who had missed the St. Louis convention because of
illness, was quite taken with the league idea: "We in Minnesota
want to do our part in realizing this vision," she said in a press
release on June 23, 1919. In September she responded quickly
when NAWSA inquired about Minnesota's interest in a series of
conferences intended to help the suffrage states organize branches. Confident that most suffragists would be eager to join the
league, Ueland asserted, "I believe Minnesota will be in the first
ranks when the work is under way." She also looked to the
University of Minnesota to help the league in organizing and
teaching "Citizenship Classes" and in training "the coming generation of University women and men" so that they in turn
would be attracted to the mission and objectives of the league.
"It may not be so easy to raise money for this as for suffrage," she
predicted, but she was prepared to confront that problem when it
arose. Writing to Theodora Winton Youmans, her Wisconsin
counterpart, Ueland suggested that the suffrage association be
kept nominally alive until the thirty-six states had ratified the
amendment, then "let the old cat die." She saw the new league as
one in which "we will not be hampered in any way by our old
constitution and by our traditions, and may I say it with all reverence and respect, without some of our workers."[5]

On September 20 Ueland appointed a Committee on Conference and Organization, chaired by Mabeth Hurd Paige, to do
the preparatory work. By October the committee was meeting
almost daily. The MWSA board agreed to transfer its assets to the
new organization for the purpose of "completing the full enfranchisement of women and increasing the effectiveness of women's
votes in furthering better government." As a preliminary step,
the committee convened a luncheon meeting of leaders of wom-
en's organizations in the tearoom of Dayton's department store in

Minneapolis on October 21 to determine their response to the league idea. Alice Winter represented the General Federation of Women's Clubs, and Nanny Jaeger the Minnesota Scandinavian Woman Suffrage Association. Most of the others were new faces from familiar organizations, such as the Minneapolis section of the National Council of Jewish Women, the League of Catholic Women, the YWCA, the Rotary Club, and the Degree of Honor.[6]

Clara Ueland spoke of her expectations that the league would enable women to use "this potential power given us . . . for the good of the state" and of her confidence that the league would marshal that power in the interest of education and legis-lation. "There is no limit to what we can accomplish," she declared. Her message was successful: "Women vied with each other . . . in their eagerness to offer the support of the organiza-tions they represented," reported the *Minneapolis Journal*.

Paige's committee worked to get the widest possible represen-tation at the organizational meeting planned for the Radisson Hotel in Minneapolis on October 28 and 29. Invitations went to fifty-five hundred members of local suffrage associations, wom-en's clubs, WCTU affiliates, thirteen fraternal women's organiza-tions, about fifteen hundred farmers' clubs, and other groups. It was apparent from the outset that the league intended to seek a broad base of membership and support—an organization for all women wanting to know how to make good use of their new vot-ing tool. A pamphlet recruiting members to the league made that purpose explicit: "It is not a woman's party. It is not a club. It does not limit its membership to certain groups. It is inclusive, not exclusive. . . . It believes with Madison that 'a people who mean to be their own governors must arm themselves with the power which knowledge gives.'" The league therefore made the education of women in government and politics its paramount consideration. And it concluded with the league's fundamental principle: "In a democracy, good government can be achieved only through good citizenship."[7]

Ueland's call to the conference proposed building an organi-zation to include all women for the "purpose [of] raising of our standards of living and the safeguarding of our cherished institutions. Together the women of the state must make wise and far-seeing plans to the end that our dreams of a democracy, in which men and women shall have an equal voice, must come true." This announcement was carefully crafted to emphasize the preservation of institutions and collaboration between the sexes.[8]

The response was impressive: More than four hundred delegates attended the conference. The group adopted a constitution and bylaws and elected Clara Ueland president after expressing appreciation for her "arduous and devoted service" to the MWSA; five other officers, six directors, and ten chairmen of congressional districts were elected to the board of directors. In place of individual membership dues, counties within each congressional district were to contribute according to specified quotas. The Minnesota League of Women Voters was off to a good financial start, with nearly six thousand dollars pledged in response to an appeal at the conference banquet. In a fitting climax to this event, three thousand men and women filled the Minneapolis auditorium to hear Carrie Chapman Catt speak on "Our Nation—What Can We Do for It?" The next day the Minneapolis Morning Tribune noted "the spirit of joyousness for the victory now in sight which pervaded the sessions."[9]

During the ten-year period when she served as the league's national president, Marguerite Wells of Minneapolis remarked that the league was an organization of women, partly because women, as new voters, needed training for political effectiveness and partly because the enfranchisement of women was its occasion. Paradoxically, she said, it was a middle-of-the-road organization and an organization of reformers. It had the most tangible of programs and the least tangible of aims. It recognized that no single political party had a monopoly on public virtue. It had a twofold mission of political education and improved legislation. League historian Louise M. Young observed that "the compass guiding the League was the public interest" and that, consistent with that compass, its lobbying activities were conducted in the open—at the front door, rather than in the back room.[10]

It was all very new, very different, and very idealistic. No one was sure how it would work or whether it would survive. Throughout the fall of 1919, Ueland deflected criticism of the proposed league—just as she had reassured people nervous over the prospect of suffrage—by saying that "the women of Minnesota are going to be a stabilizing influence. They believe in law and order; they do not believe in revolution." She also took pains to reassure the jittery other gender that both men and women could make a balanced contribution to the well-being of the state, that the league's purpose was "to have more beauty in the lives of all the citizens of Minnesota." To those who worried that the league would become a women's party, she said, "It is the middle ground where the altruistic thought of the national parties may find congenial soil and grow for the ultimate betterment of state and nation."[11]

The Minnesota league got off to a running start in November with a five-day "Short Course in Citizenship for Women Voters" organized by the General Extension Division of the University of Minnesota. An NAWSA press release indicated that Minnesota's university had "gone further in cooperation than . . . any other," referring to the three other states where leagues had similar efforts under way. Registrations for the day program were limited to three hundred participants and for the evening lectures to six hundred, but demand stretched the latter figure to eight hundred. Every member of the state board enrolled in the course, as did women from throughout the state. (Individuals could register for the entire course for a fee of $3.00 or pay $1.00 for the evening sessions only.) Eminent scholars from the university addressed three separate topics during each of the day programs, which were held in the law school auditorium from two o'clock to four-thirty. The topics included political ethics, the constitution of Minnesota, public speaking, securing legislation in Minnesota, problems of Americanization, state governmental issues and state institutions, public health, illiteracy, and parliamentary practice. In the evening, classes were held in the Minneapolis mayor's reception room in City Hall, with presentations on a wide range of topics—the city as a social and political problem, food as a policy issue, city governmental structure and organization, the national executive branch and its work, welfare and recreation, the national judiciary, freedom of speech, and the United States as a world power. The professors reported that the intelligence of the women was unusually high; bookstores reported "great stimulation" in sales on governmental subjects; newspapers carried stories on the sessions, and a Minneapolis newspaper editorialized, "Why not for men, too?"[12]

Citizenship schools outside the Twin Cities followed upon the organization of county and district leagues throughout the state. Organizers worked in all ten congressional districts to set up conferences modeled after the state meeting held in October. Ueland participated in four of those meetings, in Faribault, Willmar, Mankato, and St. Cloud. Following the organization of the districts, the counties were then organized. Emily R. Knuebuhl, the newly selected political education director (she had been a principal of three grade schools in Minneapolis), held citizenship schools in fifty-three of the eighty-six counties and in sixty-six towns.[13]

This massive dose of political education set the stage for an impressive organizational campaign. By the end of its first year, the Minnesota league had chairmen in every congressional district, representation in all but four of the counties, and an estimated fourteen thousand members. The state organization inherited the MWSA's office headquarters in the Essex Building in downtown Minneapolis and added new staff members; by January both the fourth (St. Paul) and fifth (Minneapolis) districts had opened offices and hired staff. Nearly 260,000 pieces of literature (posters, leaflets, and so forth) had been distributed throughout the state. The Minnesota league's organizing strategy was so effective that the national league's 1921 convention recognized it as a "banner" state.[14]

Given the sophistication of this effort and the accompanying enthusiasm, it is not surprising that nearly fifty Minnesota women attended the NAWSA Victory Convention and the first annual con-

The Essex Building, Minneapolis, 1913

gress of the League of Women Voters in Chicago in February 1920.
Indeed, Minnesota had the largest number attending from outside
the Chicago area. The 546 delegates were joined by uncounted
numbers of alternates and thousands of visitors—a group so large
that not even standing room was available at the public meetings.
The *Minneapolis Morning Tribune* called the meeting "the most
important ever held by women of the United States." And so it
was—a truly extraordinary gathering of talented women, including presidents of women's organizations and of women's colleges,
scholars, physicians, attorneys, social workers, teachers, directors
of settlement houses, society leaders, and the ubiquitous women
volunteers. President Woodrow Wilson sent a telegram acknowledging that the suffragists' "great work is so near its triumphant
end that you can merge into a League of Women Voters to carry
on the development of good citizenship and real democracy."[15]

Although the suffrage victory was still six months away, everyone at the convention was confident of the outcome. After all, they were only three states short of the necessary number for ratification. Carrie Chapman Catt, concluding her victory speech, enjoined her audience, "You've won! . . . rejoice, applaud, and be glad!" The minutes of the convention recorded that at these words "joy unconfined burst forth." Two thousand women let loose their emotions in nearly one hour of cheering, standing on chairs, parading, singing, shouting, and waving banners and flags. The Republican elephant and the Democratic donkey marched arm in arm to receive Catt's congratulations. Clara Ueland rang the victory bell, and Maud Stockwell carried the banner at the head of the Minnesota delegates as they marched around the hall.[16]

The suffrage women soon got down to setting up the machinery for dissolving NAWSA (a step finally taken in 1925) and elevating the league to the status of a new and independent society. Six Minneapolis suffragists played prominent roles in the process. Clara Ueland chaired a group that established the boundaries of the regional divisions, and she also led committee discussions on American citizenship. Attorney Mabeth Hurd Paige served as secretary of the committee on the unification of laws relating to women. Alice Ames Winter was vice-chairman of the child welfare committee, and Mabel S. Ulrich, a physician, chaired the social hygiene committee. Jessie M. Marcley, who later chaired the state league's committee on efficiency in government, served on the convention resolutions committee, Vivian Thorp on the press committee. Other Minnesotans sharing the limelight included Anna Dickie Olesen, who was one of six speakers at the ratification banquet, and Maria Sanford and Ethel Hurd, both of whom spoke at events honoring suffrage pioneers.[17]

From among ten names presented by the nominating committee, the delegates chose four to constitute the executive board. The four women were asked to agree among themselves who would serve as chairman, vice-chairman, secretary, and treasurer. None volunteered herself to be head of the new organization, but Maud Wood Park became the first choice of the other three. She had impressive credentials as NAWSA's chief lobbyist, she had fewer family commitments, and she lived closest to Washington. Her colleagues persuaded her to accept the office, and she reluctantly did so, serving with distinction as the national league's first president until 1924. In addition to the four officers, the delegates also elected national directors from each of the seven regions and three at-large directors. Mabeth Hurd Paige was elected to the national board as a director representing region five, which included Minnesota, Iowa, Wisconsin, North and South Dakota, Montana, and Wyoming. The league was now ready for business, armed with a final resolution from NAWSA that declared:

> Whereas millions of women will become voters in 1920 and whereas the low standards of citizenship found among men clearly indicate the need of education in the principles and ideals of our government and methods of political procedures, therefore be it resolved, that the National League of Women Voters be urged to make political education of the new women voters (but not excluding men) its first duty in 1920.[18]

Clara Ueland had been approached for the position as regional director now held by her friend Mabeth Paige, but she had other ideas. She wrote to Andreas from Chicago: "I know how you feel about my doing so much public work and I think, myself, I better have something of a vacation. So I have been firm in my decision not to accept the office. And when I get home I will take steps to get rid of some of the Minnesota responsibility." It was a decision, as her daughter Brenda noted, that required "all her serene good judgement and sense of fairness." Clara kept her promise to Andreas. In May 1920 she resigned as state league president, and Marguerite Wells was chosen to replace her.[19]

Marguerite, the first of four children (three girls and one boy) grew up in Jamestown, North Dakota, where she was an enterprising tomboy—the founder and only girl member of a stamp collectors' union, a baseball association, a fire company, and a militia. She persuaded her father to take her to the caucus of his political party, where she hid her sex in a boy's cap and slicker. When Wells entered Smith College as a member of the class of 1895, she was the first North Dakota girl to attend an eastern college. In 1902 her family moved to Minneapolis, and her father, Edward Payson Wells, prospered from an investment business and other commercial activities. Marguerite joined the suffrage movement during Ueland's presidency—her first task was sorting piles of literature in the basement of the organization's headquarters, but she quickly rose in the ranks, becoming Ueland's legislative assistant. Brenda Ueland described Wells as "a brilliant, slender and charming spinster, high-minded and formidably erudite. She was thin and lively, and rather like a beautiful and delicate bird with her fine salient little nose and her quickly turning head." After serving twelve years as Minnesota president, Wells headed the national league from 1934 to 1944. She would be the last league president who had participated in the suffrage movement.[20]

Though Ueland stepped down from the presidency, she did not shy away from other league responsibilities. At the same May meeting where her resignation was accepted with regret, the directors elected Ueland to the board, appointed her as chairman of the Legislative Council, and named her honorary president, posts she would hold until her death. Anticipating the organization of the league, Ueland had formed the Legislative Council in May 1919 to serve as a coalition of women's groups committed to social reform. In 1920, its first full year of operation, the council consisted of representatives of sixteen organizations, including the Minnesota Federation of Women's Clubs, the National Council of Jewish Women, the Women's Trade Union League, the Women's Co-operative Alliance (a major group organized to prevent juvenile delinquency and to protect the morals of children and young women), the Woman's Club of Minneapolis, and the League of Catholic Women. Other members were the chairmen of the league's own standing committees, such as women in industry, living costs, education, child welfare, legal status and law enforcement, and social hygiene.[21]

The council identified current issues, held briefings with experts, and named subcommittees to conduct intensive study of each issue. Members then brought recommendations for action to the associations they represented for discussion and decision. After six months of study and research, the council brought to the league convention in December 1920 nine legislative proposals, all of which were endorsed as the league's action agenda for the 1921 legislative session. Even though the member organizations generally concurred with the recommendations, they were free to dissent, adopting only those that they considered compatible with their own interests. The fact that they could so frequently agree on a program of legislative action indicated the high priority that women's groups attached to their chosen issues.[22]

By the end of the 1921 session, Ueland and her colleagues in the Legislative Council had successfully championed seven of the nine measures: a five-dollar increase in the monthly pension maximum for mothers of dependent children; a bill enabling the state to accept the provisions of the federal Sheppard-Towner Maternity- and Infancy-Protection Act, which provided federal grants-in-aid to support centers for child hygiene and prenatal care; a street trades bill forbidding children under twelve from selling newspapers; an amendment to the school compulsory-attendance law; and three bills making women eligible to serve on juries. A bill providing for an eight-month minimum school term (there was no minimum, only a maximum of ten months) was the only defeat, losing in the House after having been unanimously passed by the Senate. An attempt to limit to eight hours the workday for women employed outside the home also passed, but it failed to become law because of a technicality that the league blamed on House opponents.[23]

Ueland described the final day of the session on April 21 as "the most tense, dramatic day I ever experienced," with the fate of two of the league-supported bills decided "in the feverish moments after midnight before the final adjournment." She arrived home after two o'clock in the morning "and realized that the winter's work was done." Six months later, in her presidential address to the league's third annual state convention, Marguerite Wells emphasized that much of its success was attributable to the influence of women in their own communities, bringing pressure to bear on their local legislators, and lobbying on the league's behalf in St. Paul under the direction of Clara Ueland. Throughout the session the state office had communicated regularly with league chairmen throughout the state, apprising them of the progress of bills and the attitudes of their legislators. League members, especially in the smaller communities, thus knew when to contact their legislators and to urge their fellow citizens to do the same. The league prepared a final report card on the roll-call votes and sent it to members as a supplement to an issue of the *Minnesota Woman Voter.*[24]

"It is wholly a new experience at the Legislature for them all to find women lobbying there, and *without personal interest,*" Clara Ueland said in 1923. "And it is a new experience for them to have to explain why they voted this way or that on a measure." The successes of the league's legislative program in that same year included a series of educational bills increasing the school term to seven months (their failure in 1921 to extend the school year to eight months may have prompted them to settle for a more conservative extension), revising state financial aids, strengthening provisions for compulsory attendance, and providing training for physical education in all public schools. The league also won a minimum wage and protection for women in industry, appropriations to implement the Sheppard-Towner Act, the regulation of dance halls, and the prohibition of itinerant carnivals. The league opposed bills repealing indeterminate sentences and excusing women from jury duty in "salacious" cases and supported a resolution favoring U.S. participation in the World Court.[25]

While many of these middle-class women were engaged in the fight to advance the economic rights of all women through protective legislation, the professional women associated with the NWP declared that power derived from equality was the best protection. Throughout the 1920s, while the principal women's organizations were aligned on the side of legislation addressing particular needs like wages and hours, the NWP agitated for the Equal Rights Amendment, which it had introduced in 1921. Claiming—with ample justification—that suffrage had been but one step in the elimination of inequality between men and women, the party proposed to level all distinctions in law between men and women. Although Wisconsin suffragists succeeded in passing a compromise equal rights law early in 1921 that preserved existing protections and privileges, and although Alice Paul, still president of the party, agreed not to contest league efforts to seek special protections for women in Massachusetts and New York, she soon stiffened her back to further concessions. Meetings between Paul and Maud Wood Park, National Consumers' League general secretary Florence Kelley, and representatives of working women in the latter part of 1921 were unsuccessful in healing the rift. As she left a meeting on December 4, Park said to Paul, "You will divide the women's movement."[26]

This division within the postsuffrage, feminist house pitted the NWP against most other women's organizations for four decades. It was built on a legacy of organizational jealousy, personal hostility, and ideological conflict. The rift between the party's agenda and that of the reformist women's groups surfaced in Minnesota in 1923 when Representative Myrtle Cain (a labor leader, NWP activist, and Farmer-Laborite from Hennepin County, who—in 1922—was among the first four women elected to the Minnesota House) and six of her male colleagues introduced an equal rights bill in the House. The three other women legislators were opposed. "This is not the time for a bill of this kind," said Hannah Kempfer, a farm wife, teacher, and Independent from Otter Tail County, "and besides, the bill is too sweeping. If there are any laws discriminatory against women these can be remedied by separate bills, not by one that takes in everything and would lead to endless litigation." Wells and Ueland sent a letter to legislators before the session began, enclosing a copy of the program developed by the Legislative Council and emphasizing their reasons for opposing the kind of "blanket" or indiscriminate coverage proposed by an equal rights bill.[27]

The league and many other women's organizations were also opposed to the equal rights bill because they feared it would jeopardize the protective legislation they had already secured. When the proposed amendment came to the floor of the Minnesota House on March 8, the first four women serving in the legislature had to take sides. Kempfer moved that it be indefinitely postponed, and her motion carried by a vote of seventy-eight to thirty. Cain voted against the motion to postpone; Kempfer and Mabeth Hurd Paige (Republican, Hennepin) voted in the affirmative; and Sue Dickey Hough (a businesswoman and Republican from Hennepin County), who was absent, said that she, too, would have voted to defeat the measure.[28]

In one meeting where Ueland spoke against this "dangerous and foolish bill," her former associate Bertha Moller, who was then head of the NWP in Minnesota, was heard to whisper, "These women are hopeless . . . living in the Middle Ages." At a 1925 celebration of the fifth anniversary of suffrage, two of the speakers—longtime Ueland friends Emily Bright and Sophie Kenyon—expressed their disappointment that women had not come together in support of the Equal Rights Amendment.[29]

As with the Minnesota league and those in other states, the National League of Women Voters was also pursuing an ambitious congressional agenda. By the time of its national convention in the spring of 1924, the league could point to several successes. The child labor amendment to the U.S. Constitution, giving Congress the power to limit, regulate, and prohibit the labor of persons under eighteen years of age, had been passed by the House and was on its way to the Senate. The Sheppard-Towner Act was in place. The Cable Act, enabling women to maintain their citizenship irrespective of marital status, had been passed. A women's bureau had been established in the U.S. Department of Labor to investigate conditions and to protect the

rights of wage-earning women, and the Bureau of Home Economics in the Department of Agriculture reflected the league's
interest in safe and low-cost food products. Even more impressive than these national legislative achievements were the 420
measures supported by state leagues that became law and the 64
measures opposed by state leagues that failed to pass. Most of the
new statutes were in the field of child welfare, but there were also
significant advances in mitigating various disabilities and discriminations affecting women.[30]

These legislative accomplishments were high points of the
league's early years as it struggled to define its mission, recruit
members, refine its organization, and raise money—struggles
common to any new group but especially critical to the league in
its role as the successor to NAWSA. For example, at the league's
founding convention in 1920, representatives of the General
Federation of Women's Clubs had expressed their concern that
the new organization would unnecessarily duplicate their own
work in civic education and on behalf of women's interests. Catt
had impatiently advised finding a way to work together, and the
convention passed a resolution that laid the basis for the organization of the Women's Joint Congressional Committee. While
Park worked hard to win and maintain the General Federation's
cooperation at the national level—especially during the presidency of Alice Winter between 1920 and 1924—friction persisted at the local level for several years. Despite this particular territorial dispute, the joint committee offered women's organizations
an effective means of achieving social and economic reforms.[31]

The league also had to cope with public surprise at the slug-
gish turnout of women voters, who did not seem to be making
the expected difference in the body politic, and with its own
disappointment that only a fraction (about a hundred thousand)
of the several million NAWSA members had chosen to join the
organization. The league also endured an attack on its loyalty,
including suggestions that Sheppard-Towner and other league-
supported legislation had been drafted in Moscow. John W.
Weeks, who had been defeated in his reelection bid to the U.S.

Members of the Minnesota League of Women Voters, Minneapolis, 1924

Senate in 1918 because Massachusetts suffragists had opposed him, had been appointed secretary of war by President Warren G. Harding. A unit within his department circulated a chart resembling a spiderweb that purported to show the interlocking directorate of women's organizations subverting the government. Park threatened Weeks (and, implicitly, the Harding administration) with political reprisals from twelve million women voters, and he ordered the charts destroyed.[32]

Even the league's successes required continuing vigilance. The Sheppard-Towner Act, a modest five-year program with an annual cost of one million dollars, gave the states money to operate programs aimed at reducing infant mortality and helping pregnant women. Even though federal aid to the states was not a new concept, Sheppard-Towner extended the reach of the federal government into the sphere of social welfare, which was previously the preserve of state and local governments or of private charities. Jealous of federal intrusion, opponents organized a campaign that proved to be obdurate and unyielding. In reality the legislation was designed simply to make sure that healthy mothers had healthy children. The bill had experienced a rough passage in its birthing, and opponents kept up a stream of invective until they succeeded in persuading Congress to terminate the act in 1929. Most damaging was the assault by the American Medical Association, which described the legislation as "socialistic" and destructive of family life, as denying patients their own doctors' services, and as an excuse for examining women for syphilis. Certain business interests and the Catholic and Lutheran churches found common cause in the opposing camp. Despite its short existence, the act did improve the health of mothers and their children, especially in rural areas. The comprehensive Social Security Act of 1935 resurrected Sheppard-Towner with many of the same provisions intact.[33]

If the health of mothers and young children was first on the list of welfare measures consuming the energies of league members, the protection of the child laborer was second. In December 1922 Clara Ueland became part of that process as Minnesota chairman of the campaign to back the proposed child labor amendment. Ueland's experience with public policy issues relating to children could be traced back to her efforts beginning in 1892 to establish kindergartens in the Minneapolis public schools. In 1916 Governor Burnquist had appointed her to the Minnesota Child Welfare Commission, which was charged with examining existing laws and proposing new ones in four areas: "defective" children, as the physically and mentally disabled were then called; dependency and neglect; delinquency; and general child welfare. Legislation growing out of the commission's work had placed Minnesota in the forefront of states with exemplary children's codes, described by one historian as "perhaps the greatest achievement in the history of Minnesota's social legislation." Even so, the code had not addressed every concern relating to children, not the least of which was the child at work.[34]

In a lengthy newspaper interview published on December 3, 1922, Ueland described the extent of child labor in the United States and its tragic consequences. One out of every twelve children between the ages of ten and fifteen was in the labor force, and American children—on average—spent less than one day in four in school. As many as five million people were illiterate, with the highest rates in regions employing the highest proportion of children. Some children worked ten hours a day, others worked from sunrise to sunset in textile mills, factories, canneries, and mines. The proposed amendment would give Congress the power "to limit, regulate and prohibit the labor of persons under 18 years of age." At its 1923 convention the national league jumped on the bandwagon of amendment supporters in response to the urging of Julia C. Lathrop, a former league official and former head of the U.S. Children's Bureau. Florence Kelley presided over a subcommittee of the Women's Joint Congressional Committee that plotted legislative strategies in support of the amendment. The Women's Joint Congressional Committee associations joined with other groups to form Organizations Associated for Ratification of the Child Labor Amendment, and both major political parties called for approval of the amendment in their 1924 party platforms.[35]

For a moment it seemed as if the amendment would become law. Pushed by women's organizations, the National Child Labor Committee, and the American Child Health Association (a Herbert Hoover initiative), Congress passed it in 1924. But as it went to the states for ratification, the opposing forces began to exercise their political muscle. A formidable group, including the National Association of Manufacturers, the U.S. Chamber of Commerce, the American Farm Bureau Federation, and southern textile interests, called the amendment "communistic" and charged that it would undermine parental authority and dilute states' rights. Several states in the South refused to ratify the amendment, but more damaging was the defeat in Massachusetts, where seventeen groups led by the league had orchestrated the campaign on its behalf. The Chamber of Commerce and the local Catholic hierarchy opposed the amendment, and in the end their arguments prevailed. State after state followed the lead of Massachusetts. By early 1925 only four states had approved the child labor amendment.[36]

In Minnesota the campaign for ratification became a major interest of the league until the House approved a resolution rejecting the amendment by a vote of sixty-eight to fifty-six on February 27; the Senate followed suit on April 14, first by voting down a recommendation for ratification by forty-two to twenty-two and then adopting the House resolution against the amendment by a vote of thirty-six to twenty-eight. In that year the league succeeded in helping to pass a comprehensive state governmental reorganization bill but, as Ueland said, "little else." She observed curtly that it was "a reactionary period." Although the child labor amendment never became a part of the Constitution, subsequent laws, such as the Fair Labor Standards Act of 1938 ("prohibiting the employment of children under sixteen in industries engaged in interstate commerce and young people under eighteen in dangerous occupations"), eventually removed the most flagrant abuses that had sparked the campaign.[37]

For four years Clara Ueland had worked on behalf of the amendment, but when it became clear that the effort had failed, she found another cause to energize league members. At the league's convention in November 1926 she told a session: "Now this is the time of energy for the World Court. . . . This is the time of night and winter for the Child Labor Amendment, and the time of night and of winter and of rest is not without its uses. . . . It is a time . . . I believe, for renewing energy, for crystallizing ideas, for gathering ourselves for a new attack." It was a typical response to what Clara Ueland no doubt regarded as a temporary defeat. "She well knew the slowness of reform but also that reform was inexorable," Brenda Ueland commented.[38]

In selecting the World Court as the target for that new attack, Ueland reflected a league priority that Catt had articulated at its 1921 national convention when she made an impassioned plea to the delegates to campaign for peace. Responding enthusiastically, they authorized the league to enter the foreign policy arena, which was "destined," as league historian Louise Young described it, "to be among the most fruitful of its intellectual dominions." Two years later the league joined the effort to have the United States become a member of the World Court, a body formally known as the Permanent Court of International Justice, which was established in 1920 by the Covenant of the League of Nations. Although U.S. reluctance to take up the responsibilities of world leadership led Congress to vote against joining the League of Nations in 1920, support in the nation remained strong for the World Court. Even some Americans opposed to membership in the League of Nations advocated that the United States participate in this new judicial body. President Harding had asked the Senate to give its consent to ratification in 1923, and, after his death that same year, President Calvin Coolidge reiterated that request. Opposition to the World Court came from those who, fearing any surrender of national sovereignty, objected to the concept of compulsory jurisdiction by an international judicial body.[39]

Clara Ueland readily associated herself with the League of Women Voters' new interest in foreign policy issues. In 1921 she agreed to chair the Minnesota league's Standing Committee on the International Reduction of Armaments in 1921. Like Catt she was not a pacifist—there is no evidence, for example, that she joined the Women's International League for Peace and Freedom, which was led in Minnesota by her friend Maud Stockwell—but she consistently deplored the use of war to settle conflicts between nations. She and Mabeth Hurd Paige probably composed the resolution sent late that year by the Minnesota league board to President Harding expressing appreciation for the arms reductions achieved at the Washington Naval Conference and foreseeing "the possibility of a plan by which wars shall be prevented, and peace maintained by international understanding."[40]

Ueland enthusiastically endorsed a Minnesota league plan to obtain a mile of signatures on a petition supporting U.S. adherence to the World Court and traveled in the summer of 1923 with league associates in the "World Court Car" to several congressional districts to gather signatures. After the signatures were obtained, "General" Clara Ueland and several hundred

Henriette T. McKnight, Grace M. Petersen, Edna Hargreaves, Marie M. McGuire, and Belle M. Purdy in Washington, D.C., December 1923, delivering the MLWV's petition supporting the World Court.

other women marched down Nicollet Avenue in Minneapolis on December 10 to celebrate the achievement. The petitions were packed in hat boxes and entrusted to a delegation headed by Henriette T. McKnight, president of the fifth district (Minneapolis) league, who traveled to Washington, D.C., and delivered them to President Coolidge and Secretary of State Charles Evans Hughes. After welcoming the delegates, Coolidge and Hughes advised them to deliver the petitions instead to the two isolationist Minnesota senators—Henrik Shipstead and Magnus Johnson—neither of whom had agreed to support U.S. participation.[41]

In 1925, as the national campaign for the World Court escalated, Clara Ueland remained optimistic that as women acquired "more influence and more power and wider knowledge," they would persist in their determination to end war: "Gathered in groups as never before and armed with power in unison, they are demanding that, one by one, the necessary steps be taken to bring about a civilization in which law and not war shall prevail." In January 1926 the U.S. Senate adopted a resolution of adherence but attached a fifth reservation enabling the United States to bar the court from rendering "advisory opinions" perceived to be adverse to U.S. interests; this reservation proved to be unacceptable to the other member nations. Later attempts to win congressional approval for membership in the World Court would also fail, leaving the United States outside this arena of international cooperation.[42]

Legislative issues, the child labor amendment, and the World Court were not the league's sole preoccupations. From the time of its founding, leaders of the League of Women Voters urged women to join and become active as well in the political party of their choice. But even the leadership did not always follow this advice. When Jessie Scott, an activist in the Democratic party and later a national committeewoman, asked Clara Ueland in 1919 for a public commitment as a Democrat, Ueland hedged, saying her sympathy had been more with the Democrats than with the Republicans, "but I am not ready to align myself with either party for the present." She was more definite in a remark she made a year later: "As for me, I would normally be a Democrat but I am strong for Hoover. Aside from liking Hoover, my strongest conviction is that I could not possibly be a Republican." When Warren Harding got the Republican nod in 1920, Clara supported his Democratic opponent, James M. Cox, also of Ohio, whom she admired as a suffrage supporter and opponent of child labor. Her apprehension about Harding made her show her political colors publicly when she volunteered to stump the state for Cox during the candidate's Labor Day visit to Minnesota.[43]

In the 1920 presidential election—the first following the ratification of the Nineteenth Amendment—twenty million women became eligible to vote. There was no upsurge in the number of those who voted, however. Both men and women were apathetic about the unexciting campaign, which pitted the two men of Ohio against each other. Minnesota women did better at voting than the national average, however: 50 percent of the women qualified to vote in the state went to the polls, as compared with only 37 percent of women nationwide. Eight women ran for national office in 1920, but the only congressional winner was Alice Mary Robertson, an Oklahoma Republican who had been against suffrage and whose opposition to the Sheppard-Towner Act had offended even the antis, many of whom supported reform legislation.[44]

Although Clara Ueland never stepped forward as a candidate herself, she was a strong advocate of electing women to public office. She had high hopes that as many as twenty women would be elected to the state legislature in 1922, but she cautioned that women candidates should not expect other women to vote for them merely because of their sex. The presence in the legislature of women possessing "ability, forcefulness, and character" would expedite programs of particular concern to women, Ueland believed. Marguerite Wells urged her colleagues in the league and other public-spirited women to take the responsibility of recruiting women to run for office. Although the league's policy precluded endorsements, "We may and should help start a movement to get women . . . of the right sort to stand for office." Wells advised that districts having vacancies or legislators with poor records offered the best opportunities for women candidates to succeed.[45]

Four of the eight women contesting for seats in the Minnesota legislature won in 1922—the first year of their eligibility for elective office. (Grace F. Kaercher, who was elected in 1922 as clerk of the state supreme court, was the first woman elected to a statewide office and the first elected as clerk of any state supreme court.) Although four was far short of the twenty women legislators that Ueland had hoped for, the good news was that, including Minnesota, ninety-eight women had been elected to legislative seats in thirty-five states, more than tripling the number elected in 1920.[46]

In the national arena, only sixteen women ran for Congress in 1922. Once again there was only one winner, Winifred Mason

Huck of Illinois, who finished the unexpired term of her father. She would be the first of a series of women taking the "coffin" route to public office by filling out terms of deceased male relatives, most frequently husbands. In that same election, Anna Dickie Olesen became the first Minnesota woman to run for the U.S. Senate. Well known and popular with women voters of all parties and well liked by her audiences, she won the public endorsement of Clara Ueland and of prominent club leaders. Olesen got off to a good start by winning a commanding victory in the Democratic primary on June 19. Her two opponents were incumbent Frank Kellogg, a poor campaigner, and Farmer-Labor challenger Henrik Shipstead, whose oratory appealed to farmers suffering in 1922 from depressed farm prices. Olesen attempted to moderate the novelty of a woman running for national political office: "I ask no consideration because I am a woman," she said. "I also ask that no one close his mind against me because I am a woman." Despite her demonstrated abilities, neither she nor other Democrats nor even Republicans could contend with the growing strength of the Farmer-Labor party, which swept Shipstead into the U.S. Senate, three congressmen into the U.S. House, twenty-four into the state senate, and forty-six members into the lower house of the legislature.[47]

There were similar disappointments on the voting front in 1922, with women showing a reluctance to go to the polls. Like most states in nonpresidential years, Minnesota experienced a decline (14 percent) in voter turnout that year from 1920 levels. Results were better, however, in smaller communities where the league made a special effort. In Graceville in Big Stone County, for example, the vote increased by 26 percent, and the women outvoted the men.[48]

Ueland continued to push the league to get more women involved in politics. In the fall of 1923 she proposed that the state league establish a committee to find ways to encourage qualified women to become candidates, and she persuaded the state board to urge league members to attend party meetings,

Minnesota Leauge of Women Voters bellringers march to get out the vote,
1924.

caucuses, and conventions so that they would become familiar
with the landscape of the political parties.[49]

In the summer of 1924 Andreas and Clara Ueland went to
Norway for an extended visit. It would be her second trip there,
and her last. Clara was impressed by the turnout of the Norwegian women, who went to the polls in large numbers without
the urging of an organization like the league. The Uelands
returned home in time for Clara to participate in the league's
national get-out-the-vote campaign in the fall presidential election. In Minnesota the centerpiece of that effort was a caravan
carrying a "Torch of Democracy" that wound eleven hundred
miles from the Canadian border to the Iowa border, urging citizens in general and women in particular to go to the polls. Clara
joined the caravan at Wells, and she was chosen as a pioneer
suffragist to present the torch to Governor Jacob A. O. Preus in

St. Paul on the day before the election. She and other caravan "evangelists" found themselves in church pulpits on Sunday mornings to preach the "gospel of citizenship." Edna Hargreaves, chairman of the Minnesota league's committee on international cooperation, noted that "if any one had ever told me that I would be moved to preach three sermons before large congregations a few years ago, I would have fainted."[50]

This unprecedented league effort to get out the vote increased the number of ballots cast for president by nearly 12 percent (but the turnout barely increased from the 50 percent of 1920), convincing league leaders that an increase in the number of those who took their civic responsibilities seriously was an everyday task that required more than exhortations at election time. Despite the energetic vote drive organized by state leagues around the country, only one woman, Mary H. Norton, a product of the New Jersey Democratic party machine, was elected to Congress, making a total of three women elected to national office in three successive elections—not a very impressive showing. Norton, however, would remain in office for twenty-six years.[51]

Efforts and exhortations did begin to produce winning women in local elections in Minnesota. A 1927 league survey revealed that 204 women had been elected to county and municipal offices: of the 70 women elected to county office, 54 were superintendents of schools; and of the 184 elected to municipal office, 51 held positions as village, town, and city clerks. Women school-board members were too numerous to include in the study, and the same was true of women holding appointive office. At last count in an earlier survey, 855 filled such positions on town boards. In keeping with the league's commitment to give women officeholders the greatest possible visibility, the 1926 league convention in Duluth included a panel featuring Representative Hannah Kempfer, Bess M. Wilson, a regent of the University of Minnesota, and Florence Stukel, a game warden from Crow Wing County.[52]

Despite the league's continuing efforts, however, women throughout the 1920s persisted in voting in lower numbers than men—in Minnesota as in the nation—and they continued to be greatly underrepresented in public office.[53]

Despite setbacks on some legislative issues and disappointments in women voter turnouts and in the election of women to high public office, the League of Women Voters could savor the fact that women were learning day by day how to use the political system and were gaining confidence that they could produce results serving the public interest. In her remarks at the Minnesota league luncheon celebrating the Nineteenth Amendment's fifth anniversary, Clara Ueland could rightly claim that women had "made good" with their vote. "They have more influence and more power and wider knowledge," Clara said. "Having the vote gives them the feeling of self respect for their privilege of helping mold the destinies of the country."[54]

Clara Ueland herself was still playing a central role within the young Minnesota League of Women Voters as the key legislative activist, as a board member, as a prominent fund-raiser, and as a catalyst in efforts on behalf of women, children and world peace. Although she had relinquished the nominal leadership of the organization, Ueland remained a commanding presence in the public life of Minnesota.[55]

11

THE FINAL DAY

*The women of her state feel that they owe
to this fine woman and her splendid
leadership a debt that can never be paid.*

Vivian Stanley Thorp, *Woman Citizen,*
September 1919

 When Clara Ueland awakened in her Minneapolis home on March 1, 1927, she readied herself with anticipation and determination for another day in the halls of Minnesota's handsome state Capitol in St. Paul. After thirty-seven years of civic activity, at the age of sixty-six, she still had a cause to argue, a case to present. On this particular Tuesday she would continue her quiet but persistent efforts to have the legislature introduce a ratification resolution on behalf of the child labor amendment to the U.S. Constitution. Two years earlier, the legislature had rejected ratification, but Ueland was not prepared to accept that defeat as the final answer when it came to protection against the economic exploitation of children.[1]

At breakfast Clara may have prepared some household lists for the servants and discussed matters with Andreas, perhaps about their children—some far away, others living nearby. Sigurd, Arnulf, and Rolf had built homes for their families on Andreas's property, and the corner acres of Calhoun Boulevard and Richfield Road now constituted a Ueland compound. Clara

Clara Ueland

Ueland must have been reassured by the success of the three daughters and four sons whom she had raised with love and attention. They were intelligent, productive citizens; several possessed artistic and athletic talents, all of them were serious about and interested in the world around them. They were also merry and witty and enjoyed good times in one another's company. More than likely, Ueland also glanced at the newspaper. A headline on the front page of the *Minneapolis Morning Tribune,* "U.S. Aids in Peace Move in Nicaragua," surely captured her attention. In a letter to Brenda a few days before, she said she hoped to get Andreas to go with her to a Foreign Policy Association dinner meeting on American relations with Mexico and Nicaragua. She would have been pleased to read an editorial approving a regional conference, sponsored by fifty educational, health, and welfare groups, to address concerns relating to the physical and moral well-being of children. She may also have scanned the society page for news of her friends.[2]

Arriving at the Capitol after an hour's streetcar ride, Ueland undoubtedly exchanged greetings with incumbent legislators. She and associates from the Minnesota league and other member organizations of the Legislative Council planned their day's work, and she went about the business of prodding and persuading. It was not a very successful morning. Sometime around noon, Ueland went to Mabeth Paige's office and succumbed to rare vitriol and even tears over an unidentified senator whose antiquated views frustrated her beyond belief. Her daughter Brenda described him as "a moss-back of an old fool with an arteriosclerotic stiff old brain that had not had a living thought for twenty years." The two good friends had lunch together before they returned to their respective legislative frays. Thinking ahead to the 1929 session, Ueland had already proposed that the league send speakers on an educational campaign on legislative issues throughout the state.[3]

Ueland left the legislature earlier than usual to keep an appointment with a physician who was looking after her wrist, which she had broken in a fall. It was late in the afternoon when she got on a streetcar in downtown Minneapolis to go home. The weather was wet, the wind was blowing, and the streets were icy. Brenda told what happened at about five o'clock when Clara got off the streetcar at Thirty-ninth Street: "Now this alighting place was under the pretty stone bridge over which the [Calhoun] Boulevard winds through woods from Lake Calhoun to Lake Harriet. . . . She walked down the Boulevard toward Lake Calhoun. There the road converged with Richfield Road which went up the gentle hill along the Ueland Pasture." As Ueland started to cross Richfield Road, she came into the path of a light truck being driven by a young electrician who lived on nearby Upton Avenue.

> He tried to slow down. He sounded his horn at 75 feet. The wheels of his truck were in frozen ruts and . . . he made a final effort to avoid her by turning sharply away from her to the right toward the Ueland driveway. Probably her arm in the sling had affected the usual flowing ease of her reflexes. . . . To his horror his front wheels spun out of the ruts but the rear ones skidded and the back of his truck dashed her to the ground. . . . Sigurd sent the terrible telegram to me, and Elsa and Anne in the East, to poor Torvald in Pittsburgh and alone.
>
> *Darling mother killed suddenly, struck by car at our driveway.*[4]

"Mrs. Andreas Ueland Killed," read the banner headline across the front page of the *Minneapolis Morning Tribune* on March 2, 1927. The fact that such a respected community leader had been the victim of a tragic accident seemed to magnify the grief felt by her family and friends and by the many others whose lives had been touched by Clara Ueland's causes and crusades. No one was more upset than the driver of the truck, who knew and respected Ueland. He was so distraught that he collapsed while being questioned by the police and had to be taken to General Hospital. A man and his son who witnessed the accident testified that the driver had made every effort to avoid it.[5]

Brenda, Anne, and Elsa took the train together from New York City to Minneapolis. On the same train was Marguerite Wells, also returning from the East, perhaps from a trustees' meeting at Smith College. During the journey Brenda recalled her last time with her mother in Brenda's Connecticut home. Clara had taken the train from New York and on the way had read a lengthy narrative of the "bombarding of the atoms" in the *New York Times:* "She had read it all, many columns of small print, and then had learned the total account with care—schoolteacher that she was—for she knew that it was a great revolutionary event in the history of physics." After dinner she gave Brenda and her five-year-old daughter, Gaby, a full explanation of this momentous happening. Brenda later wrote about that visit, concluding with these words:

> I, as always, experienced a happy carefree bliss that she was there for two days. How interesting, how heartening and delightful to have her! It was very mysterious. When she was there (alas, it was not so with many mothers) one felt light-hearted, freed, debonair, cozy, confident, talkative to the Nth power. Why was it? Well you were in the presence of a great soul and not an ordinary soul. Clear, golden life and intelligence poured from her and released whatever there was of it in yourself and flooded all surrounding space.[6]

Anne may have thought about her mother's recent description of home during the holidays: "The world was as beautiful as a miracle—a damp snow fell and it turned a little cold[,] freezing a shining bejewelled covering on every branch and twig. Minnesota never was so lovely." Clara's last letter to Elsa had included a political note, "I am going to the Legislature tomorrow as usual.

We are having hard sledding with our Welfare measures, a reactionary and extra-economical spirit holds this part of the country."[7]

When the daughters reached home, they helped Andreas with the funeral arrangements. "It was queer," recalled Brenda, "it seemed cheerful and a relief for us to be talking so, in such ordinary voices, such as at a gathering when the children have come home for the holidays. But at something, Father suddenly began to cry. His voice came in loud, adult sobs, his chest heaving. But he stopped in just a minute, just a second or two. This made the most heart-breaking impression."[8]

Clara Ueland's funeral was held on Saturday, March 5, in the chapel at Lakewood Cemetery, less than a mile from her home. Despite her displeasure with the humanistic focus of the Minneapolis Unitarian Society, she had not turned her back on Unitarianism. Frederick M. Eliot, the minister of Unity Church in St. Paul, officiated. Clara, who was an expert gardener, would have admired the flowers that adorned the chapel but would have deplored their overabundance. A modest though confident woman, she also would have been embarrassed by the review of her life and the outpouring of tributes from her friends. In the days following her death, journalists, longtime friends, associates, and even political foes spoke to the qualities of her life and leadership. Lillian E. Taaffe, a reporter who had covered many of Ueland's civic activities for the *Minneapolis Tribune*, wrote that she was "Minnesota's best known and best loved leader of leaders" among pioneer suffragists, "an outstanding figure in the state for more than a half century, and the most notable woman . . . at the state legislature" on behalf of suffrage and ratification. Calling her "a natural leader," Charles B. Cheney of the *Minneapolis Journal* added: "For about 20 years Mrs. Ueland had been the best known and most influential woman in public life in Minnesota." A headline in the *Journal* referred to her as a "feminist general," but an editorial in the *St. Paul Pioneer Press* suggested that she "regarded herself not primarily as a feminist but as a participant in the busy world of politics."[9]

Women who had worked closely with Clara in the suffrage movement perhaps knew her better than anyone outside the family. Carrie Chapman Catt recalled that period of intense effort and sacrifice in her own tribute:

> The passing of Mrs. Ueland leaves a sad gap in the old band of suf-frage veterans. She was a spirited factor in the genial comradeship that kept the campaign going without pause, a faithful follower, a bold leader, and an untiring prophet of the cause. . . . Mrs. Ueland was a heroine whose step never wavered when the torrent of oppo-sition roared loudest. There never was a call to which she did not give quick and sturdy response. . . . That kind of moral courage is rare, and characterizes the great—the makers of history. A greater soul has gone than Minnesota now recognizes; another day, it will build her a monument.[10]

A public memorial service was held at the Capitol on March 20. Among the organizers were Jane Humbird Burr and Jose-phine Sarles Simpson of the league and Florence Carpenter, whom Ueland held in high regard but who had been an oppo-nent in the suffrage drama. Despite a "blinding snow storm," according to the *Minneapolis Morning Tribune*, "pioneer workers associated with Mrs. Ueland . . . came out to pay her tribute—nothing could keep them from having a part in the great memo-rial to their 'chief'—a memorial never before staged for any pri-vate citizen in Minnesota." The event, which drew two thousand people, was the first such service broadcast by wcco radio. Still another first was an act passed unanimously by both houses of the legislature permitting a tablet in Ueland's honor to be placed in the Capitol as a permanent memorial.[11]

Although the service included many speakers, the remarks of Ole Sageng, Ueland's old friend in the suffrage battle, were most eloquent. She was, he said,

> a woman of strong and earnest convictions but she was wholly free from that narrowness of view which often manifests itself in an intolerant or even disrespectful attitude toward those who hold a

different opinion. She realized that we cannot hope to solve the problems of our political democracy if we are not big enough to qualify as citizens of a genuine democracy of thought. . . .

She loved justice. In her political and social philosophy that word was not a thing to parade for effect in idle declarations. It was a reality to be translated by her personal efforts as far as she could into the environments and the lives of the helpless, the weak and the erring.[12]

The commission for the bronze memorial tablet was awarded to Louise Cross, a young Minneapolis sculptor who had studied at the Minneapolis School of Art and at the Art Institute of Chicago. It was unveiled in the Capitol rotunda on April 4, 1928.[13]

Andreas Ueland with Arnulf's children, Andrea and Arnulf, Jr., Easter 1927

As part of its response to Ueland's death, the Minnesota League of Women Voters sponsored a drive to raise money for a fellowship at the University of Minnesota in her name. On July 12, 1929, the university accepted a gift of contributions totaling more than eleven thousand dollars for the establishment of a Clara Ueland Fellowship "to prepare a young woman for leadership in the service of good government."

Ueland's family had its own adjustments to make. Although Andreas continued to practice law, he was less busy now that Sigurd and Rolf had joined his practice. In 1930, four years after her divorce, Brenda and her daughter, Gabrielle (named for Andreas's father, Ole Gabriel), moved to Minneapolis to live with Andreas in the big house. Brenda stayed and cared for him until he died three years later. His book, *Recollections of an Immigrant,* which was mostly completed before Clara's death, was published in 1929. In his review of the book, historian Theodore C. Blegen wrote that

> many Minnesotans will feel a faint regret here, for Minnesota is proud both of the judge and of Mrs. Ueland—and indeed of the entire Ueland family. Mrs. Ueland's name and character are written into the broad story of the struggle for social betterment in Minnesota; and the reader, though conscious throughout of the ubiquitous influence of this remarkable woman, would gladly have forgiven the judge if he had permitted himself to speak more freely of his family.[14]

"In Memoriam" is the one chapter that Andreas devoted to Clara. Its seven pages mostly consist of a brief description of her interests and the circumstances of her death, together with lengthy excerpts from the speeches of the memorial service. At the end of the chapter, Andreas wrote:

> I used sometimes to say to her, half seriously and half in fun, quoting Browning:
> Grow old with me!
> The best is yet to be.
> It held good to the First of March, 1927.[15]

Reflecting in his book about the fifty-seven years since his emigration to America, Andreas wrote: "The strongest memories are of the wife, and of the home she and I made, and of the children from earliest infancy until they now promise to bring the family in all worthy things of life to higher levels than I have reached." Andreas Ueland died on July 30, 1933, at the age of eighty-one. Brenda remembered "his bravery, gallantry, swagger, truculence, vigor; his beauty, his humor, irony, fight, his integrity. Never in his life did he say anything he didn't mean."

What manner of woman was Clara Ueland? What was there about her that prompted both women and men to be so enthusiastic in their praise? Even discounting the exaggerated rhetoric that sometimes inflates an individual's life after death, people's response to Ueland demonstrated that she possessed special qualities that set her apart as a human being and as a leader. Having grown up with a passive and dependent mother, she had learned to do for herself. Her experience as a young teacher helped develop her capacity for caring and intensified her commitment to provide equal educational opportunities for children of diverse backgrounds. As a wife, she became an efficient manager of a large household. She created a supportive environment for her children and encouraged them to be daring in thought and activity. Membership in the Peripatetics honed her intellectual skills, and her work to bring kindergartens to the public schools established her reputation as a woman who made things happen.

The demands on Ueland for leadership seemed never ending. She set an example of responsibility and hard work and expected the same of her associates. They were eager to please her, and she treated her friends and coworkers with kindness and consideration—even if she was sometimes impatient when their performances fell short of her expectations. Clara was unassuming, generous in giving credit where it was due, and quick to express her appreciation for a job well done. No wonder that women liked working with her. She was an intelligent, competent woman who knew how to achieve goals and to have a good time in the process. Although her leadership of the Minnesota Woman Suffrage Association represented the pinnacle of her political life, it was neither the end nor the sum of her civic career. Josephine Simpson provided a partial litany of some of Ueland's other activities:

> better sanitary care of school buildings, medical inspection in the public schools, the establishment of a Juvenile Court, a Tag Day

for the benefit of Visiting Nurses, a pure milk supply, the abate-
ment of smoke, public playgrounds, cleaner streets, early Christmas shopping, the closing of shops on Christmas Eve, and the
Saturday half holiday for employees, better lodging houses for
working women, the abolishment of billboards, securing women
on the school board, the abolishment of the Red Light District,
the promotion of better drama, especially for High School students, and a pure water supply for Minneapolis.[16]

Above all, Ueland was a good and decent woman. Brenda,
remarking on the atypical character of her mother's great political power, conjured the memory of candidates for state office
seeking to persuade Clara to back them:

> This amused us (we could see the man gravely talking to her, in the
> sunlight on the front porch) because she was so unlike a political
> boss. Instead of a cigar and conniving, there was naïve, clear dis-
> interested goodness. That is, if it were proposed to have a play-
> ground downtown that would have cut the value of Father's court
> house lot in two, she would be very much interested in it. A play-
> ground. A good idea. Of course, this was a family joke, but it tells
> how she was.[17]

Soon after Clara's death, Minnesota league president Marguerite Wells described her as a person "whose sympathy flowed
no more freely for those she sought to protect than for those who
sometimes opposed her, a woman whose unwavering activity in
behalf of the public interest was never marred by malice nor
bitterness." Friends and foes alike were impressed with Clara
Ueland's civility in discourse and in deed. The ability to disagree
without being disagreeable and the recognition that every woman
and man has a right to her or his opinion and to express that
opinion freely were key values in her understanding of the good
life. The fact that her opponents treated her with courtesy and
respect was evidence of her ability to listen but not to capitulate.[18]

Like many women of her time, Clara was serious and earnest
when such behavior was called for, but she also enjoyed the

lighthearted side of work and friendships. Suffrage supporters and their families looked forward to the several fund-raising parties given over the years at the Ueland home. Hope McDonald commented on the "brilliancy and gayety" of the last of these suffrage garden parties. Clara especially liked the gatherings at Jane Burr's St. Paul home or at the Minnesota Club, where they could talk about the day's events "after some of our exciting sessions" at the legislature. The camaraderie of women working together was part of the joy of doing what they did—it was not all serious business, for there were anecdotes to be told, experiences to be related, and laughter to be shared. Frances Perkins, who served as the country's first woman cabinet member, once observed that "women learned to like each other in that suffrage movement." Historians Dorothy and Carl J. Schneider concluded that "part of what kept them toiling away through such discouragements and for so long was the sheer fun of it."[19]

Despite her gentle manner, however, Ueland could give and receive criticism. Women who left the MWSA for the NWP, for example, were obviously distressed over what they regarded as Ueland's conservative and conventional leadership. Ueland herself remarked of the Kansas woman who chaired the council of state presidents in the year of transition from suffrage to the League of Women Voters that she "was unequal to her position. . . . as a speaker and propagandist she is a failure." Yet her judgments were based not on petty vitriol but on the high standards she demanded of others, no less than of herself.[20]

Clara Ueland was a woman of conviction. She declared herself to be a Woodrow Wilson Democrat even though she spent most of her years in Minnesota working with progressive-minded Republicans, as well as with contrarians of both parties who tried her soul but seldom exhausted her patience. She was a Unitarian who went elsewhere when new ministers did not fit her definition of Unitarianism, but she was loyal in her opposition. She was a feminist who believed that women must make and take opportunities to do for themselves and to speak for themselves in achieving fuller lives and larger liberties.

Clara Ueland fit comfortably into that era of Progressive politics within which suffrage flourished and finally succeeded. One element of Progressivism was the elevation of a state of civic virtue that was characterized by high moral standards and by the desire for basic societal reforms. In many respects, Ueland personified that civic virtue. Although her interests were broad, she seized suffrage as the issue of her time and gave it her Minnesota signature. She did not work alone to achieve this goal, of course, but she functioned as a leader not fearful of the task or arrogant in its undertaking. Moving women to heights they could scarcely imagine, she gave them a chance to prove themselves in the public realm and finally to enjoy their hard-won success.

REFLECTIONS

 It has been commonplace to conclude that suffrage was in one sense a failure, promising so much and delivering so little. Most Americans anticipated a great transformation from such a stunning victory. Along the way to winning the vote women had gained other rights—the right to own property, to possess their wages and earnings, to make contracts and bring suits, and to have equal guardianship of their children. Because of these gains, and because the achievement of suffrage seemed to represent the climax of women's ambitions, other areas of deprivation and discrimination against women were ignored or dismissed as inconsequential.

Suffragists did not necessarily subscribe to the proposition that the enfranchisement of women would advance their causes or solve the nation's ills. As early as 1907 Maud Stockwell had predicted that the woman's vote "will not bring the millennium; it will not insure prohibition; it will not purify politics; it will not curb the corporations. . . . Women do not base their plea for the ballot on the good they promise to do with it, but upon the fact that they are justly entitled to it." She added that a woman had the same right as a man to use the vote foolishly and that many women would probably do so. Ethel Hurd was of the same mind: "We anticipate many mistakes and sad blunders, but hope wisdom will come with experience." As MWSA president, Clara Ueland cautioned in 1915 that while suffrage would serve in the long run as an influence "on the side of good," it did not promise to "correct all evils."[1]

Despite the cautionary notes of these Minnesota leaders, all three would have been pleased with the assessment made by Marguerite Wells a decade later. Responding to the criticism that suffrage had failed to live up to expectations, Wells identified positive results: "I did not realize before suffrage was won how different from men's was the contribution women might make to American political life, nor how great would be the need of their new and different contribution." Wells mentioned in particular the efforts of women in expanding the commitment of government to programs of public welfare and their leadership in ridding the world of "the scourge of war."[2]

The public, as well as some suffragists, had other expectations: a high turnout of women who would vote cohesively and the election of large numbers of women to office. (During the struggle for the vote, suffragists seldom spoke of women holding public office.) While the turnout proved to be varied and the numbers of elected women few, significant postsuffrage policy reforms supported by women did in fact become law because decision makers feared the consequences of the first two expectations.[3]

In the years after suffrage, many roadblocks still impeded women's progress. While women had greater access to educational opportunities, their actual enrollment in colleges and universities declined from 1920 to 1930 by nearly 4 percent. Job opportunities were limited to female occupations, and even in the fields they dominated—like education—women were often denied top positions. During the Great Depression of the 1930s women lost ground in professions such as law and medicine by a measure of nearly 2 percent. Equal opportunity in the workplace, to say nothing of more equitable pay, stayed a distant dream. The achievement of suffrage also did not halt the physical and mental abuse of women, who kept to themselves until the 1970s the full extent of battering in the home and harassment on the job.[4]

Achieving the right to vote turned out to be not the final step but rather one in a series of steps in the arduous journey of women seeking equality and individuality. While suffrage by itself did not transform women's lives, "it was," historian Ellen Carol DuBois observed, "the first independent movement of women for their own liberation." It also represented a commitment to gaining control over their own lives and constituted "a major change in the condition of those lives."[5]

After 1920 women's interests and activities in the public realm became diversified and would never again attain the unity associated with the campaign to pass the Nineteenth Amendment. Lacking suffrage as a centerpiece, the women's movement experienced a letdown and an understandable slackening of momentum. Some of the women who were energized by the suffrage movement chose to follow in the footsteps of the National League of Women Voters. A few found partisan politics a more appropriate outlet, even in a decade in which the presidencies of Warren Harding and Calvin Coolidge diminished the integrity and the role of government. Other women gravitated to other organizations or pursued other interests or simply rested and caught their breath. The postsuffrage decade witnessed women trying on different roles, exercising a new cultural language, and struggling to define their goals. Common purpose eluded the movement as the National Woman's Party and the National League of Women Voters engaged in a continuing quarrel over the best way to advance women's interests, whether by a sweeping equity amendment or by specific protective legislation.

One cannot conclude that the women's movement was merely dormant in the 1920s and 1930s, however, without overlooking the significant organizational and legislative achievements of those decades. While certain organizations active in the suffrage enterprise declined in vigor or influence, others changed their operations, and new associations emerged. Name a cause or issue, and there were sure to be women involved and probably leading the way. The suffrage campaign had produced many experienced executive alumnae who had the skills and drive to head large national organizations. In the contrasting worlds of the Roaring Twenties and the Depression Thirties and beyond, extraordinarily large numbers of women were actively engaged through their associations in the political process. Common cause, however, was hard to achieve among groups whose specificity in mission and membership intensified the diversities of race, ethnicity, class, and politics among women.[6]

Minnesota women followed the same course of dispersal and fragmentation. Maud Stockwell became the first president of the Minnesota chapter of the Women's International League for Peace and Freedom, serving in that capacity from 1922 to 1934. Josephine Simpson's longtime interest in the Women's Co-operative Alliance, an organization designed to help young people and to prevent delinquency, led to her subsequent involvement as a member of the advisory board of the Birth Control League. Josephine Schain, who served on the national staff of the National League of Women Voters, assisted Carrie Chapman Catt with her new organization, the National Committee on the Cause and Cure of War, which held its first conference in 1925. In the years that followed, Schain had a distinguished career in international affairs. Disarmament and the child labor amendment engaged the support of Bertha Moller, who also enrolled in law school at the University of Minnesota in 1921 "to seek legal equality for women." Younger women like Vivian Thorp, Henriette McKnight, and Marguerite Wells, who had joined the movement in its last years, became leaders in the MWSA's successor organization. These leading Minnesota suffragists—even though they went their separate ways—did not, in Ueland's words, allow "great causes . . . to languish."[7]

The antis also made important contributions to their communities. Lavinia Gilfillan shared Josephine Simpson's interest in the Women's Co-operative Alliance, serving for about four years as vice-president. Florence Carpenter continued her service as a trustee of Wells College and was active in a variety of social service agencies. Once the vote was won, she did her civic duty and went to the polls: While her husband always voted Republican, Carpenter always voted for the Democrats. Despite the diversity of individual and organizational activity, women found unifying themes in their commitment to maternal and child health programs and to better working conditions for women.[8]

From the 1930s through the 1950s, American women's roles and experiences reflected both acceptance and rejection of their growing social equality. With the arrival of the Great Depression, a renewed feminist consciousness was aroused as women had to deal with unintended singleness, childlessness, and employment. Women had to find work to help support the family, but most of the jobs available to them were part-time, seasonal, and marginal. World War II brought women out of the home and into field and factory, but after 1945 they had to make way for returning servicemen. The decade of the 1950s was witness to a hyperbole of domesticity, with women being defined almost exclusively as wives and mothers (never mind that women were entering the labor force in greater numbers than ever before). But this surface tranquillity was prelude to the storm of the 1960s and the resurgence of a movement that articulated the new expectations of womankind.[9]

Women active in this movement called themselves feminists. *Feminism*, it might be noted, was not a word used in the nineteenth century, but it has been grafted, as Nancy F. Cott observed, "onto the history of women's rights." The term originated in France in the 1880s and made its way into popular parlance in the United States in about 1913, when it was used to convey the idea that women's issues included the whole range of women's concerns; it would have been a useful description for the goals inscribed in Elizabeth Cady Stanton's Declaration of Sentiments. Those opposed to suffrage tended to use the term pejoratively, impugning *feminism* with all kinds of dire consequences contrary to the values and virtues of American society. Minneapolitan Ella Pennington implied as much in an essay (probably written in 1917) opposing woman suffrage: "Feminism may not be a part of Suffrage; but who will deny that Suffrage is a part of Feminism? Many of the Suffrage leaders are Feminists; they have led followers to Suffrage and are now leading them to Feminism, the 'Ballot' being a mere way station."[10]

Distinct parallels between the nineteenth-century suffrage experience and twentieth-century feminism can be found in three areas: their origins, the schisms that divided them, and the opposition of women to suffrage and to feminism. Both movements originated in struggles for equal rights for African Americans—abolition in the 1800s and civil rights in the 1960s. Young white and African-American women who had been inspired by the idealism of the civil rights struggle became dispirited by their experiences with both black and white men who expected women to play traditional and subservient roles. ("The only position for women in [the Student Nonviolent Coordinating Committee] is prone," said Stokely Carmichael in 1964.) Black women, who constituted the backbone of the civil rights movement, remained understandably preoccupied with racial prejudice, but white women responded with a heightened awareness of the discrimination that had been leveled at them. Women began to organize, and activists startled the nation at the 1968 Miss America contest as they filled a "freedom trashcan" with symbols of their constraints (girdles, bras, and hair curlers) and subjugation (women's magazines).[11]

Somewhat earlier, middle-aged, middle-class women (suffrage types, if you will) came into the movement energized by the publication in 1963 of Betty Friedan's *The Feminine Mystique*. Friedan identified the "problem that has no name," the growing frustration of these educated women unhappy with their lot as mothers and homemakers and uneasy with their rusting minds. Those women who did work, usually compelled by economic necessity, were trapped in dull and menial jobs. Women's concerns about jobs, opportunities, and choices had prompted President John F. Kennedy to create the Commission on the Status of

Women in 1961, chaired by Eleanor Roosevelt. Although the resulting document was temperate in tone, it clearly established the existing patterns of discrimination against women. By 1967 similar commissions had been appointed in all the states. (In 1963 Governor Karl F. Rolvaag established the Minnesota Governor's Commission on the Status of Women and appointed as its chairman Viola H. Hymes, a member of both the president's commission and the Minneapolis school board and a former president of the National Council of Jewish Women.) All these studies produced an increasing body of evidence about sex discrimination that gave rise to the call for legislative remedies. At the national level, the Equal Pay Act of 1963 (enacted eighteen years after it was first proposed), Title VII of the Civil Rights Act of 1964, which added "sex" to the prohibitions of discrimination in employment, and Title IX of the Higher Education Act (passed in 1972), which prohibited discrimination in federally funded programs (including women's athletics), were important landmarks. Minnesota passed a Fair Employment Practices Law in 1955 and enlarged that legislation with a State Act Against Discrimination in employment and housing in 1961.[12]

A second parallel between the two waves of the women's movement can be found in the schisms that operated within each. Movements are seldom blessed by a consistent ideology, and both nineteenth- and twentieth-century feminism have been marked by deep disagreement. During the 1870s, the substantive schism emerged over the "Negro-only" or "woman-too" content of the Fourteenth Amendment. In 1914 strategic differences prompted the congressional committee of NAWSA to split off from the parent organization, reconstituting itself first as the Congressional Union and then in 1917 as the NWP. These differences over strategy were intensified by the party's provocative decision to picket the White House and the Capitol and by its introduction of partisanship into what had been a nonpartisan campaign. Members of the NWP were regarded as the radical feminists of their day and NAWSA members as the more traditional and mainstream American women.[13]

The conflict persisted after 1920 when the NWP introduced the Equal Rights Amendment, reviving old arguments over similarities and differences. Although there have been plentiful quarrels over strategies and tactics, the most divisive emerged over what historian Steven M. Buechler has termed "the premise of equality and the presumption of difference." Opponents of the ERA, including working women who valued the protective legislation put in place by the National League of Women Voters and other reformers, invoked women's differences. Supporters of the amendment—mostly NWP members—believed more in similarities and thus opted for equality. This issue—what historian Ann Snitow called "the feminist divide"—has been the most contentious and persistent controversy throughout the various stages of the women's movement. By the 1970s virtually all ERA holdouts became converts: Times had changed, and court decisions (many of them initiated by the petitions of working women) found that "protections" of women could now be interpreted to have violated their civil rights with sex segregation and the "feminization" of occupations leading to inequities of pay, mobility, and status.[14]

In his study of the parallels between the earlier struggle for women's rights and the contemporary feminist movement, Buechler concluded that "the ultimate success of the suffrage movement was due in part to its ability to argue for the vote on the grounds of both equality and difference, suggesting that these two standpoints are not always incompatible." Women have demonstrated a political aptitude for making the best of both possible worlds, and their success is often linked to their ability to accommodate a range of ideological differences.[15]

A third parallel between the two peak periods of women's activism is the commonality between the women who supported and opposed suffrage and between the latter-day feminists and their opposites "voicing antifeminist views." According to critic Susan Faludi, these latter-day opponents internalize the message of the women's movement and quietly incorporate "its tenets of self-determination, equality, and freedom of choice into their private behavior." Polls consistently revealed that women supported efforts to improve their lives, whether or not they were willing to accept the label of "feminist."[16]

Naomi Wolf, a Rhodes Scholar and provocative young writer, has written that feminism "should mean . . . nothing more complicated than women's willingness to act politically to get what they determine that they need." And what do women need? The question has as many answers as there are women. Because women are as diverse as the races, cultures, religions, and classes they represent, feminism has many faces and many perspectives. "We must," Wolf wrote, "reclaim feminism as that which makes women stronger in ways that each woman is entitled to define for herself."[17]

Complicating the assessment of the twentieth-century women's movements is the mixed record of women in politics—their behavior as voters, their turnout at the polls, and their interest in pursuing public office. The male political establishment held its collective breath during the first elections after the ratification of the Nineteenth Amendment, anticipating that great numbers of women would vote alike. In the years between 1920 and 1960, women did not go to the polls in great numbers, nor did they vote as a bloc. But the potential threat held good for long enough in the early 1920s for women to initiate, support, and implement an impressive record of reforms. Another five decades would pass before women would once again amass such an impressive legislative record. The political successes of the women's movement of that later period were grounded in a heightened public awareness, increased organizational activity, and membership growth in some of the newer women's groups. But the most dominant political symbol of the time—the Equal Rights Amendment, passed by Congress in 1972—failed to be ratified even after the March 1979 deadline for ratification had been extended to June 1982. In the years that followed, the ERA, like the failed child labor amendment, was destined to have its goals realized in part, if not yet in whole, by legislation, by executive orders, and by judicial interpretation.[18]

Voter turnout of both women and men has varied over the decades. In the heyday of Progressivism, from 1896 to 1920, men voted in declining numbers, and that decline intensified in the 1920s. In those same early years after suffrage, women tended not to vote—as men did not vote—when the issues were not compelling or the candidates were not inspiring. But the absence of women from the voting booth was most noticeable in those environments where sex role differences were most visible: in the South and among immigrant, rural, and poor populations. Women did not begin to go to the polls in significant numbers until the presidential years of Franklin D. Roosevelt, as a result of both the Depression and the efforts of Eleanor Roosevelt—and the activist women with whom she worked—to enlist women as voters. It was not until 1964, however, that a gender gap began to emerge, with women expressing a marginal preference for Democratic candidates over Republicans. Since 1980 the gender gap has widened because women were outvoting men and because men were moving from the Democratic to the Republican party. Observers credited the increase in voter turnout among women to their growing numbers in the workplace.[19]

The expectation that large numbers of women would be elected to public office, like the anticipation of a great turnout of women voters, proved to be illusory. Very few women even contended for state and national legislative seats, and, except for local offices, they rarely won elections. Despite Clara Ueland's high hopes that twenty women would be elected to the Minnesota legislature in 1922, that goal was not reached until 1980. In 1992, seventy-two years after winning the vote (and 144 years after beginning to fight for it), women tripled their numbers in the U.S. Senate from two to six and almost doubled their numbers in the U.S. House from twenty-eight to forty-seven. In Minnesota fifty-four women held legislative seats (27 percent of the total) in 1993, eleven more than in 1991. Nevertheless, that advance has proved to be the exception to the rule. The prevailing trend for women winning higher office is slow but sure.[20]

Women like Clara Ueland had viewed suffrage as a way of expressing women's individuality and a means of increasing women's power and ability to effect change in the political arena, especially in meeting the needs of women and children. In her postsuffrage days with the League of Women Voters and the Legislative Council, Ueland was an activist and champion of the underdog. The issues that consumed women of her era are issues that receive the support of women today. They are still interested in changing the face of politics, still concerned about the well-being of women and children, and still involved with a host of diverse policies, ranging from international affairs to education to health care. Ueland's sympathy with working women and poor children was rooted in the poverty of her own childhood. Her active participation in educational affairs stemmed from her seven years of experience as a schoolteacher. Her commitments were stimulated by her intellectual exchanges with Andreas, by her education in the Peripatetics, and by her peers in the causes they championed. Her suffrage involvement derived not only from friends but also from her articulate and enthusiastic daughters.

Clara Ueland's kind are alive and well and active in Minnesota. In 1994 the *Minnesota Women's Press* celebrated its tenth anniversary. The Minnesota Women's Consortium, organized in 1980, counted well over one hundred women's groups among its members fourteen years later. Many of these member associations had been founded to attend to new needs identified by women in the 1960s and 1970s, and their efforts to persuade legislators to adopt the consortium's annual economic action plan was similar to the work of the Legislative Council in the 1920s. Indeed, some of the consortium members could trace their roots back to that earlier period. Whether new or old, they shared a common problem: how to keep going when the supply of volunteers had been depleted by the large numbers of women in the work force.

Despite her occasional ventures of support for the bolder rhetoric and tactics of the suffrage era, Ueland was at heart a moderate. The essence of her belief was that women need the same rights as men because they, too, are human; they also require special treatment because they are different. She always resisted attempts to polarize the issue, to accept female stereotypes of the moment, and to force women to make what she regarded as false choices between rights and families—or to agitate for a sham equality that implied that the two sexes should be treated as identical when in fact they were not. Although most suffrage women were homemakers who did not necessarily reject the idea of home as "woman's place," they also saw women as individuals who should be able to choose whether they wanted to be in factories, offices, universities, political parties, medical centers, police forces, or other places that best suited their interests and their talents. Although Ueland's inclination was to support conventional means to achieve progress for women, she admired and sought to emulate some of Alice Paul's more flamboyant tactics—parades and street speaking, for example—which commandeered the attention of the media.

Clara Ueland recognized that although some men resisted efforts to expand opportunities for women, others provided support and leadership in the campaign to remove the injustices impeding women's progress. She did not regard men as a class, and—refusing to cast them in a single mold—she treated them with equal courtesy, aware that even political foes might become friends and allies.

However much she might have empathized with the women who felt they were victimized by society's inequities, Ueland would not have wasted her time or energy on anger. It was not an acceptable expression in her life. Nor was submission: In Clara Ueland's world, the meek did not inherit the earth. Her response would have been to employ all her resources of power and persuasion to find a workable solution to end the oppression of women. Ueland's contemporaries continued their struggle for political power without the head start enjoyed by succeeding generations who have gained not only a greater measure of political power but economic power as well. The mileposts are increasingly visible: women outvoting men; more women than

men graduating from college and more of those women intend-
ing to pursue graduate or doctoral degrees; women making up
almost half of the work force; and women-owned businesses
employing more workers than the companies making up the
Fortune 500. "We have seen in the past two decades," wrote
historian and critic Garry Wills in 1993, "a sharper change in
the ideal and practice of equality for women than occurred in the
preceding two millennia—it is the most basic social change of
our time."[21]

The suffrage campaign in Minnesota—like those in the
other states—left a legacy to the nation: the expansion of
human rights, a commitment to advocacy and reform, and a
cadre of women who led diverse organizations that gave voice to
the aspirations of their members. While other women's groups
also acquired power and status by virtue of the vote, the direct
descendant of suffrage was the League of Women Voters, which
continues to work on behalf of what Ueland once described as
"the ultimate betterment of state and nation." Politicians
respected and sometimes feared the league for its careful, nonpartisan examination of issues; other organizations have looked
to it for leadership; citizens learned to trust the league as one of
the nation's best-known civic educators. Its record on behalf of
a wide range of policy innovations and reforms is admired and
envied. And if the advancement of women has been marred by
occasional setbacks, it has nevertheless been on course, thanks
to the remarkable women who have inspired other women to
follow suit. Clara Ueland was one of those extraordinary women
who remained confident that women would win in the end and
would take their places with men as equal partners in the
business of life.[22]

NOTES

NOTES TO PREFACE

1. The ratification of the Nineteenth Amendment on Aug. 26, 1920, occurred after Ueland's resignation as league president two months earlier.
2. Carolyn G. Heilbrun, *Writing a Woman's Life* (New York: W. W. Norton & Co., 1988), 16–17.
3. Quotation from an unspecified women's rights convention.
4. See, for example, Eileen Lorenzi McDonagh, "The Significance of the Nineteenth Amendment: A New Look at Civil Rights, Social Welfare, and Woman Suffrage Alignments in the Progressive Era," *Women and Politics* (1990), vol. 10, no. 2, p. 59–94.
5. Gerda Lerner, *The Majority Finds Its Past: Placing Women in History* (New York: Oxford University Press, 1979), 35.

NOTES TO PROLOGUE

1. The quotation is from one of the resolutions composed by Elizabeth Cady Stanton at the first women's rights convention in Seneca Falls, N.Y., July 19–20, 1848. See also *The Woman Suffrage Year Book: 1917*, ed. Martha G. Stapler (New York: National Woman Suffrage Publishing Co., 1917), 27–42.
2. *History of Woman Suffrage*, by Elizabeth Cady Stanton et al. (6 vols.; Rochester: N.Y.: Susan B. Anthony; New York: National American

Woman Suffrage Assn., 1881–1922) is a major source used in the research and writing of this book. For the quotation from the account of the national convention of 1901, see vol. 5, p. 3 (NAWSA, 1922). See also the chapters on "Minnesota" by Sarah B. Stearns, 3:649–61 (Anthony, 1886), Julia B. Nelson in 4:772–82 (Anthony, 1902), and Maud C. Stockwell, 6:317–25 (NAWSA, 1922).

3. *Minneapolis Tribune*, May 31, 1901, p. 5; Elisabeth Griffith, *In Her Own Right: The Life of Elizabeth Cady Stanton* (New York: Oxford University Press, 1984), 50–58; Judith Wellman, "The Seneca Falls Women's Rights Convention: A Study of Social Networks," *Journal of Women's History* 3 (Spring 1991): 28–29. On the women's rights organizations, see Chapter 1. Anthony had pleaded with Stanton to prepare one of her customary rousing messages on suffrage, but Stanton stubbornly clung to her denunciation of canon law and did not win delegates to her views; Stanton et al., *History* 5:3, 5n1; *Minneapolis Tribune*, May 31, 1901, p. 5.

4. Mary Gray Peck, *Carrie Chapman Catt: A Biography* (New York: H. W. Wilson Co., 1944), 85–110.

5. Rhoda R. Gilman, *The Story of Minnesota's Past* (St. Paul: Minnesota Historical Society Press, 1991), 171–72; Dorothy Schneider and Carl J. Schneider, *American Women in the Progressive Era, 1900–1920* (New York: Facts on File, 1993; reprint, New York: Anchor Books, 1994), 243. On the changing roles of women, see Louise A. Tilly and Joan W. Scott, *Women, Work, and Family* (New York: Holt, Rinehart & Winston, 1978).

6. Stanton et al., *History* 5:15.

7. Stanton et al., *History* 5:14.

8. Stanton et al., *History* 5:3, 7–8, 6:678.

9. *Minneapolis Journal*, May 31, 1901, p. 6.

10. Stanton et al., *History* 5:6.

11. *Minneapolis Journal*, June 1, 1901, p. 2; *Minneapolis Tribune*, June 1, 1901, p. 10. In her unpublished biography, "Clara Ueland of Minnesota" (1967, typescript, Minnesota Historical Society Collections, St. Paul [hereafter MHS]), Brenda Ueland quoted an unidentified newspaper account describing her mother as "the young and beautiful Mrs. Andreas Ueland in yellow brocade" (p. 107). William D. Gregory was president of Gregory, Jennison, and Co.

12. B. Ueland, "Clara," 104–7 (Maud Stockwell quote, p. 105).

13. The Seneca Falls Declaration stated, with what Gerda Lerner described as "considerable exaggeration," that "the history of mankind is a history of repeated injuries and usurpations on the part of man toward woman, having in direct object the establishment of an absolute tyranny over her"; *Majority Finds Its Past*, 27, 29.

NOTES TO CHAPTER 1

Epigraph: Jane Grey Swisshelm, *Crusader and Feminist: Letters of Jane Grey Swisshelm, 1858–1865*, ed. Arthur J. Larsen (St. Paul: Minnesota Historical Society, 1934), 33.

1. Ellen Carol DuBois, *Feminism and Suffrage: The Emergence of an Independent Women's Movement in America, 1848–1869* (Ithaca, N.Y.: Cornell University Press, 1978), 32–33.

2. Anne Firor Scott, *Making the Invisible Woman Visible* (Urbana: University of Illinois Press, 1984), 282–83; Addams quoted in William L. O'Neill, *Feminism in America: A History*, 2d rev. ed. (New Brunswick, N.J.: Transaction Publishers, 1989), 34.

3. Griffith, *In Her Own Right*, 37–39. The Stanton quote about Mott is from Anne Firor Scott, *Natural Allies: Women's Associations in American History* (Urbana: University of Illinois Press, 1991), 54. See also Alma Lutz, "Stanton, Elizabeth Cady," in *Notable American Women, 1607–1950: A Biographical Dictionary*, ed. Edward T. James et al. (3 vols.; Cambridge: Belknap Press of Harvard University Press, 1971), 3:342–43; Dorothy Sterling, *Ahead of Her Time: Abby Kelly and the Politics of Antislavery* (New York: W. W. Norton & Co., 1991), 112. Steven M. Buechler proposed alternative dates of origin for various phases of the women's movement: distinct sentiments (early to mid-1840s), networks of people acting on those sentiments (1848 and continuing for the next dozen years), and independent organizations (after the Civil War with the formation of two national women's associations); *Women's Movements in the United States: Woman Suffrage, Equal Rights, and Beyond* (New Brunswick, N.J.: Rutgers University Press, 1990), 20–21.

4. Griffith, *In Her Own Right*, 42–52; Wellman, "Seneca Falls Women's Rights Convention," 24–27. Stanton would have four more children born in 1851, 1852, 1856, and 1859—five boys and two girls in all; *In Her Own Right*, 228–29.

5. Griffith, *In Her Own Right*, 53; for the text of the declaration, see Anne Firor Scott and Andrew MacKay Scott, *One Half the People: The Fight for Woman Suffrage* (Philadelphia: Lippincott, 1975; reprint, Urbana: University of Illinois Press, 1982), 56–59; Stanton et al., *History of Woman Suffrage*, 2d ed. (Rochester, N.Y.: Susan B. Anthony, 1889), 1:70–73, 804.

6. Stanton et al., *History* 1:70–73.

7. Griffith, *In Her Own Right*, 54–57. The quote is from the declaration. The resolution read, "That it is the duty of the women of this country to secure for themselves their sacred right to the elective franchise"; Stanton et al., *History* 1:72.

8. DuBois, *Feminism and Suffrage*, 46–47 (quote, 47); Eleanor Flexner, *Century of Struggle: The Woman's Rights Movement in the United States* (Cambridge: Belknap Press of Harvard University Press, 1959), 75–76. In the nineteenth century, the singular *woman*, as Nancy F. Cott explained, "symbolized, in a word, the unity of the female sex. It proposed that all women have one cause, one movement." By the twentieth century, as Cott noted, the "woman movement" sounded both ungrammatical and archaic. Although "feminism" came into vogue after 1910, "women's movement" (plural) also became a term of common usage; *The Grounding of Modern Feminism* (New Haven, Conn.: Yale University Press, 1987), 3–10. More recently Flora Davis has suggested that "women's movements" might be the most appropriate term to describe the diversity that characterized both the campaign for suffrage and the second wave of feminism that emerged in the 1960s; *Moving the Mountain: The Women's Movement in America since 1960* (New York: Simon & Schuster, 1991), 11.

9. Anthony, whose family resided in Rochester, N.Y., was in Seneca Falls as the houseguest of Amelia Bloomer, whose name brought fame to a liberating but nonetheless controversial form of dress; Alice Felt Tyler, *Freedom's Ferment: Phases of American Social History to 1860* (Minneapolis: University of Minnesota Press, 1945), 459.

10. Griffith, *In Her Own Right*, 74; Flexner, *Century of Struggle*, 89.

11. Stanton et al., *History* 1:39; Sterling, *Ahead of Her Time*, 1–3; David Morgan, *Suffragists and Democrats: The Politics of Woman Suffrage in America* ([East Lansing]: Michigan State University Press, 1972), 13; Grimké quoted in Emily Hahn, *Once upon a Pedestal: The Fascinating and Informal Chronicle of the American Woman's Struggle to Stand on Her Own Two Feet* (New York: Thomas Y. Crowell Co., 1974), 89. Buechler noted that discrimination by some abolitionists prompted

the formation of "a number of specifically female anti-slavery societies"; *Women's Movements*, 46. Dorothy Sterling, Kelly's biographer,
attributed the failure to document Kelly's achievements to her own
inherent modesty, to the bias of male historians, and to her alliance
with the Lucy Stone wing of the suffrage movement, which Stanton
and Anthony chose to downplay in their history; *Ahead of Her Time*,
4–5, 43–44. In the dedication of Volume 1 of the Stanton et al.,
History, Stanton, Anthony, and Gage "inscribed" the history to the
memory of nineteen women, including Wollstonecraft, Wright,
Mott, Martineau, and the Grimké sisters, "Whose Earnest Lives and
Fearless Words, in Demanding Political Rights for Women, have
been, in the Preparation of these Pages, a Constant Inspiration."
Anne Firor Scott suggested that Mary Wollstonecraft initiated the
ideology, Sarah Grimké provided its most systematic statement, and
that the Seneca Falls convention "codified the principles of the
cause"; *Natural Allies*, 54.

12. Morgan, *Suffragists and Democrats*, 13; Mary Foulke Morrisson,
"Preliminary Agitation," in National American Woman Suffrage
Assn., *Victory, How Women Won It: A Centennial Symposium,
1840–1940* (New York: H. W. Wilson Co., 1940), 10; Flexner,
Century of Struggle, 64; Tyler, *Freedom's Ferment*, 434–35; Mott quoted in Griffith, *In Her Own Right*, 91. Stone went one step further
than most feminists of the 1840s and 1850s who chose not to use
their husbands' names, a practice initiated by Maria Weston
Chapman and happily applauded by Elizabeth Cady Stanton;
women who followed her lead came to be known as "Lucy Stoners."
See Sterling, *Ahead of Her Time*, 222, 301.

13. Sterling, *Ahead of Her Time*, 346–47.

14. "American Anti-Slavery Anniversary," *National Anti-Slavery
Standard* (New York), May 13, 1865, p. 2, quoted in DuBois,
Feminism and Suffrage, 59; Mary Foulke Morrisson, "That Word
Male," in NAWSA, *Victory*, 50. Charles Sumner told the suffragists
that he had spent nineteen pages of foolscap trying to get rid of the
word "male," without success; Sterling, *Ahead of Her Time*, 346.

15. DuBois, *Feminism and Suffrage*, 170–80; Sterling, *Ahead of Her Time*,
348.

16. DuBois, *Feminism and Suffrage*, 162–64, 174; Louis Filler, "Stone,
Lucy," in James et al., *Notable American Women* 3:388–89. Lucy
Stone has been described as "puritanically conservative" while
Stanton was a social radical and Anthony somewhere in between;

Ellen Carol DuBois, "Making Women's History: Activist Historians of Women's Rights, 1840–1940," *Radical History Review* 49 (Winter 1991): 70. DuBois also said of the *History of Woman Suffrage* that "nothing in the annals of American reform" was quite like it, "a prolonged deliberate effort on the part of activists to ensure their place in the historical record . . . a product of Stanton's broad philosophical range, Anthony's organizational abilities, and Matilda Joslyn Gage's historical sensibilities"; *Feminism and Suffrage*, 63.

17. Alice S. Rossi, "Equality between the Sexes: An Immodest Proposal," in *The New Feminism in Twentieth-Century America*, ed. June Sochen (Lexington, Mass.: D. C. Heath & Co., 1971), 89–90; Laura Ballard, "What Flag Shall We Fly?," *Revolution*, Oct. 27, 1870, p. 264, quoted in O'Neill, *Feminism in America*, 19. O'Neill observed that NWSA was the only women's organization of its time that placed the source of the "woman's question" on the family system, from which, it asserted, all other inequities derived; *Feminism in America*, 21. The failure to gain suffrage in Kansas in 1867 convinced Stone and Blackwell that their primary task was to build grassroots support through state suffrage campaigns; Flexner, *Century of Struggle*, 149–50, 152–54. Anne Firor Scott, however, believed that the conventional wisdom suggesting conflict between the two organizations over means—state amendments versus a federal amendment—has been exaggerated, that "either would have welcomed any degree of enfranchisement"; *Natural Allies*, 137.

18. Flexner, *Century of Struggle*, 157; Ida Husted Harper, *A Brief History of the Movement for Woman Suffrage in the United States* (New York: National American Woman Suffrage Assn., 1914), 17; Stearns, "Minnesota," in Stanton et al., *History* 3:661.

19. Harper, *Brief History*, 12–13, 16.

20. The General Federation of Women's Clubs, organized in 1890, grew from half a million to more than two million members in twenty years. See Morgan, *Suffragists and Democrats*, 20–21; Sara M. Evans, *Born for Liberty: A History of Women in America* (New York: Free Press, 1989), 140–43; A. F. Scott, *Making the Invisible Woman Visible*, 282. Scott quoted Jane Cunningham Croly, who believed that when the history of the nineteenth century came to be written, "women will appear as organizers and leaders of the great . . . movements among their own sex for the first time in the history of the world," a fact Croly regarded as one of the central changes of a century characterized by revolutionary social change; Anne Firor Scott, "On Seeing and Not Seeing: A Case of Historical Invisibility," *Journal of*

American History 71 (June 1984): 7–21 (Croly quote, p. 13). See also Croly, *The History of the Woman's Club Movement in America* (New York: H. G. Allen & Co., 1898).

21. The other chief negotiator was Rachel Foster Avery, one of "Aunt Susan's nieces," as the many young women who gravitated to Anthony were called. See Griffith, *In Her Own Right*, 197–99, 203–18 (Anthony quote, p. 218); Alma Lutz, "Anthony, Susan Brownell," and "Stanton, Elizabeth Cady," in James et al., *Notable American Women* 1:55, 3:346–47. Stanton's radicalism is the reason she seemed to take second place to Anthony in the minds of succeeding generations of suffragists. Lucretia Mott, Stanton's mentor, had died in 1880, and Lucy Stone, who served as chair of NAWSA's executive committee, died in 1893; Frederick B. Tolles, "Mott, Lucretia Coffin," and Filler, "Stone, Lucy," in *Notable American Women* 2:592–95, 3:390. Grace Greenwood, a writer and pioneering suffrage enthusiast reporting for the *Philadelphia Press* on the National Woman's Suffrage convention early in 1869, described the three pioneers: "Indeed, it seems to me that while Lucretia Mott may be said to be the soul of the movement, and Mrs. Stanton the mind, the 'swift, keen intelligence,' Miss Anthony, alert, aggressive, and indefatigable, is its nervous energy—its propulsive force"; Stanton et al., *History* (Rochester, N.Y.: Susan B. Anthony, 1881), 2:361.

22. On Harriet Bishop, see Winifred D. Wandersee Bolin, "Harriet E. Bishop: Moralist and Reformer," in *Women of Minnesota: Selected Biographical Essays*, ed. Barbara Stuhler and Gretchen Kreuter (St. Paul: Minnesota Historical Society Press, 1977), 7–19; J. Fletcher Williams, *A History of the City of Saint Paul to 1875* (St. Paul: MHS, 1876; reprint, MHS Press, Borealis Books, 1983), 152, 169; Stanton et al., *History* 3:650; Lucile M. Kane and Alan Ominsky, *Twin Cities: A Pictorial History of Saint Paul and Minneapolis* (St. Paul: MHS Press, 1983), 6–7.

23. William Watts Folwell, *A History of Minnesota*, corrected eds. (St. Paul: Minnesota Historical Society, 1969), 4:333–34; Maud C. Stockwell, "Suffrage in Minnesota," in Mary Dillon Foster, comp., *Who's Who among Minnesota Women* (N.p.: Privately published, 1924), 316; Stanton et al., *History* 3:650. The convention, which was split apart by partisan politics, nevertheless was able to put together a constitution through the efforts of a joint committee consisting of five Democrats and five Republicans, and Minnesota's application for statehood was signed by President James Buchanan on May 11, 1858; Theodore C. Blegen, *Minnesota: A History of the*

State (Minneapolis: University of Minnesota Press, 1963; reprint, 1975), 223, 229.

24. Abigail McCarthy, "Jane Grey Swisshelm: Marriage and Slavery," in Stuhler and Kreuter, *Women of Minnesota*, 47; St. *Paul Press* quoted in Swisshelm, *Crusader and Feminist*, 133n10.

25. A *Pioneer Press* (St. Paul and Minneapolis) article of Jan. 27, 1884, eulogized Swisshelm as a "tiger" in her time; Swisshelm, *Crusader and Feminist*, 21, 33, 53–54 (quote, p. 30). See also *Daily Pioneer and Democrat* (St. Paul), Feb. 25, 1860, p. 3; *Daily Minnesotian and Times* (St. Paul), Feb. 25, 1860, p. 4; Jane Grey Swisshelm, *Half a Century*, 3d ed. (Chicago: Jansen, McClurg & Co., 1880), 4, 217.

26. Ethel Edgerton Hurd, *Woman Suffrage in Minnesota: A Record of the Activities in Its Behalf since 1847* (Minneapolis: Minnesota Woman Suffrage Assn., 1916), 25; William Anderson and Albert J. Lobb, *A History of the Constitution of Minnesota, with the First Verified Text* (Minneapolis: University of Minnesota, 1921), 229. In 1858 Stearns had recruited twelve girls to petition the University of Michigan to admit women. The university denied that request, but finally began admitting women in 1869; Stanton et al., *History* 3:526–28, 649.

27. Minnesota, House of Representatives, *Journal* (hereafter *House Journal*), 1868, p. 41, 47; St. *Paul Pioneer Press*, Jan. 24, 1868, p. 2; Hurd, *Woman Suffrage*, 25.

28. Stanton et al., *History* 3:650–51. Hurd indicated that a Minneapolis group was also organized by Stearns in 1868 (*Woman Suffrage*, 1), but Stearns in her chapter on Minnesota in *History* (3:649–61) made no reference to a Minneapolis group by name; she did, however, refer to the organization of a suffrage club in Kasson in 1872 (p. 652) and the subsequent formation by her of societies before 1883 in St. Paul and Minneapolis (p. 658).

29. *House Journal*, 1870, p. 166; Minnesota, Senate, *Journal* (hereafter *Senate Journal*), 1870, p. 210; Faith Rochester, "From Minnesota," *Woman's Journal* (Boston and Chicago), Apr. 2, 1870, p. 99, extracts of Minnesota interest, typescript, MHS. A similar strategy was in place when gender was added to Title VII of the 1964 Civil Rights Bill in hopes of defeating it; O'Neill, *Feminism in America*, 313.

30. Stanton et al., *History* 3:651; Glenda Riley, *The Female Frontier: A Comparative View of Women on the Prairie and the Plains* (Lawrence: University Press of Kansas, 1988), 166–67 (quoting Swisshelm in the *Woman's Journal*).

31. *House Journal*, 1875, p. 426; *Senate Journal*, 1875, p. 210; Stanton et al., *History* 3:652–53; Folwell, *History of Minnesota* 4:334–35; newspaper clipping, Oct. 25, 1919, roll 18, frame 74, microfilm edition, Minnesota Woman Suffrage Assn. Records, MHS (hereafter MWSA Records; each citation carries reference to the document's location on the microfilm edition, thus: 18:74).

32. U.S. Census Office, *Twelfth Census of the United States, Taken in the Year 1900* (Washington, D.C.: The Office, 1901), Population, pt. 1, p. 2–3; Folwell, *History of Minnesota* 3:72; Minnesota, Secretary of State, *Legislative Manual* (hereafter *Legislative Manual*), 1901, p. 237–38.

33. Joseph Stipanovich, *City of Lakes: An Illustrated History of Minneapolis* (Woodland Hills, Calif.: Windsor Publications, 1982), 77, 80, 89; Blegen, *Minnesota*, 287; Kane and Ominsky, *Twin Cities*, 81.

34. Gilman, *Story of Minnesota's Past*, 96–97, 145; U.S. Census Office, *Report on the Population of the United States at the Eleventh Census: 1890* (Washington, D.C.: GPO, 1895), pt. 1, p. 198, and *Thirteenth Census of the United States, Taken in the Year 1910* (1913), Population 2:959; *Legislative Manual*, 1901, p. 237–39.

35. Here and following paragraph, Kane and Ominsky, *Twin Cities*, 84; Bertha L. Heilbron, *The Thirty-second State: A Pictorial History of Minnesota* (St. Paul: Minnesota Historical Society, 1966), 201–15; Daniel J. Boorstin, *The Americans: The Democratic Experience* (New York: Random House, 1973), 101; Stipanovich, *City of Lakes*, 115; *Walker Art Center: A History* ([Minneapolis]: The Center, 1985), 3.

36. Here and following paragraph, Kane and Ominsky, *Twin Cities*, 83–85; Heilbron, *Thirty-second State*, 232, 233, 246–62. Andreas Ueland, along with William H. Dunwoody, Calvin G. Goodrich, and Thomas Lowry, was one of the founders of the Minnekahda Club in Minneapolis; David A. Lanegran and Ernest R. Sandeen, *The Lake District of Minneapolis: A History of the Calhoun-Isles Community* (St. Paul: Living Historical Museum, 1978), 63.

37. Stipanovich, *City of Lakes*, 103–5. In 1911 Andreas Ueland began his long association with the financial community when he became general counsel of the Scandinavian-American National Bank, which evolved into the Midland National Bank and Trust Company. In 1911 he assumed a similar position with the Federal Reserve Bank in Minneapolis; Andreas Ueland, *Recollections of an Immigrant* (New York: Minton, Balch & Co., 1929), 213.

38. Lincoln Steffens, *The Shame of the Cities* (New York: McClure, Phillips & Co., 1904), 64–65. Charles B. Cheney suggested that Edward E. Smith's service in the legislature was simply a prelude to his becoming "as near the definition of a boss as anyone ever did in Minnesota"; *The Story of Minnesota Politics: High Lights of Half a Century of Political Reporting* ([Minneapolis: Minneapolis Tribune], 1947), 43. See Carl H. Chrislock, *The Progressive Era in Minnesota: 1899–1918* (St. Paul: Minnesota Historical Society, 1971), 48–49, for details on Smith's influence, especially during the administration of Governor Adolph O. Eberhart.

39. Folwell, *History of Minnesota* 3:172; Gilman, *Story of Minnesota's Past*, 168.

40. G. Theodore Mitau, *Politics in Minnesota* (Minneapolis: University of Minnesota Press, 1960), 6; Roger Butterfield, *The American Past: A History of the United States from Concord to the Nuclear Age*, rev. ed. (New York: Simon & Schuster, 1957), 313; Chrislock, *Progressive Era in Minnesota*, 9, 14. John Lind returned to private life, joining Andreas Ueland's law firm in 1901 as one of a series of partners who had distinguished careers. Ueland's first partnership was with Arthur J. Shores, who became a counsel for Amalgamated Copper in its New York office, and with Andrew Holt, who became an associate justice of the Minnesota Supreme Court. Lind worked with Andreas until 1914, when he was asked by President Woodrow Wilson to represent the U.S. in the controversy with Mexico. In 1921 the oldest Ueland son, Sigurd, joined the firm and followed in his father's footsteps as counsel to the Federal Reserve Bank. In 1924 the third son, Rolf, began the practice of law with his father and brother. Arnulf, the second son, went to work for the Midland National Bank and ultimately became president; A. Ueland, *Recollections*, 85–86.

41. Stanton et al., *History* 3:653–54; Theodore Christianson, *Minnesota: The Land of Sky-tinted Waters: A History of the State and Its People* (Chicago: American Historical Society, 1935), 2:37. Dr. Adaline Williams was also elected in St. Charles, but because of a challenge she had to run and be elected a second time before she was duly installed as a member of the school board. Davis was elected by the legislature to the U.S. Senate and served from 1887 to 1900. As chairman of the Senate Foreign Relations Committee, he played a pivotal role in the decisions surrounding U.S. involvement in the Spanish-American War and in the peace negotiations that followed;

Barbara Stuhler, *Ten Men of Minnesota and American Foreign Policy, 1898–1968* (St. Paul: Minnesota Historical Society, 1973), 20–31.

42. *House Journal*, 1877, p. 431–32; *Senate Journal*, 1877, p. 439; *Legislative Manual*, 1985–86, p. 44; [Emily H.] Bright, "Experiences in Minnesota," typescript, [1914], Political Equality Club of Minneapolis Records, MHS; Warren Upham and Rose Barteau Dunlap, comps., "Minnesota Biographies, 1855–1912," *Collections of the Minnesota Historical Society* 14 (1912): 259.

43. Stanton et al., *History* 3:650, 657. In the twentieth century such a home would be called a battered women's shelter.

44. *House Journal*, 1879, p. 92, *1881*, p. 318, *1885*, p. 251, 348, *1891*, p. 946, *1893*, p. 850; *Senate Journal*, 1879, p. 260, *1893*, p. 487–88; Stanton et al., *History* 3:655; Bright, "Experiences in Minnesota," Political Equality Club of Minneapolis Records, MHS.

45. Newspaper clipping, Oct. 25, 1919, 18:74, MWSA Records. The views on the "woman question" of Kate, Donnelly's equally colorful spouse, were not known, but her forceful personality may have contributed to his sympathy with the issue; Gretchen Kreuter, "Kate Donnelly versus the Cult of True Womanhood," in Stuhler and Kreuter, *Women of Minnesota*, 20–33.

46. Stanton et al., *History* 3:657.

47. Julia Wiech Lief, "A Woman of Purpose: Julia B. Nelson," *Minnesota History* 47 (Winter 1981): 310.

48. Stanton et al., *History* 4:773, 777; *Minneapolis Morning Tribune*, May 10, 1916, p. 4 (quoting Carrie Chapman Catt). Suffragists joined with the campaign of the Minnesota Federation of Women's Clubs to establish free libraries in the state; Linda Lounsbury, "The Woman Suffrage Movement in Minnesota," 35–36, unpublished manuscript, 1982, in private collection; Folwell, *History of Minnesota* 4:335. Bright suggested that the other amendment was a stratagem of the liquor dealers, but Lounsbury speculated that it may have been prompted by fears of radical social change stemming from the rising power of the Populist movement. Both are probably correct; Bright, "Experiences in Minnesota," Political Equality Club of Minneapolis Records. Before that time, voters accepted three-quarters of submitted changes. From 1900 to 1981 the percentage dropped to 42 percent and then rose slightly in subsequent years, largely because many of those recent amendments proved to be relatively uncontroversial; Betty Kane, "Amending Our State Constitution: Continuity through Ordered Change," *Legislative Manual*, 1981–82, p. 2–7; see also 1989–90, p. 45.

49. In the 1890s women ministers occupied pulpits of Congregational, Universalist, Christian, and Wesleyan Methodist churches; Stanton et al., *History* 4:779–81.

50. Stanton et al., *History* 3:657, 772–73; Hurd, *Woman Suffrage*, 32–35.

51. Stanton et al., *History* 3:650, 657–59. Hurd reported that records were incomplete for the years 1883 to 1890; *Woman Suffrage* 10.

52. Stanton et al., *History* 4:773. Lounsbury noted that in 1898, MWSA regarded the southern part of the state as being both more populous and "homogeneous," and she suggested that this "was probably a code word for English-speaking or native born"; "Woman Suffrage Movement," 38n2.

53. See, for example, Stanton et al., *History*, various volumes, and Hurd, *Woman Suffrage*, 10–16; Ethel Edgerton Hurd, "A Brief History of the Minneapolis Political Equality Club," 2, 5, typescript, Apr. 15, 1921, Political Equality Club of Minneapolis Records, MHS.

NOTES TO CHAPTER 2

Epigraph: Brenda Ueland, *Strength to Your Sword Arm: Selected Writings* (Duluth: Holy Cow! Press, 1993), 182.

1. Kane and Ominsky, *Twin Cities*, 81; Jane Grey Swisshelm, "Letter from Minnesota," Oct. 27, 1870, in *Woman's Journal* extracts, MHS. Information on the Ueland family and home came primarily from the following memoirs: A. Ueland, *Recollections*; Brenda Ueland, *Me* (New York: G. P. Putnam's Sons, 1939; reprints, St. Paul: Schubert Club, 1983, Duluth: Holy Cow! Press, 1994); and Sigurd Ueland, "Sense and Senility: (A Commonplace Biography)" (1971, unpublished manuscript, photocopy in MHS). The most valuable source of information is Brenda Ueland's 1967 unpublished biography of her mother, "Clara Ueland of Minnesota."

2. S. Ueland, "Sense and Senility," 11.

3. B. Ueland, *Me*, 13–14, 17, 24–25, and "Clara," 423. Information on the appearance of the Uelands was provided by their daughter-in-law Margaret L. Ueland and granddaughter Gabrielle McIver in separate conversations with the author, Dec. 29, 1992; notes in author's possession.

4. This and subsequent material relating to the early years and family background of Clara Hampson are taken from B. Ueland, "Clara"; see especially p. 1–6, 9–14.

5. "Miss Wells [sic] Address at the 5th Annual Convention of the Minnesota League of Women Voters[,] Wednesday, Nov. 5, 1923," state convention 1923, League of Women Voters of Minnesota Records, MHS (hereafter LWVM Records). In 1946 the Minnesota League of Women Voters changed its name to the League of Women Voters of Minnesota; see chapter 10, note 3, below. See also B. Ueland, "Clara," 9.

6. B. Ueland, "Clara," 13–14; Rolf Ueland and Margaret L. Ueland, comps., "The Lineal Ancestors, Descendants and Other Relatives of Anne, Elsa, Brenda, Sigurd, Arnulf, Rolf and Torvald Ueland," 1973–76, unpublished manuscript, photocopy in author's possession.

7. B. Ueland, "Clara," 14; R. Ueland and M. Ueland, "Lineal Ancestors," 2; A. Ueland, Recollections, 39. Maud Conkey, who married Sylvanus A. Stockwell, was a longtime suffrage activist and one of Ueland's predecessors as MWSA president; quoted in "Clara," 16.

8. B. Ueland, "Clara," 9, 17, and Me, 14; S. Ueland, "Sense and Senility," 13.

9. A. Ueland, Recollections, 3, 11–12, 22–25; Knut Gjerset, History of the Norwegian People (New York: Macmillan Co., 1915), 2:478; Karen Larsen, A History of Norway (Princeton, N.J.: Princeton University Press for the American-Scandinavian Foundation, 1948), 417–18. Ole Gabriel was married twice. By his first wife, Marthe, he had nine children, and by his second wife, Anne Ollestad, four children, including Andreas; R. Ueland and M. Ueland, "Lineal Ancestors," 2. Houston and Fillmore counties and the Red River Valley were favored locations for Norwegian immigrants; June Drenning Holmquist, ed., They Chose Minnesota: A Survey of the State's Ethnic Groups (St. Paul: Minnesota Historical Society Press, 1981), 4.

10. A. Ueland, Recollections, 29, 32–33, 35; S. Ueland, "Sense and Senility," 12.

11. A. Ueland, Recollections, 38–39; Carlton C. Qualey and Jon A. Gjerde, "The Norwegians," in Holmquist, They Chose Minnesota, 222, 227, 228; Odd S. Lovoll, The Promise of America: A History of the Norwegian-American People (Minneapolis: University of Minnesota Press in cooperation with the Norwegian-American Historical Assn., 1984), 104–5, 143–44; Wyman Smith, [History of the First Unitarian Society, Minneapolis], Jan. 20, 1965, photocopy of typescript, 1–2, 5–6, MHS.

12. The Odin Club was founded in 1898 (following a club to create a Scandinavian "high life") and existed until 1930. It "entertained

important guests and cultivated social activity." At one time there were as many as three hundred members; Lovoll, *Promise of America*, 192; A. Ueland, *Recollections*, 38–39, 136–37.

13. A. Ueland, *Recollections*, 39, 59–60; B. Ueland, "Clara," 22.

14. George E. Warner and Charles M. Foote, comps., *History of Hennepin County and the City of Minneapolis* (Minneapolis: North Star Publishing Co., 1881), 647; *Rushford Star*, Oct. 2, 1879, Mar. 25, 1880, June 12, 1884; *Minneapolis Tribune*, Mar. 24, 1880; author to Hennepin County, Minn., vital records office, Sept. 7, 1994, office to author, ca. Sept. 8, 1994—both in author's possession; entries for Ohlhouse family in U.S. 1870 and Minnesota 1875 censuses for Rushford, Fillmore County. Elizabeth Nissan, an emeritus professor at the University of Minnesota, remembered that her father and other friends of Andreas knew of his earlier marriage. Whatever the reason, Andreas chose not to speak or write about Anna, and present-day Ueland family members have only a vague knowledge of that short-lived union; author's conversations with Elizabeth Nissan (then ninety-six years old), Margaret L. Ueland, Harriet Ueland, and Andrea Brainard, 1993–95, notes in author's possession.

15. B. Ueland, "Clara," 16–18.

16. A. Ueland, *Recollections*, 35–36, 50; Kathryn Ericson, "Triple Jeopardy: The Muus vs. Muus Case in Three Forums," *Minnesota History* 50 (Winter 1987): 301–5.

17. A. Ueland, *Recollections*, 50–51; *Evening Journal* (Minneapolis and St. Paul), Nov. 7, 1881.

18. B. Ueland, "Clara," 27–29, 34; A. Ueland, *Recollections*, 50, 53–54, 174. Nelson served as a state senator, 1875–78, U.S. representative, 1883–89, governor, 1893–95, and U.S. senator, 1895–1923; W. F. Toensing, comp., *Minnesota Congressmen, Legislators, and Other Elected State Officials: An Alphabetical Check List, 1849–1971* (St. Paul: Minnesota Historical Society, 1971), 71, 86; *Dictionary of American Biography*, s.v. "Nelson, Knute."

19. B. Ueland, "Clara," 32; A. Ueland, *Recollections*, 54, 57; Gilman, *Story of Minnesota's Past*, 146.

20. B. Ueland, "Clara," 29–30; A. Ueland, *Recollections*, 60–61. Andreas had purchased land in an area known as the Cottage City Addition of Minneapolis, which was the former site of a Dakota Indian village established in 1828 by Lawrence Taliaferro, the U.S. Indian agent at nearby Fort Snelling; Margaret L. Ueland, "The Ueland Family and

Their Homes on Interlachen Terrace, Minneapolis," 1988, type-script, photocopy in author's possession; *Minneapolis Tribune*, July 22, 1953, p. 5.

21. *Minneapolis Tribune*, July 22, 1953, p. 5; Brenda Ueland quoted in her obituary, *Minneapolis Star and Tribune*, Mar. 7, 1985, p. 1; B. Ueland, "Clara," 62.

22. S. Ueland, "Sense and Senility," 16, 25; B. Ueland, "Clara," 62.

23. The girls and their birth dates were Anne (1886), Elsa (1888), Dorothy (1889), and Brenda (1891); the boys were Sigurd (1893), Arnulf (1895), Rolf (1899), and Torvald (1902); genealogical infor-mation about Andreas and Clara Ueland's children, Oct. 13, 1987, photocopy of typescript in author's possession; M. Ueland, "Ueland Family"; B. Ueland, "Clara," 53, 71–72.

24. B. Ueland, "Clara," 75–77, and *Me*, 36.

25. B. Ueland, *Me*, 36, *Strength*, 182, and "Clara," 68–69, 112–13.

26. B. Ueland, "Clara," 77–78.

27. U.S. Census Office, *Twelfth Census of the United States, Taken in the Year 1900* (Washington, D.C.: The Office, 1902), *Population*, pt. 2, p. clviii; B. Ueland, *Me*, 51, *Strength*, 132–33, and "Clara," 72; Marguerite N. Bell, *The Lives and Times of Just Molly: An Auto-biography* (Minneapolis: Golden Valley Press, 1980), 22; S. Ueland, "Sense and Senility," 19.

28. B. Ueland, "Clara," 479–80; Stanton et al., *History* 4:779. In 1876 a number of women had been elected to school boards in the first year of their eligibility to vote in Minnesota school elections and to be board members; *History* 3:653; *Minneapolis Journal*, Mar. 2, 1927, p. 1, 6.

29. Material on Nanny Jaeger, Josephine Simpson, and Alice Winter is taken from the Minnesota Biography Project Files, MHS, and Foster, *Who's Who among Minnesota Women*, 150, 298, 347. Additional material about Jaeger comes from the Hans Mattson and Family Papers, and about Simpson from the David Ferguson Simpson and Family Papers (photocopy of scrapbook, 1–12)—both MHS. Winter was appointed by President Warren G. Harding in 1921 to serve on the advisory committee for a conference on the limitations of arma-ments, an activity that she regarded as the highlight of her career. She was later rumored to have been considered for a position in President Herbert Hoover's cabinet. For information about Winter, see Carl H. Chrislock, *Watchdog of Loyalty: The Minnesota Commis-*

sion of *Public Safety during World War I* (St. Paul: Minnesota Historical Society Press, 1991), xi, 107; Marguerite N. Bell, *With Banners: A Biography of Stella Louise Wood* (St. Paul: Macalester College Press, 1954), 47–48; [Clara Ueland] to state chairmen of National Council of Defense, May 22, 1918, 9:279, "Organization and Conference of the League of Women Voters, Minneapolis, October 28 and 29, 1919," program, 14:227—both MWSA Records; Jeannette Ludcke, *You've Come a Long Way, Lady!: The Seventy-five Year History of the Woman's Club of Minneapolis* ([Minneapolis]: The Club, [1982?]), 416–17; Minnesota Federation of Women's Clubs, *Annual Report,* 1920–21, p. 8, copy in MHS.

30. Stella Louise Wood, "History of the Kindergarten Movement in Minnesota," in *History of the Kindergarten Movement in the Mid-Western States and in New York: Presented at the Cincinnati Convention, Association for Childhood Education, April 19–23, 1938,* p. 42–46, copy in Macalester College Archives, St. Paul. Eventually the reactionary forces of the Prussian government banned kindergartens as their emphasis on the democratic ideal of free growth for the individual and their "tendency toward the emancipation of women, was considered politically dangerous"; Bell, *With Banners,* 27, 48; B. Ueland, "Clara," 63–64, 69–70, 84.

31. Bell, *With Banners,* 7, 46–50, and *Just Molly,* 156; B. Ueland, "Clara," 78. Stella Wood had a long career as a pioneering and distinguished early-childhood educator.

32. Wood, "History of the Kindergarten Movement," Edith Achsa Stevens, "A Sketch of Stella Louise Wood's Life and Services to Children," undated typescript—both in Macalester College Archives. The school merged with Macalester College in 1949.

33. Raymond B. Bragg, *The Career and Influence of Henry M. Simmons, 1841–1905* ([Minneapolis?]: Privately published, [1944?]), 7, 11, 22; A. Ueland, *Recollections,* 62–63; Smith, [History], 1–2, 5–6.

34. B. Ueland, "Clara," 87, 176, and *Strength,* 184–85; Smith, [History], 4.

35. B. Ueland, "Clara," 216, 217, 225; author's interview with Margaret L. Ueland, Feb. 13, 1992, notes in author's possession. Brenda Ueland had similar theological reservations, according to Khoren Arisian, a minister with the Minneapolis society during the last years of her longtime membership; conversation with the author, Dec. 7, 1992, notes in author's possession. See also Paul R. Lucas, "The Church and the City: Congregationalism in Minneapolis, 1850–1890," *Minnesota History* 44 (Summer 1974): 61, 69.

36. B. Ueland, "Clara," 109–10, 246–47, and Me, 90–91, 93; S. Ueland, "Sense and Senility," 19.

37. [Clara Ueland] to Elizabeth Hauser, May 29, 1917, 8:278, MWSA Records; B. Ueland, "Clara," 247; Minneapolis Sunday Tribune, Jan. 3, 1915, second section, 9; Minneapolis Journal, Jan. 4, 1915, p. 12.

38. S. Ueland, "Sense and Senility," 13.

39. Peripatetics, The Peripatetics of Minneapolis ([Minneapolis: The Club, 1990]), 8; Andrea Brainard, "Charter Members: Lavinia Gilfillan, Clara Ueland, Alice Winter, and Florence Carpenter," 4, paper presented at Peripatetics meeting by Clara Ueland's granddaughter, Oct. 16, 1989, photocopy of typescript in author's possession; Theodora Penny Martin, The Sound of Our Own Voices: Women's Study Clubs 1860–1901 (Boston: Beacon Press, 1987), 1. As historian Anne Firor Scott phrased it, "Literary clubs for 'self-culture' proliferated as if some very contagious virus was loose in the female population"; Natural Allies, 113.

40. Brainard, "Charter Members," 4–5; yearbooks for 1893–94, 1912–13, 1913–14, 1914–15, 1916–17, 1921–22, Peripatetics Records, MHS; Peripatetics, yearbook, 1920–21, copy in MHS.

41. Martin, Sound of Our Own Voices, 175. Anne graduated from Wells College, Elsa from the University of Minnesota (with graduate work at Columbia University), Brenda spent her first three years at Wells but graduated from Barnard College; B. Ueland, Me, 83, 99, 103, and "Clara," 215.

42. B. Ueland, Me, 34, and "Clara," 46–49, 59, 159–60; S. Ueland, "Sense and Senility," 96–97.

43. B. Ueland, "Clara," 155, 158–59.

NOTES TO CHAPTER 3

Epigraph: B. Ueland, "Clara," 171.

1. Here and following paragraph, Butterfield, American Past, 288–89, 312, 314–5; Time-Life Books, This Fabulous Century: Sixty Years of American Life, vol. 1, 1900–1910 (New York: Time-Life Books, 1969), 6, 231, 255, 259.

2. Here and following paragraph, This Fabulous Century 1:38, 156, 177; Stanton et al., History 4:778.

3. B. Ueland, Strength, 69.

4. D. Schneider and C. Schneider, *American Women*, 15; Cott, *Grounding of Modern Feminism*, 129; [Minnesota] Commission on the Economic Status of Women, *Minnesota Women in the Twentieth Century* (St. Paul: The Commission, 1990), 4–5. By 1990 Minnesota women constituted almost 69 percent of the state's labor force; data supplied by Cheryl Hoium, commission staff member, in conversation with author, 1993, notes in author's possession.

5. This is the central thesis of Aileen S. Kraditor's *The Ideas of the Woman Suffrage Movement, 1890–1920* (New York: Columbia University Press, 1965; reprint, Garden City, N. Y.: Doubleday & Co., 1971). See also Ethel Klein, *Gender Politics: From Consciousness to Mass Politics* (Cambridge: Harvard University Press, 1984), 14. Jane Addams is credited with articulating "the ideal expression of the new philosophy" in an article that appeared in the *Ladies' Home Journal* in 1909. Other women were expressing similar thoughts; *Ideas of the Woman Suffrage Movement* (1971 edition), 52–65, 68–71; Evans, *Born for Liberty*, 153–54.

6. Marjorie Bingham, "Keeping at It: Minnesota Women," in *Minnesota in a Century of Change: The State and Its People since 1900*, ed. Clifford E. Clark, Jr., (St. Paul: Minnesota Historical Society Press, 1989), 441. A best-selling novel about a women's club in the fictional town of Waynesboro, Ohio, from 1868 to 1932 is particularly entertaining and instructive. See Helen Hooven Santmyer, " . . . *And Ladies of the Club*" (New York: G. P. Putnam's Sons, 1984); *Current Biography Yearbook 1985*, p. 357–60.

7. John E. Haynes, "Reformers, Radicals, and Conservatives," in Clark, *Minnesota in a Century of Change*, 361–62; Richard Hofstadter, *The Age of Reform: From Bryan to F.D.R.* (New York: Vintage Books, 1955), 5; Bernard A. Weisberger, "The Party of the People," *American Heritage*, May–June 1992, News section, 20; quotation from Martin Ridge, *Ignatius Donnelly: The Portrait of a Politician* (Chicago: University of Chicago Press, 1962; reprint, St. Paul: Minnesota Historical Society Press, Borealis Books, 1991), 295–96. Ridge's book is a useful guide to Minnesota's role and Donnelly's leadership in the rise and fall of the People's party in the state.

8. Arthur M. Schlesinger, Jr., *The Crisis of the Old Order, 1919–1933*, vol. 1 of *The Age of Roosevelt* (Boston: Houghton Mifflin Co., 1957), 17; Weisberger, "Party of the People," 22; Haynes, "Reformers, Radicals, and Conservatives," in Clark, *Minnesota in a Century of Change*, 362. Chrislock marked the beginning of the decline of Populism with the 1896 election defeat of William Jennings Bryan, free

silver, and the People's party, and the return of prosperity in 1897; *Progressive Era*, 10–11.

9. Chrislock wrote that Lind, after becoming governor in 1899, "professed a loose allegiance to the Democratic party which did not preclude his support of opposition candidates if they seemed more worthy than their Democratic rivals"; *Progressive Era*, 9, 14.

10. Eric F. Goldman, *Rendezvous with Destiny: A History of Modern American Reform* (New York: Alfred A. Knopf, 1952), 83; Schlesinger, *Crisis of the Old Order*, 18; Hofstadter, *Age of Reform*, 5, 135, 137. Many of the Populist proposals came into effect during the Progressive Era. For example, four amendments to the U.S. Constitution were enacted: the income tax, direct election of U.S. senators, prohibition, and woman suffrage; Chrislock, *Progressive Era*, 199. In Minnesota, Norwegian Americans, many of whom had emigrated from their home country to protest established political and religious authority, found Progressive politics to be compatible with their own beliefs. These supportive attitudes were reflected in the votes of legislators representing districts populated by substantial numbers of Norwegians; Marte Sheeran, "Woman Suffrage and the Minnesota Legislature, 1907–1919," p. 4, 7, typescript, [1975?], photocopy in MHS.

11. Folwell, *History of Minnesota* 3:247–49; Christianson, *Minnesota* 2: 255, 258–59; S. Ueland, "Sense and Senility," 71–72; information about Arnulf Ueland, Minnesota Biography Project Files, MHS.

12. Folwell, *History of Minnesota* 3:260. The only other Democratic governor serving before Clara Ueland's death in 1927 was Winfield S. Hammond, and he, too, died in office (in 1915 after serving less than one year); Chrislock, *Progressive Era*, 18–19, 20–21, 37, 60, 87–88; Mitau, *Politics in Minnesota*, 8–10.

13. Chrislock, *Progressive Era*, viii, 3, 55, 119. Like most generalizations, this one has important exceptions, some of which are described in Sheeran, "Woman Suffrage," 3–5. See also Suzanne Lebsock, "Women and American Politics, 1880–1920," in *Women, Politics, and Change*, ed. Louise A. Tilly and Patricia Gurin (New York: Russell Sage Foundation, 1990), 45–46; Maud C. Stockwell, "Minnesota—Organization," Political Equality Club of Minneapolis Records, MHS.

14. Lebsock, "Women and American Politics," in Tilly and Gurin, *Women, Politics, and Change*, 42; D. Schneider and C. Schneider, *American Women*, 98–100; A. F. Scott, *Natural Allies*, 121.

15. Martin, *Sound of Our Own Voices*, 175; Evans, *Born for Liberty*, 4, 140; A. F. Scott, *Natural Allies*, 1–4, 178; Alexis de Tocqueville, *Democracy in America* (New York: Vintage Books, 1954), 2:114–15.

16. Farmer had read *The Conquest: The True Story of Lewis and Clark* (Chicago: A. C. McClurg & Co., 1902), a novel by Eva Emery Dye, and was inspired by the story of Sacajawea; Eugenia B. Farmer, untitled history of the Political Equality Club of St. Paul, placed with club minutes for Sept. 28, 1916, vol. 1, Political Equality Club of St. Paul Papers, MHS. See also Susan S. Chapin, "The St. Paul Political Equality Club," 9:473–74, MWSA Records; Hurd, *Woman Suffrage*, 12; *Minnesota Bulletin* (Minneapolis and Red Wing, Minn.: Minnesota Woman Suffrage Assn.), Mar. 1905, Oct. 1907, Oct. 1908, copies in MHS.

   The first staff member of the settlement house was given the title of "resident" because she did indeed reside in the house. Soon after Margaret M. Pentland's hiring, she organized a mothers' club; in one of her reports to the board of directors, she indicated the club was to have talks on "Women as citizens"; Pentland, reports to president and board of directors, monthly reports, Nov. 14, Dec. 10, 1904, Jan. 9, 1905—all Neighborhood House Assn. Records, MHS.

17. According to some accounts, it was presumed that the Woman Suffrage Club of Minneapolis was organized by Sarah Stearns in 1868. Stearns made no reference to that activity; Stanton et al., *History* 3:650–51, 6:317. Records of the early years were lost when a fire destroyed the residence of the club secretary. The name was changed to the Political Equality Club of Minneapolis in 1897; Hurd, "Brief History," 1, 2, 3, 4, 8, in club records, MHS.

18. Marguerite M. Wells, "Minnesota Calls the Roll," *Minnesota Woman Voter* (Minnesota League of Women Voters), Nov. 1929, p. 5; Lounsbury, "Woman Suffrage Movement," 40.

19. The organization was usually called the Scandinavian Woman Suffrage Association. See Nanny Mattson Jaeger, report about SWSA, 1915, woman suffrage material: press releases, resolutions, etc., Luth and Nanny Mattson Jaeger Papers (hereafter Jaeger Papers), MHS; Hurd, "Brief History," and *Woman Suffrage*, 12; *Minnesota Bulletin*, Oct. 1908; information about Potter and Peck, Minnesota Biography Project Files, MHS. Potter was then a professor of English at the university, but in 1909 she became an extension lecturer in the College of Education. She served for a brief period as corresponding secretary of the association and was active in the General Federation of Women's Clubs and the Women's Trade Union

League. Her friend and associate Mary Peck, who also taught English at the university, abandoned her career in education to work for suffrage full time. Peck's decision was probably influenced by her admiration for Carrie Chapman Catt, who became a close friend. Robert Booth Fowler, author of *Carrie Catt: Feminist Politician* (Boston: Northeastern University Press, 1986), wrote, "There can be no question that the center of Peck's adult emotional life was Catt" (p. 53–56). Peck's biography of Catt, as Fowler suggested, has merit because it was written by an intimate, but it suffers from the effort Peck admittedly made to be impersonal (p. xv). He allowed that Peck got it partially right when she observed of Catt, "The only way for you to live was to fill your life so full of work you could not think of unhappy things. Your idea of hell is probably a place where there is nothing to do but think" (p. 44).

20. Hurd, "Brief History," 19; B. Ueland, "Clara," 105; D. Schneider and C. Schneider, *American Women*, 106. For reporters' impressions of suffragists, see *Minneapolis Tribune* and *Minneapolis Journal*, May–June 1901. Hurd, in addition to organizing the SWSA, was the mainstay of the Political Equality Club of Minneapolis. Ripley had been MWSA president from 1883 to 1888; information about Ripley in Minnesota Biography Project Files, MHS.

21. Information about Maud Stockwell, Minnesota Biography Project Files, MHS; Foster, *Who's Who among Minnesota Women*, 311; B. Ueland, "Clara," 105, 178.

22. Sylvanus Stockwell also served in the Minnesota legislature from 1923 to 1925 and from 1929 to 1939—he was last elected at age eighty-one. Information about Emily Bright, Alfred Bright, and Stockwell, Minnesota Biography Project Files, MHS; B. Ueland, "Clara," 106.

23. B. Ueland, "Clara," 163–64.

24. Here and following two paragraphs, Hurd, *Woman Suffrage*, 12; B. Ueland, "Clara," 163–64, 178, 185, 233.

25. B. Ueland, "Clara," 235, 238–44.

26. Clark A. Chambers, "Ueland, Clara Hampson," in James et al., *Notable American Women* 3:499; information about Ueland and Josephine Simpson, Minnesota Biography Project Files, MHS; Ludcke, *You've Come a Long Way, Lady!*, 7–14, 23, 27.

27. B. Ueland, "Clara," 243–44; unidentified and undated newspaper clipping, 17:703, MWSA Records. Ueland's name last appeared in the membership roster published in the club's yearbook for 1919–20.

Before her resignation, Clara used her position, as head of the club's Department of Arts and Letters, to pursue her interest in immigrant arts and crafts. Soon after the Minnesota legislature created the Minnesota State Art Society (sometimes called the Minnesota State Art Commission) in 1903, she had apparently been appointed to the governing board. Hope McDonald reported that Clara had been on the first governing board. Because society reports are incomplete, it is impossible to be precise about the length of Ueland's service. She may have been appointed before 1912, but that is the first time her name appears. The incomplete society records at the MHS contain no record of society members (only the director) before 1912, when Ueland's name appeared on the letterhead; it appeared again in 1917, after which there is a gap in annual reports. If McDonald was correct, Ueland would have been appointed by Governor Samuel Van Sant in 1903 or 1904; if her initial year was 1912, she would have been appointed by Governor Adolph O. Eberhart. See McDonald, "Early Years and Work," *Minnesota Woman Voter*, Mar. 1927 (Clara Ueland memorial issue), 4; Minnesota State Art Society, annual reports and correspondence, 1912–17, State Art Society records, Minnesota State Arts Board Records, Minnesota State Archives, MHS.

Few museums in the country then exhibited these humble crafts—woodcarving, cabinet- and metalwork, embroidery, lacemaking, pottery, rug and textile weaving. On her 1909 trip with Andreas to Norway and Sweden, Ueland collected examples of contemporary crafts to show to Minnesota artists. A year later she initiated, under Woman's Club auspices, an annual exhibit of immigrant arts and crafts. According to Brenda, Clara spent the month of July 1912 traveling to many towns throughout the state on behalf of the State Art Society's effort to revive products of the "wonderful ancestral good taste of the immigrants"; see "Clara," 244–45. The society's annual report for 1912 reflected the emphasis given not just to the exhibition of works of art but also to the "encouragement of arts and crafts and household industries" as being of "the greatest importance in its relation to the industry and happiness of the people."

As a result of Ueland's dual role with the Woman's Club and the State Art Society, coupled with the interest and involvement of the state Federation of Women's Clubs, the project expanded into a yearly exhibition and sale of fine and applied arts at the Minnesota State Fair. Ueland, who chaired the Department of Arts and Letters for five years and served with the Society for at least six years, conceptualized the project and made it a success, which contributed substantially to the preservation of these artifacts and to the pride in their work experienced by immigrants and their descendants. See Woman's Club of Minneapolis, *Yearbook, 1907–8*, p. 3, 13–15, *1910*, p. 3, 9–11, *1911*, p. 3, 9–11, *1913*, p. 3, 16–18, copies in MHS; Chambers, "Ueland, Clara Hampson," in James et al., *Notable American Women* 3:8–99; Minnesota State Art Society, annual report, 1912.

28. B. Ueland, "Clara," 247.

29. B. Ueland, "Clara," 197–98, 212.

NOTES TO CHAPTER 4

Epigraph: "Mrs. Andreas Ueland, President, Minnesota Woman Suffrage Association," dated by cataloger [1916?], 10:240, MWSA Records. Ueland probably made this statement in 1914 when she became MWSA president.

1. *Minneapolis Tribune*, Sept. 18, 1913, p. 8; meeting minutes, Sept. 17, 1913, 15:196–98, MWSA Records.

2. *Minneapolis Tribune*, Sept. 18, 1913, p. 8; Equal Suffrage Assn. of Minneapolis (ESAM) board minutes, Sept. 22, 1913, 15:199–200, MWSA Records; *Minneapolis Journal*, Sept. 17, 1913, p. 12.

3. *Minneapolis Tribune*, Sept. 18, 1913, p. 8; ESAM meeting minutes, Sept. 17, 1913, 15:249, MWSA Records.

4. *Minneapolis Tribune*, Sept. 18, 1913, p. 8.

5. The communities included Austin, Excelsior, Grand Rapids, Luverne, Mankato-St. Peter, Marshall, Pipestone, Redwood Falls, and Tracy; there were also neighborhood clubs in St. Paul. Some of the town clubs were not new but had been dormant and were revived by Lutz and her coworkers. See Hurd, *Woman Suffrage*, 13–14, 17; "Suffrage Clubs Affiliated with the Minnesota Woman Suffrage Association," [1912?], 9:436–37, MWSA Records; Alpha H. Boostrom to "Dear Sir," Jan. 2, 1913, Minnesota Equal Franchise League (MEFL) Papers, MHS.

6. Executive board minutes, Dec. 9, 1912, 14:489, "Report of the Minnesota Equal Franchise League," [ca. Dec. 1912], 9:439—both MWSA Records; Hurd, *Woman Suffrage*, 14; Boostrom to "Dear Sir," Jan. 2, 1913, MEFL Papers. Peyton was an attorney then teaching at Humboldt High School in St. Paul; executive board minutes, Sept. 16, Oct. 24, 1912, 14:472, 482; information about Theresa Peyton, Minnesota Biography Project files, MHS.

7. Here and following paragraph, Ruth McCormick to Theresa B. Peyton, Mar. 20, 1914, [Peyton] to Doris Stevens, Mar. 20, 1915, MEFL Papers; Sophie G. Kenyon to [Anna Howard] Shaw, Mar. 10, 1913, 1:164–66, MWSA Records.

8. Executive board minutes, Apr. 9, June 4, 1913, Jan. 24, Mar. 7, 1914, 14:506, 511, 537, 543, MWSA Records; Jane Bliss Potter to Theresa Peyton, Apr. 10, 1913, Mar. 5, 1914, MEFL Papers; Hurd, *Woman Suffrage*, 14; Lounsbury, "Woman Suffrage Movement," 64.

9. *Minneapolis Journal*, Sept. 17, 1913, p. 12; *Minneapolis Morning Tribune*, Sept. 18, 1913, p. 8; ESAM minutes, Sept. 17, Dec. 19, 1913, 15:196, 207, MWSA Records.

10. *Minneapolis Journal*, Sept. 17, 1913, p. 12; Lounsbury, "Woman Suffrage Movement," 51, 80; Kraditor, *Ideas of the Woman Suffrage Movement*, 3.

11. No civic or cultural organization of any significance—including suffrage groups—went untouched by "the very beautiful, high-minded" Emily Noyes; Sherna Gluck, ed., *From Parlor to Prison: Five American Suffragists Talk about Their Lives* (New York: Vintage Books, 1976; reprint, New York: Octagon Books, 1976), 47. Other material on the life of Noyes, here and below, is taken from her obituary, *St. Paul Pioneer Press*, Sept. 10, 1930, p. 1, and from a brief essay on Noyes sent to the author by Rhoda R. Gilman, Apr. 1994.

12. Foster, *Who's Who among Minnesota Women*, 358.

13. After suffrage had been achieved, the club changed its name to the Everywoman Progressive Council and turned its attention to "the promotion of political and economic equality and social justice to the negro, co-operation between white and colored women and men, training of local colored women leaders and fostering the recognition of negroes who have achieved success"; Foster, *Who's Who among Minnesota Women*, 101. Conde Hamlin of the *St. Paul Pioneer Press* was in the audience and helped Francis get the position; Judy Yaeger Jones, "Nellie F. Griswold Francis," in *Women of Minnesota: Biographies and Sources* ([St. Paul: Women's History Month, 1991]), 12–15; B. Ueland, "Clara," 399; undated list of officers, Everywoman Suffrage Club, 9:435, MWSA Records. Francis was also president of the Minnesota State Federation of Colored Women and chairwoman of the press department of the National Association of Colored Women's Clubs.

14. The Workers' Equal Suffrage Club may have become the Minneapolis Workers' Equal Suffrage League, which Fanny Fligelman (later

Brin) served as president in 1912. In 1913 the Women Workers' Suffrage Club was organized with Gertrude Hunter as president; Hurd, *Woman Suffrage*, 12, 14; Stanton et al., *History* 6:320.

15. Biographical information about Alice Paul is taken from Linda G. Ford, *Iron-jawed Angels: The Suffrage Militancy of the National Woman's Party, 1912–1920* (Lanham, Md.: University Press of America, 1991), 15–18, 24, 27. See also Inez Haynes Irwin, *The Story of the Woman's Party* (New York: Harcourt, Brace & Co., 1921), 7, 18, 28–29, 36–37, 47–48, 66–67. Flexner put the number of marchers at five thousand; *Century of Struggle*, 263.

16. Suffrage parade committee minutes, Apr. 1, 1914, 15:228–29, mwsa Records.

17. *Minneapolis Journal*, May 3, 1914, pt. 1, p. 1, 3, 14; B. Ueland, "Clara," 264.

18. Twenty-eight years later—in 1942—that young parade participant became president of the Minnesota League of Women Voters. Helen Holmes Jones, daughter of David Percy Jones (twice mayor of Minneapolis) and Alice Gale, married Philip S. Duff in 1920 and reared a family of three sons and one daughter. After 1944 Helen ("Honey," as she was known to friends) Duff joined forces with the Minnesota Republican Workshop and worked in the first of Harold E. Stassen's many presidential campaigns, both activities indicative of the moderate-progressive Republicanism she espoused. She continued to attend Republican caucuses well into her nineties; "Account of Suffragette Parade," from Duff's journal as read by her daughter, Molly Duff Woehrlin, at Duff's funeral service, Apr. 14, 1988, photocopy in author's possession.

19. *Minneapolis Tribune*, May 3, 1914, pt. 1, p. 1; Ole O. Sageng to [Clara] Ueland, May 5, 16:104, Maria L. Sanford to Ueland, May 11, 16:106—both 1914, mwsa Records. Elizabeth Cady Stanton deplored these perceptions of suffragists as "sour old maids, childless women, . . . divorced wives"—perceptions that persisted through the years; Griffith, *In Her Own Right*, 51. One analysis of eighty-nine suffragists born between 1792 and 1886 revealed that three out of four were married at least once. Stanton was incorrect in one respect because 16 percent of those marriages had resulted in divorce. The average age at the time of marriage was twenty-four, a figure somewhat above the national pattern but also skewed by the marriage of one "doughty suffragist" at the age of eighty-seven. Of the sixty-seven who married, fifty-three had children; some had six to eight,

which was typical of nineteenth-century families, but the average was three, "well below the national norm for the time." Aside from family size and divorce, suffragists were notable because of their educational attainments. More than 50 percent had been to some institution of higher learning; others had the benefit of independent study with fathers or husbands, frequently in the law; A. F. Scott and A. M. Scott, "The Suffragists: A Collective Sketch," in *One Half the People*, document 10, p. 164–65.

20. Suffrage parade committee minutes, May 6, 26, 1914, 15:240–42, MWSA Records. The two largest parades had been in Philadelphia, with twenty-five thousand women participants, and in Boston, with nine thousand; Ruth McCormick to "Dear Madam President," May 15, 1914, MEFL Papers.

21. *Minneapolis Tribune*, Aug. 7, 1914, p. 7.

22. Beginning in 1900, the suffragists held an open house at the Minnesota State Fair for twenty years; Stanton et al., *History* 6:322. See also executive board minutes, June 20, July 16, Oct. 3, 1914, 14:559–61, 568, MWSA Records; "A Word to Suffragists about Your Girl and Mine," advertisement, [Feb. 1915?], MEFL Papers.

23. Hurd wrote to Shaw, "We then would have a committee representing women popular in society and club work, strong financially, a splendid board"; Nov. 2, 1909, 1:75, MWSA Records.

24. ESAM board meeting minutes, Oct. 8, 1914, 15:251, "Mrs. Andreas Ueland," 10:240—both MWSA Records. A year later, on Nov. 22, 1915, ESAM was transformed into the Hennepin County Woman Suffrage Association (part of the political design). Ueland served as a vice-president until the organization's demise in 1920; ESAM meeting minutes, Nov. 22, 1915, 15:313.

25. Executive board minutes, special meeting, Oct. 24, 1914, 14:574–75, ESAM board minutes, Sept. 25, 1914, 15:248—both MWSA Records. Ueland's immediate predecessor was her good friend Emily Bright, who stepped down because of what Clara described as "a very sad accident in Mrs. Bright's family." Bright, who otherwise might have continued in office and succeeded in bringing some order out of the prevailing chaos, returned to action as a MWSA board member after a brief absence; minutes of the 33rd annual convention, Oct. 16–17, 1914, 15:124, 135, "Mrs. Andreas Ueland," 10:240, Ueland to MWSA secretary, [Nov. 6, 1914], 1:211, executive board minutes, May 5, 1915, 14:603.

26. Lounsbury, "Woman Suffrage Movement," 72; "Dear Suffragist," [1915?], 16:147, executive board minutes, Jan. 2, 1915, 14:586—both MWSA Records.

27. Clara Ueland to "Dear Suffragist," Aug. 5, 1915, 1:291, executive board minutes, Dec. 1, 1915, 14:636, "Mrs. Rene E. Hamilton Stevens," press release, [1915], 10:234—all MWSA Records.

28. Clara Ueland to "Dear Suffragist," Nov. 23, 1915, 1:372, MWSA Records. The first "Dear Suffragist" communication, indicating that subsequent letters would be sent "from time to time," was issued on Aug. 5, 1915; 1:291.

29. Newspaper clippings, 17:470–76, flyers, [Aug. 20, 1915], 16:238–39, MWSA Records.

30. Fowler, Carrie Catt, 28–29; Gertrude Foster Brown, "A Decisive Victory Won," in NAWSA, Victory, 107–20. In a letter to Shaw, Ethel Hurd approved her decision, saying, "Your place in the struggle is on the platform where you have no peer"; Dec. 9, 1915, 1:380, MWSA Records.

31. The twelve suffrage states in 1916 were Wyoming, 1890; Colorado, 1893; Idaho, 1896; Utah, 1896; Washington, 1910; California, 1911; Oregon, 1912; Arizona, 1912; Kansas, 1912; Illinois (presidential suffrage), 1913; Montana, 1914; Nevada, 1914. See "The Electoral Thermometer," in NAWSA, Victory, 161–62.

32. Peck, Carrie Chapman Catt, 261; Flexner, Century of Struggle, 279–82.

33. Eleanor Flexner, "Catt, Carrie Clinton Lane Chapman," in James et al., Notable American Women 1:309–13; Flexner, Century of Struggle, 275; statement of appreciation from Minnesota to be included in gift booklet for Catt, undated (probably for a NAWSA convention, possibly 1919 or 1920), 1:46, MWSA Records. When Mrs. Frank Leslie died in 1914, she left her estate of nearly $1 million to Catt to use on behalf of suffrage. Contested by Leslie relatives, the money did not come into Catt's hands until 1917, but when it did, it provided valuable resources for staffing national headquarters and for the publication of Woman Citizen, NAWSA's principal organ of communication. Control of such a sum clearly added to Catt's clout and effectiveness as the national leader of NAWSA; Fowler, Carrie Catt, 117–19, 142–45.

NOTES TO CHAPTER 5

Epigraph: Lavinia Coppock Gilfillan, "The Disadvantages of Equal Suffrage," in Papers and Proceedings of the Eighth Annual Meeting of the Min-

nesota Academy of Social Sciences, general topic "Women and the State," ed. J. F. Ebersole ([Mankato, Minn.]: Published for the Academy by the Free Press Printing Co., 1915; hereafter "Women and the State"), 176.

1. Newspaper clipping, 17:734, MWSA Records. This was true of antis around the country. Flexner described them as being, almost without exception, "ladies of means and social position"; *Century of Struggle,* 296. Anne Firor Scott pictured them as mirror images of the suffragists "except that they were a little richer, and a little more linked to the mercantile and manufacturing elite"; *Natural Allies,* 139. In the first quarterly statement of the Minnesota Associations Opposed to the Further Extension of Suffrage to Women, membership totals for St. Paul were listed as 1,300, including 800 wage earners, and more than 700 for Minneapolis; Minnesota Associations Opposed to the Further Extension of Suffrage to Women, undated statement (sometime after 1914), 14:328.

2. The debate was part of a two-day program recorded in Ebersole, "Women and the State"—especially see p. 142, 158; see also Minnesota Academy of Social Sciences annual meeting, Dec. 3–4, 1914, program, 16:138, MWSA Records; B. Ueland, "Clara," 277. Josephine Schain served as education chair until mid-1913. It is not clear what prompted her to leave the board.

3. B. Ueland, "Clara," 261; "A Protest against Statutory Suffrage for Minnesota Women," [Jan. 6, 1917], 14:401–3, "Some of the Women in Minnesota Opposed to Woman Suffrage," [ca. after 1914], 14:327, MWSA Records; Charles B. Cheney, "Women Had a Tough Fight to Get the Right to Vote," *Minneapolis Morning Tribune,* Dec. 5, 1946, p. 4; Carol A. Subialka, "The Ideology of Minnesota's Woman Suffrage Movement: 1910–1920," senior thesis, Department of History, University of Minnesota, 1987, p. 19, copy in MHS.

4. Foster, *Who's Who among Minnesota Women,* 118.

5. B. Ueland, "Clara," 129, 277, 282, 290–92; John William Leonard, ed., *Woman's Who's Who of America: A Biographical Dictionary of Contemporary Women of the United States and Canada: 1914–1915* (New York: American Commonwealth Co., 1914), 162, copy in MHS. Anne's attachment to a young man of whom the senior Uelands disapproved had prompted them to look at colleges far from home.

6. Peck, *Carrie Chapman Catt,* 409–10; Fowler, *Carrie Catt,* 47.

7. [Florence Welles] Carpenter, "The Disadvantages of Equal Suffrage," in Ebersole, "Women and the State," 191. See Kraditor, *Ideas of the*

Woman Suffrage Movement, 12–37, for an elaboration of the arguments used by antisuffragists.

8. Carpenter, 186–91, Gilfillan, 176–78—both "Disadvantages," in Ebersole, "Women and the State."

9. Gilfillan, 174, 180–85, Carpenter, 191–93—both "Disadvantages," in "Women and the State."

10. Josephine Schain, "The Advantages of Equal Suffrage," in "Women and the State," 160, 162, 163, 164, 165, 169.

11. [Clara Hampson] Ueland, "The Advantages of Equal Suffrage," in "Women and the State," 142.

12. C. Ueland, "Advantages," in "Women and the State," 142, 145.

13. C. Ueland, "Advantages," in "Women and the State," 146–48.

14. C. Ueland, "Advantages," in "Women and the State," 148, 149, 155.

15. Stanton et al., *History* 5:678–79; A. F. Scott, *Natural Allies,* 139–40. In the great debate of 1914 at the University of Minnesota, Gilfillan claimed that societies were organized in twenty-six states; "Disadvantages," in "Women and the State," 183. The figure of twenty-six also comes from Buechler, *Women's Movements,* 183. In *One Half the People,* the Scotts wrote that by 1917 NAWSA membership had grown to two million (p. 39). In *American Women,* the Schneiders wrote that membership "surged in 1917 to two million" (p. 170). In 1918 the antisuffrage association moved its headquarters to Washington, D.C.

16. [Ella Lawler] Pennington, "Woman the Helpmate," undated pamphlet, 14:239, 243, MWSA Records.

17. *St. Paul Pioneer Press,* Jan. 31, 1915, section 3, p. 6.

18. Lebsock, "Women and American Politics," in Tilly and Gurin, *Women, Politics, and Change,* 44–45; Chrislock, *Progressive Era,* 2–3.

19. Christine A. Lunardini, *From Equal Suffrage to Equal Rights: Alice Paul and the National Woman's Party, 1910–1928* (New York: New York University Press, 1986), 173; Irwin, *Story of the Woman's Party,* 35; Kraditor, *Ideas of the Woman Suffrage Movement,* 163–64. The wording of the Anthony amendment as first introduced into Congress on Jan. 10, 1878, by Anthony's close friend Sen. Aaron A. Sargent of California is the wording of the Nineteenth Amendment; Stanton et al., *History* 3:75; Flexner, *Century of Struggle,* 173. McCormick was the daughter of famed politico Mark Hanna, the longtime Republican boss who had engineered William McKinley's election to the presidency over the popular William Jennings Bryan.

The initiative and referendum were popular reforms advanced during the Progressive Era.

20. Morgan, *Suffragists and Democrats*, 90–91. Delegates to the 1914
NAWSA convention were divided over the issue, and the debate over
the merits of the amendment continued throughout 1915; Young, *In
the Public Interest*, 20.

21. Executive board minutes, Apr. 3, 14:595, Katharine Gregory Camp
to [Maud] Stockwell, Apr. 10, 14:598—both 1915, MWSA Records;
Kraditor, *Ideas of the Woman Suffrage Movement*, 163–71.

22. Kraditor, *Ideas of the Woman Suffrage Movement*, 114; Carpenter,
"Disadvantages," in Ebersole, "Women and the State," 186–87;
Flexner, *Century of Struggle*, 219.

23. Morgan, *Suffragists and Democrats*, 23; Griffith, *In Her Own Right*,
206.

24. Anne Firor Scott, "Addams, Jane," 1:16–22, Louise C. Wade, "Kelley,
Florence," 2:316–19, Christopher Lasch, "Breckinridge, Sophonisba
Preston," 1:233–36, and Allen F. Davis, "Starr, Ellen Gates,"
3:351–53—all in James, *Notable American Women*. Addams, along
with Starr, founded the pioneering Hull House in Chicago in 1889.

25. B. Ueland, "Clara," 191A.

26. Lebsock, "Women and American Politics," in Tilly and Gurin,
Women, Politics, and Change, 48.

27. Kraditor, *Ideas of the Woman Suffrage Movement*, 124–28; Flexner,
Century of Struggle, 363n1; O'Neill, *Feminism in America*, 153–55;
Lerner, *Majority Finds Its Past*, 60–61.

28. Buechler, *Women's Movements*, 148; Christine Bolt, *The Women's
Movements in the United States and Britain from the 1790s to the 1920s*
(Amherst: University of Massachusetts Press, 1993), 208; Kraditor,
Ideas of the Woman Suffrage Movement, 105–28; Griffith, *In Her Own
Right*, 206; Naomi Black, *Social Feminism* (Ithaca, N.Y.: Cornell
University Press, 1989), 32–33. The effort to reach out to these new
citizens was intensified with the outbreak of World War I and the
inauguration of an intensive "Americanization" campaign conducted by the government and voluntary associations such as NAWSA.
(The significant effort on the part of suffragists to promote literacy
and to provide civic education could be viewed as the precursor of
the voter-education projects of the League of Women Voters.) This
more sympathetic (if still patronizing) outlook by middle-class suffragists encouraged foreign-born and working women—perceiving

that their interests could be advanced by suffrage—to join forces with the mainstream suffrage groups.

29. League of Women Voters of Minnesota, *Indians in Minnesota*, 2d ed. (St. Paul: The League, 1971), 6; news bulletin, July 23, 1917, 10:262, MWSA Records.

30. Chrislock, *Progressive Era*, 32. In 1920 there were 8,809 Negroes in Minnesota, with Indians a close second (also 0.4 percent) in a total population of 2,387,125; U.S. Bureau of the Census, *Fourteenth Census of the United States*, vol. 3, *Population* (Washington, D.C: GPO, 1922), 19, 36. The amendment providing for "Equal Manhood Suffrage" had to go before Minnesota voters two times before it was passed in 1868; Folwell, *History of Minnesota* 3:7–8. According to one account, at the time of passage only forty-two Negroes in the state were estimated to be eligible to vote; Louise R. Noun, *Strong-minded Women: The Emergence of the Woman-Suffrage Movement in Iowa* (Ames: Iowa State University Press, 1969), 85n. The Democrats' proposal to extend suffrage to married women was ignored as "too frivolous for notice"; *History of Minnesota* 4:333–34. Article 7 of the original Minnesota constitution established four categories of citizens: white U.S. citizens; foreign-born individuals declaring their intention to become citizens; "civilized" mixed bloods; and Indians found competent by a district court; Anderson and Lobb, *History of the Constitution of Minnesota*, 123–24.

31. Nanny Jaeger, undated item, woman suffrage material, Jaeger Papers, MHS. Woman suffrage was granted by Finland in 1906, by Norway in 1913, by Denmark in 1915, and by Sweden in 1921; Stanton et al., *History* 6:771, 776, 778, 783; clippings, 17:353, 725, MWSA Records; Sheeran, "Woman Suffrage," 6–7. "It is the German communities in this state which are most difficult," wrote one woman of German descent to a suffragist in New Ulm; [probably Clara M. Heckrich] to Mrs. M. A. Bingham, Jan. 9, 1919, 5:78–79.

32. Unidentified and undated newspaper clippings, 17:662, 722, "State Organizer" [probably Rene E. H. Stevens] to Anna Himrod, Jan. 15, 1919, 5:149, [Clara Ueland] to Mrs. J. W. Andrews, Oct. 18, 1918, 3:852–53—all MWSA Records. See also Barbara Stuhler, "Fanny Brin, Woman of Peace" (p. 284–300) and information about Cain in Arvonne S. Fraser and Sue E. Holbert, "Women in the Minnesota Legislature" (p. 262–63)—both in Stuhler and Kreuter, *Women of Minnesota*; Judy Yaeger Jones, "Eleanore Harriet Bresky," in *Women of Minnesota: Biographies and Sources* ([St. Paul: Minnesota Women's History Month, 1991]), 6–8. Brin became president of the National

Council of Jewish Women and served for many years as that organi-zation's representative on Carrie Chapman Catt's National Commit-tee on the Cause and Cure of War. Cain, business agent for the Telephone Operators Union, was among the first group of women elected to the legislature in 1922. Bresky was an attorney.

33. Clara Ueland, president's address, MWSA convention, Dec. 4, 1916, 8:166, MWSA committee to Douglas Greeley, June 5, 1916, 1:774, MWSA Records. In her study of the ideology of the suffrage movement in Minnesota, Carol Subialka found only these two references re-vealing some identification with that "superior" strain of suffragist thought; there were probably others never recorded for posterity; "Ideology," 16.

34. Robert L. Morlan, *Political Prairie Fire: The Nonpartisan League 1915–1922* (Minneapolis: University of Minnesota Press, 1955; re-print, St. Paul: Minnesota Historical Society Press, Borealis Books, 1985), 25–34.

35. Morlan, *Political Prairie Fire*, 215–16; *Nonpartisan Leader* (Minneapolis), Mar. 15, 1920, p. 7; Arthur Warner, "The Farmer Butts Back," *The Nation*, Aug. 28, 1920, p. 240–41. The Sept. 6, 1920, issue of the *Nonpartisan Leader* reported that all Nonpar-tisan League states ratified the Nineteenth Amendment—and reprinted the text of the league's telegram to the Tennessee legis-lature urging a favorable vote (p. 10). The Oct. 4 issue has an arti-cle urging all women members to vote (p. 12). These, and the occa-sional earlier references to suffrage, all appeared on the women's page. Suffrage finally broke out of the women's page with an edito-rial in the Oct. 18 edition, which contained another exhortation urging women to go to the polls on election day (p. 3). In the new introduction to the reprint edition of *Political Prairie Fire*, Larry Remele noted that the book's original index contained no men-tion of women (p. xiv).

36. Editorial, *Farmer's Wife* (St. Paul), July 1919, p. 31.

37. Executive board minutes, Apr. 4, 29, 1914, 14:550, 553–54, MWSA Records. Jane Bliss Potter's initial motion was passed, but Nanny Jaeger felt that an enthusiastic welcome should accompany the ap-proval. Both motions passed with one dissenting vote, that of Ethel Hurd.

38. B. Ueland, "Clara," 262. Ueland took her recommendations for com-mittees to the executive board, including her name as legislative chair; board minutes, Nov. 4, 1914, 14:577–78, MWSA Records.

NOTES TO CHAPTER 6

Epigraph: Unidentified newspaper clipping, 17:662, MWSA Records.

1. In 1907 a resolution for a state amendment emerged from the Senate elections committee, but it was defeated in the Senate and never came before the House; Stanton et al., *History* 6:324.

2 *Senate Journal,* 1911, p. 920, *1913,* p. 130–31; *House Journal,* 1913, p. 369–70; Stanton et al., *History* 6:324; Hurd, *Woman Suffrage,* 25–29; *Minneapolis Journal,* Feb. 11, 1913, p. 1, 2; unidentified newspaper clipping, 18:74, "Minnesota," [post-1915], 9:15—both MWSA Records.

3. Here and following two paragraphs, *St. Paul Pioneer Press,* Jan. 27, 1915, p. 1, 4.

4. *St. Paul Pioneer Press.* Jan. 27, 1915, p. 4; [Lavinia] Gilfillan, "Address before the Elections Committee of Senate of Minnesota," 1915, 14:334, MWSA Records. Historian Gerda Lerner has observed that "as members of families, as daughters, and wives," patrician women were often "closer to actual power than many a man." Historian Linda Colley added, "They did not have to vote or strive for public office to win access to the political center: They were already there by virtue of who they were, of who their families were, and of whom they married. For these women, there was no gulf between the public and private spheres. The two often converged, not least because their social life was an integral part of political life"; Colley, "Women and Political Power," *Wilson Quarterly* 16 (Spring 1992): 52.

5. *Minneapolis Morning Tribune,* Mar. 5, 1915, p. 1, 12.

6. *Minneapolis Morning Tribune,* Mar. 5, p. 12, *St. Paul Pioneer Press,* Mar. 5, p. 6—both 1915. Another well-known opponent was Sen. Winslow W. Dunn, attorney for the Theo. Hamm Brewing Company of St. Paul, who worked actively for twenty-two years against all suffrage legislation. Sullivan was in the anti camp for ten years; Stanton et al., *History* 6:325.

7. *St. Paul Pioneer Press,* Mar. 5, 1915, p. 6; B. Ueland, "Clara," 298–301. On a motion to reconsider, Robert C. Dunn of Princeton changed his yea vote to a nay vote, increasing the final margin of defeat to two; *Senate Journal,* 1915, p. 479–80.

8. *House Journal,* 1915, p. 939, 1070, 1182, 1219, 1491; Clara Ueland to Mary Sumner Boyd, undated (probably Jan. or Feb. 1916), 1:413, MWSA Records. Except for Putnam, the principal supporters had all

been born in Scandinavian countries—Larson in Sweden, and Sageng and Wefald in Norway.

9. "Statement of the Minnesota Woman Suffrage Association On Suffrage Bills Now Before The Legislature," [1919], 9:23–24, MWSA Records; Folwell, *History of Minnesota* 4:335.

10. Chrislock, *Progressive Era*, 85–87, and *Watchdog of Loyalty*, 11. The executive board decided to send McFadden and a Miss Doherty to the labor union convention in Winona; the two women may have been members of one of the suffrage groups designed to attract working women, the Wage Earner's League or the Workers' Equal Suffrage Club; board meeting minutes, July 10, 1915, 14:615, MWSA Records; *Labor Review* (Minneapolis), July 23, 1915, p. 1, 2.

As with many institutions, organized labor did not always harmonize what it professed with what it practiced. Although the Federation of Labor at the same convention had considered a resolution to hire a woman organizer, it adopted instead a substitute requesting the American Federation of Labor to send a woman organizer to Minnesota as the need arose—the presumption being that there would not be enough women in the work force to justify a full-time organizer; *Labor Review*, p. 1.

11. *Labor Review*, July 30, 1915, p. 4. There is no mention of any action on county option in the minutes of meetings of the Hennepin County Woman Suffrage Association or in the minutes of the MWSA executive board; minutes, 15:320–718, MWSA Records.

12. "Labor's Position on Woman Suffrage," *New Republic*, Mar. 11, 1916, p. 152; according to a story in the *Duluth Herald* (Dec. 18, 1915, p. 9), the article was written by Sen. Richard Jones of Duluth. See also *Labor Review*, July 21, 1916, p. 1, 2.

13. ESAM board minutes, Oct. 2, 1915:303, 1915 MWSA convention minutes, 15:167–69, MWSA Records.

14. *Minneapolis Labor Review*, July 20, 1917, p. 1, 2, 3, July 19, 1918, p. 2.

15. Lounsbury, "Woman Suffrage Movement," 78.

16. Lounsbury, "Woman Suffrage Movement," 73. Communications from Ueland and the office staff and reports to the MWSA from local organizers constitute a sizable part of the existing MWSA records. See rolls 1–7 (1916–21), which also contain other materials.

17. Executive board minutes, Dec. 1, 1915, 14:636, "President's Report of Year's Work for National Association, January–August 1916," 14:662–69, Clara Ueland to Rene E. H. Stevens, July 5, 1916, 2:8,

and Aug. 26, 1916, 2:200, and Sept. 28, 1916, 2:236, report, Mar. 19, 1919, 14:781—all MWSA Records; B. Ueland, "Clara," 336; MWSA "Dear Suffragist" letter, [June 1916], correspondence, 1916, Ole O. Sageng Papers, MHS; Flexner, *Century of Struggle*, 290–91; Lounsbury, "Woman Suffrage Movement," 73. New York voters did not approve that referendum, but a second attempt, in the fall of 1917, would succeed. Many of the women became prominent in suffrage circles, including Jane Bliss Potter, Bertha Moller, and Florence Monahan. Other organizers who served for shorter periods were Grace Randall, Mabel H. Guise, and Anne E. Forrestal.

18. Rene E. H. Stevens to [Clara] Ueland, Aug. 29, 1916, 2:204–5, unidentified and undated newspaper clipping, 17:684, Stevens to [Edith Drake Briggs], Aug. 6, 1916, 2:173–74, Ueland to [Bertha C.] Moller, Oct. 4, 1916, 2:243, Moller to Ueland, Oct. 10, 1916, 2:251—all MWSA Records. Stevens spent most of her time in Minnesota until ratification of the Nineteenth Amendment by the legislature.

19. Bertha C. Moller to [Clara] Ueland, Aug. 3, 1917, 2:702, and Aug. 7, 1917, 2:706, and Sept. 1, 1917, 2:734, Moller to "Dear fellow suffragists at headquarters," Oct. 22, 1916, 2:274–77, Moller to Maria McMahon, Feb. 28, 1917, 2:434–35—all MWSA Records.

20. *Evening Tribune* (Albert Lea), Jan. 28, p. 5, *Minneapolis Morning Tribune*, May 9, p. 1, 3—both 1916. The first meeting was held in Chicago in May 1912. Representatives of seventeen states, including Minnesota, attended. Subsequent conferences were held in St. Louis, Des Moines, Indianapolis, Minneapolis, and Columbus, Ohio. A meeting scheduled for Sioux Falls, S.Dak., was usurped by a special meeting convened by Catt at the time of the Indiana state convention in Apr. 1918 to plan action on the federal amendment that appeared to be near passage. By 1919 there seemed to be no need for a conference, as victory was clearly in sight; Stanton et al., *History* 5:667–71; Peck, *Carrie Chapman Catt*, 243.

21. Time-Life Books, *This Fabulous Century*, vol. 2, *1910–1920*, p. 23.

22. Dolores De Bower Johnson, "Anna Dickie Olesen: Senate Candidate," in Stuhler and Kreuter, *Women of Minnesota*, 231, 235–41; [Clara Ueland] to [Anna Dickie] Olesen, May 20, 1916, 1:657, Ueland to Mrs. John L. Pyle, Apr. 3, 1918, 8:313, Ueland to Nellie McClung, May 5, 1919, 6:141, petition forms, 1:688, 693–736—all MWSA Records. In 1922 Olesen ran on the Democratic ticket for U.S. Senate, losing in the three-way race to Farmer-Laborite Henrik

Shipstead, who defeated the Republican incumbent, Frank B. Kellogg.

23. B. Ueland, "Clara," 337. The *St. Paul Daily News* (June 7, 1916, p. 3) reported forty thousand; the *Minneapolis Morning Tribune* (June 8, 1916, p. 3) reported five thousand; the *Chicago Tribune* estimate of ten thousand is quoted in B. Ueland, "Clara," 339.

24. B. Ueland, "Clara," 343.

25. Henriette McKnight to "Dear Suffragist," May 29, 1916, 1:748, report by Katherine Louise Smith, [undated], 8:3—both MWSA Records; *Minneapolis Morning Tribune*, June 12, p. 4, June 15, p. 3—both 1916.

26. B. Ueland, "Clara," 345–46; *St. Paul Pioneer Press*, June 16, 1916, p. 4.

27. "Report of the Vice-President for the Year 1916," [1917], 2:351–52, Kenyon listed as first vice-president on the 1916 MWSA convention program, 14:149, [Ethel E. Hurd] to [Eugenia B.] Farmer, Apr. 28, 1916, 1:604–5—all MWSA Records.

28. At the same annual convention, Ueland also reported that the special lecture on "Democracy and Equal Suffrage" by Fola La Follette—daughter of U.S. Sen. Robert M. La Follette, Sr., of Wisconsin—on Feb. 16 at a noon meeting in the Shubert Theatre renewed their hopes and restored their confidence. Reflecting on that day, she observed, "How much more profitable it is to do a spectacular striking thing than to attempt an ordinary every-day affair, that makes no appeal to the imagination." The trip to Pipestone by auto, she reflected, "was a sort of a triumphant tour," and the conferences there and in Albert Lea both proved to be successful. Ueland also reported on another meeting at which suffrage leaders had plotted a complex legislative strategy supporting a bill for presidential suffrage through legislation rather than a state amendment. They were also proceeding with organizational planning, raising money, circulating literature, and expanding their press work; president's address, 1916, 8:95–100, "Fola LaFollette [sic] Lecture, Feb. 16, 1916," report, 15:352—both MWSA Records.

29. Clara M. Heckrich to Mary Sumner Boyd, Apr. 5, 1917, 2:470, executive board minutes, Mar. 7, 1914, 14:743—both MWSA Records; *House Journal*, 1917, p. 96.

30. Betty Kane, "Amending Our State Constitution" in *Legislative Manual*, 1981–82, p. 2, 8–10.

31. "Statement . . . On Suffrage Bills," [1919], 9:23–24, report of legislative work for 1917, [ca. 1918], 9:398—both MWSA Records; *House*

Journal, 1916 & 1917, p. 95, 489, 522–23; *Senate Journal*, 1916 & 1917, p. 86, 997–98.

32. Report of legislative work for 1917, [ca. 1918], 9:398–99, unidentified newspaper clipping, 17:798—both MWSA Records; *Minneapolis Morning Tribune*, Mar. 30, p. 1, 9, *Minneapolis Journal*, Mar. 30, p. 19—both 1917.

33. *St. Paul Daily News*, Apr. 6, Apr. 10—both 1917, p. 10. The bill was sponsored by William I. Nolan and Willis I. Norton of Minneapolis, Claude E. Southwick of Wells in Faribault County, Theodore Christianson of Dawson in Lac qui Parle County, and Adolph Larson of Sandstone; *House Journal*, 1916 & 1917, p. 136; *Senate Journal*, 1916 & 1917, p. 1186, 1189. The three votes are also reported in a note from Clara Ueland to Mary Sumner Boyd, [Apr. 9, 1917?], 2:471; see also report of legislative work for 1917, [ca. 1918], 9:398—both MWSA Records.

34. Minnesota report, "Minutes of Suffrage Convention," [1911?], 1:85–87, MWSA Records. According to this same report, seventy-eight women voted in a Turkish election in Feb. 1910.

35. Speech at auditorium, Minneapolis, May 2, 1914, typescript, in correspondence, Apr.–July 1914, Sageng Papers, MHS. The enlightened attitude held by Sageng might have been shaped by the fact that his daughters outnumbered his sons, six to two; *Legislative Manual*, 1953, p. 12.

36. B. Ueland, "Clara," 423. With his controversial Populism behind him, Sageng was referred to in one editorial as "the last tall tree in the vanished Populist forest"; *Minneapolis Morning Tribune*, Apr. 15, 1914, p. 6.

NOTES TO CHAPTER 7

Epigraph: Irwin, *Story of the Woman's Party*, 284.

1. Lunardini, *From Equal Suffrage to Equal Rights*, 13–15; Sidney R. Bland, "Burns, Lucy," in *Notable American Women: The Modern Period*, ed. Barbara Sicherman and Carol Hurd Green (Cambridge: Belknap Press of Harvard University Press, 1980), 124–25.

2. O'Neill, *Feminism in America*, 127; Bolt, *Women's Movements*, 186–87; Midge Mackenzie, *Shoulder to Shoulder: A Documentary* (New York: Alfred A. Knopf, 1975), 137.

3. Mackenzie, *Shoulder to Shoulder*, ix, x; Ford, *Iron-jawed Angels*, 32; Eleanor Flexner, "Blatch, Harriot Eaton Stanton," in James et al., *Notable American Women* 1:172.

4. Bolt, *Women's Movements*, 202; Lunardini, *From Equal Suffrage to Equal Rights*, 20–21. By 1912 Paul had received her doctorate from the University of Pennsylvania and Burns had returned from England.

5. Lunardini, *From Equal Suffrage to Equal Rights*, 21–30; genealogical information about Andreas and Clara Ueland's children, in author's possession; Irwin, *Story of the Woman's Party*, 30; Flexner, *Century of Struggle*, 264.

6. Irwin, *Story of the Woman's Party*, 35, 37; Lunardini, *From Equal Suffrage to Equal Rights*, 6.

7. As a southerner, Clay believed suffrage was a matter for state, not federal, action; Lunardini, *From Equal Suffrage to Equal Rights*, 35–36, 45, 46, 49.

8. Anna Howard Shaw to "Dear Member of the Executive Council," Jan. 22, 1914, folder: July 1913, Mar. 1914, MEFL Papers, MHS; Young, *In the Public Interest*, 19–20; Buechler, *Women's Movements*, 56; Flexner, *Century of Struggle*, 265–67.

9. Lunardini, *From Equal Suffrage to Equal Rights*, 262–63; "Splendid Advance in Minnesota," *The Suffragist* (Washington, D.C.), July 10, 1915, p. 5; *Minneapolis Journal*, June 28, 1915, p. 6. From Nov. 15, 1913, through July 1, 1916, *The Suffragist* was the official organ of the Congressional Union for Woman Suffrage; from July 8, 1916, through Mar. 3, 1917, for both the Union and the NWP; and from Mar. 10, 1917, onward, the publication of the NWP.

10. "Splendid Advance in Minnesota," July 10, 1915, p. 5, "Deputation in Minnesota," Aug. 14, 1915, p. 6—both in *The Suffragist*. Gertrude Hunter and Josephine Schain also served as organizers. In 1916 Hunter was in charge of the campaign against President Wilson and Democratic congressional candidates in Wyoming; Lunardini, *From Equal Suffrage to Equal Rights*, 64, 66.

11. "Deputation in Minnesota," Aug. 14, 1915, p. 6, "Suffrage Deputation in Minnesota," July 31, 1915, p. 6—both in *The Suffragist*.

12. "Deputation in Minnesota," *The Suffragist*, Aug. 14, 1915, p. 6.

13. "Federal Work in Minnesota," Oct. 30, 1915, p. 4, Elsa Ueland, "Minnesota Deputation to Congressman Anderson," Aug. 28, 1915, p. 8—both in *The Suffragist*; Bruce L. Larson, *Lindbergh of*

Minnesota: A Political Biography (New York: Harcourt Brace Jovan-
ovich, 1971), 205–6.

14. 1915 MWSA convention minutes, Oct. 7–8, 1915, 15:165, Emily H.
Bright, report on NAWSA conference of June 7–8, 1915, [Oct. 8,
1915], 15:170–74, Sophie Kenyon to executive board, June 11,
1915, 14:609–10—all MWSA Records. At the Aug. meeting of the
executive board, Maud Stockwell, apparently in response to potshots
in Minnesota, moved that no publicity be given to any public criticism of the Congressional Union. The motion passed without dissent; board minutes, Aug. 7, 1915, 14:618.

15. Irwin, *Story of the Woman's Party*, 116–17; "Hearing before the House
Judiciary Committee," *The Suffragist*, Dec. 25, 1915, p. 5.

16. B. Ueland, "Clara," 317–19. Brenda thought that this letter gave a
good idea of her mother's "notions of wisdom and leadership."

17. B. Ueland, "Clara," 219.

18. [Clara Ueland] to Rene E. H. Stevens, July 13, 1916, 2:31–32, MWSA
Records; Lounsbury, "Woman Suffrage Movement," abstract, 2;
"Hearing before the House Judiciary Committee," Dec. 25, 1915,
p. 5, "Minnesota," Jan. 29, 1916, p. 7, "Mrs. Field Reaches Journey's
End," Mar. 11, 1916, p. 10—all in *The Suffragist*.

19. Evans, *Born for Liberty*, 167; Peck, *Carrie Chapman Catt*, 241. Just
before Congress adopted the Nineteenth Amendment in 1919,
women could vote for 339 out of 531 presidential electors; A. F.
Scott and A. M. Scott, *One Half the People*, 168.

20. "Voting Women Launch a Woman's Party," *The Suffragist*, June 10,
1916, p. 6–8; Bolt, *Women's Movements*, 243–44. Flexner explained
that, except in Illinois where women could vote only for president
and consequently had their votes counted separately, there was no
way to gauge how women voted in congressional contests. The NWP
claimed success, however, arguing that Wilson's election was due to
the support of Progressives, labor, and farmers ("all presumably
male!"); *Century of Struggle*, 277.

21. Irwin, *Story of the Woman's Party*, 194; Rosalind Rosenberg, *Divided
Lives: American Women in the Twentieth Century* (New York: Hill &
Wang, 1992), 72; Lunardini, *From Equal Suffrage to Equal Rights*,
99–100.

22. "National Conventions of the Congressional Union and the
Woman's Party," Jan. 31, 1917, p. 7, "Conventions of Woman's Party
and the Congressional Union," Mar. 10, 1917, p. 4–5—both in *The*

Suffragist. Martin, from Nevada, ran again in 1920 and devoted the rest of her life to women's causes; Kathryn Anderson, "Martin, Anne Henrietta," in Sicherman and Green, *Notable American Women*, 459–60.

23. "Suffrage Sentinels Resume Picket," p. 5, "The First Drive on the Sixty-fifth Congress," p. 8—both in *The Suffragist*, Apr. 7, 1917; Fowler, *Carrie Catt*, 151. Jane Bliss Potter was among those picketing the Capitol.

24. Irwin, *Story of the Woman's Party*, 208–11. Burns asserted that the pickets were simply "asking free Russia to speak to a deaf Executive on our behalf"; see "The Woman's Party Appeals to the Russian Mission," *The Suffragist*, June 23, 1917, p. 7.

25. Lunardini, *From Equal Suffrage to Equal Rights*, 128–29.

26. See, for example, [George] H. Partridge to [Clara] Ueland, Oct. 15, 1917, 2:858; see also press release of statement approved by MWSA conference, [1917], 10:253—both MWSA Records. A list of signers, beginning with "Mrs. Andreas Ueland," can be found in an untitled statement, [ca. June 27, 1917], 8:178. Also see *Minneapolis Tribune*, Nov. 18, 1917, section 1, p. 10; Lounsbury, "Woman Suffrage Movement," 67–68.

27. 1917 convention minutes, Nov. 16–17, 1917, 3:56–57, [Clara Ueland] to Mrs. D. N. Ackerman, Nov. 19, 1917, 3:62, press release of statement approved by MWSA conference, [1917], 10:253—all MWSA Records; "National Woman's Party," *The Suffragist*, Aug. 31, 1918, p. 2. Bertha Moller had resigned from the MWSA executive board in July, and Ueland—in addition to her presidential and legislative duties—assumed Moller's congressional-liaison responsibilities; board minutes, July 7, 1917, 14:715; Mary Christine Pruitt, "'Women Unite!' The Modern Women's Movement in Minnesota," Ph.D. diss., University of Minnesota, 1987, p. 62, copy in MHS.

28. Buechler, *Women's Movements*, 208; Thomas C. Pardo, ed., *The National Woman's Party Papers, 1913–1974; A Guide to the Microfilm Edition* (Glen Rock, N.J.: Microfilming Corporation of America, 1977), 5.

NOTES TO CHAPTER 8

Epigraph: Clara Ueland, address, [Nov. 16, 1917, convention], 8:101–2, MWSA Records.

1. Schlesinger, *Crisis of the Old Order*, 34–35. California's vote for Wilson gave him a winning margin of twenty-three electoral votes. The men of Minnesota elected one new Republican senator, Frank Kellogg of St. Paul, and two new Republican representatives, Ernest Lundeen and Harold Knutson from the fifth and sixth congressional districts, respectively. In the Republican primary, Kellogg had beat out an impressive array of contenders, including former Governor Adolph Eberhart, incumbent Sen. Moses E. Clapp, and retiring Rep. Charles A. Lindbergh; Stuhler, *Ten Men*, 42, 54, 57, 102.

2. "Mrs. Ueland's Report on Minnesota Congressmen," [undated], 9:68–69, MWSA Records. Ueland acted as the congressional chairman after Bertha Moller resigned; executive board minutes, July 7, 1917, 14:715.

3. Maud Wood Park, *Front Door Lobby*, edited by Edna Lamprey Stantial (Boston: Beacon Press, 1960), 175.

4. Butterfield, *American Past*, 356; *Minneapolis Morning Tribune*, Apr. 5, p. 1, Apr. 6, p. 1, 3—both 1917; *Congressional Record* (hereafter *Cong. Rec.*), 65th Cong., 1st sess., 1917, 55, pt. 1:118–20, 261, 412–13; Franklin F. Holbrook and Livia Appel, *Minnesota in the War with Germany* (St. Paul: Minnesota Historical Society, 1928), 1:52. Four of Minnesota's ten congressmen voted against the war: three Republicans (Charles Davis, Harold Knutson, Ernest Lundeen) and one Democrat (Carl Van Dyke).

5. Park, *Front Door Lobby*, 77; Flexner, "Catt, Carrie Clinton Lane Chapman," in James et al., *Notable American Women* 1:311. Rep. Ernest Lundeen of Minnesota's fifth congressional district also reported that Rankin's vote had been dignified and restrained—tears were a "newspaper myth"; Hennepin County Woman Suffrage Assn. board of directors meeting minutes, Apr. 18, 1917, 15:597, MWSA Records.

6. *St. Paul Daily News*, Apr. 1, 1917, p. 1, 6; *Cong. Rec.*, 64th Cong., 1st sess., 1916, 53, pt. 14:497–506. Charles A. Lindbergh [, Sr.], *Why Is Your Country at War: And What Happens to You after the War, and Related Subjects* (Washington, D.C.: National Capital Press, 1917), 76–78; Stuhler, *Ten Men*, 38–39.

7. Chrislock, *Watchdog of Loyalty*, 20–22, 40–51, 58, 234–35, 242–45. This is the best single account of the Minnesota Commission of Public Safety. See also Holmquist, ed., *They Chose Minnesota*, 10–11.

8. Minutes of special meeting of executive board, Feb. 17, 1917, 14:693–95, MWSA Records.

9. B. Ueland, "Clara," 349; unidentified newspaper clipping, 17:800, MWSA Records. For an overview of the conflict with Mexico, see Thomas A. Bailey, A Diplomatic History of the American People, 9th ed. (Englewood Cliffs, N.J.: Prentice-Hall, 1974), 554–62.

10. B. Ueland, "Clara," 369, and Me, 163–65, 167–70, 288, 312–16, 385. Kenneth Taylor succeeded in finding a treatment for soldiers suffering from gas-gangrene poisoning, and by war's end was a colonel in charge of U.S. Army medical activities in the Balkans, Palestine, and Poland.

11. B. Ueland, "Clara," 376, and Me, 167. Elsa, who had received an M.A. degree from Columbia University and had been teaching in Gary, Indiana, would spend the rest of her career as head of Carson College; B. Ueland, "Clara," 370–76; undated newspaper clipping (probably July or Aug. 1916), 17:696, MWSA Records; Rheta Childe Dorr, "I'd Like My Daughter in This Orphan Asylum," Hearst's International Combined with Cosmopolitan, July 1926, p. 74–75, 205. In Apr. 1916 Brenda had married Wallace Benedict, former husband of Crystal Eastman (1881–1928), who was a suffragist and feminist identified with the militant wing of the woman's movement. See Crystal Eastman, Crystal Eastman on Women and Revolution, edited by Blanche Wiesen Cook (New York: Oxford University Press, 1978), 1–4, 9–10.

12. S. Ueland, "Sense and Senility," 35–36; B. Ueland, Me, 171, 172, and "Clara," 391.

13. B. Ueland, "Clara," 381, 393, 400, 402; author's conversation with Andrea Brainard, Jan. 29, 1995, notes in author's possession; Minneapolis Journal, Jan. 13, 1918, Sporting section, 1. Sigurd was also married that same summer, to Julie Plant of Minneapolis.

14. The headline read, "Suffragists Will Offer to Fill Vacancies If War Comes"; Minneapolis Morning Tribune, Mar. 27, 1917, p. 1. See also Clara Ueland to "Dear Suffragist," Apr. 27, 1917, 2:479–81, MWSA Records.

15. Report of corresponding secretary [Maud Stockwell], Oct. 1916–Oct. 1917, 2:759–60, executive board minutes, Sept. 17, 1918, 14:763— both MWSA Records. The term "War Baby" was used by Vivian Stanley Thorp in an MWSA press release; releases, Mar. 22, May 18, [Aug.], 1918, 10:299, 305, 312.

16. Report of corresponding secretary, Oct. 1916–Oct. 1917, 2:759, press release, May [1917], 2:485, executive board minutes, June 2, 1917, 14:711, Clara [M.] H[eckrich] to [Bertha C.] Moller, May 8, 1917,

2:506–7, report by Effie McCollum Jones, May 5–7, 1917, 2:503–4, Jones to Heckrich, June 14, 1917, 2:602—all MWSA Records.

17. Executive board minutes, Feb. 3, 1917, 14:689–90, May 5, 1917, 14:707, July 7, 1917, 14:715, Clara Ueland to Florence Monahan, July 23, 1917, 2:666, report of corresponding secretary, Oct. 1916–Oct. 1917, 14:125—all MWSA Records.

18. Clara Ueland to "Dear Suffragist," June 20, 1917, 2:610, Ueland to M. Eleanor Wilson, July 30, 1917, 2:684, Bertha C. Moller to Ueland, July 16, 1917, 2:651—all MWSA Records.

19. Report of corresponding secretary, Oct. 1916–Oct. 1917, 2:759–60, executive board minutes, Apr. 7, 1917, 14:701—both MWSA Records; Senate Journal, 1916 & 1917, p. 997–98, 1189.

20. Clara Ueland, address, [Nov. 16, 1917, convention], 8:102, MWSA convention, Nov. 1917, minutes, 14:738—both MWSA Records. Ueland, "While We Wage War," Woman Citizen, Oct. 27, 1917, p. 413; Stanton et al., History 6:761. Actually, "full emancipation" was an exaggeration. The 1917 law did not take effect until Feb. 6, 1918, and extended suffrage to English women over thirty years of age who met other stipulations of status and property. In Nov. 1918 women were given the right to be parliamentary candidates, but they did not receive full suffrage until 1928; Bolt, Women's Movements, 240.

21. Clara Ueland to "Dear Suffragist," July 19, 1917, 2:658, annual report for 1917, [about Jan. 1918], 14:739–40—both MWSA Records; Time-Life Books, This Fabulous Century 2:222.

22. Report of corresponding secretary, Oct. 1916–Oct. 1917, 2:759–60, MWSA Records; "A Woman Citizen Building," Woman Citizen, Oct. 27, 1917, p. 413; president's address, May 15, 1918, "Number" (about chain parties), undated—both in press releases, resolutions, etc., woman suffrage material, Jaeger Papers; Karal Ann Marling, Blue Ribbon: A Social and Pictorial History of the Minnesota State Fair (St. Paul: Minnesota Historical Society Press, 1990), 101–2. The building was given to the Minneapolis Council of Americanization in 1919 and renamed the American Citizen Building. Later it was sold and then torn down. See Clara Ueland's invitation to dedication of Woman Citizen Building, Sept. 3, 1917, 2:728, report of joint meeting of MWSA and Minneapolis Council of Americanization, Aug. 1, 1919, 7:4–5, 10, executive board minutes, Aug. 2, 1919, 14:811, Ueland to [Vivian] Thorp, Jan. 17, 1920, 7:579, 584; author's conversation with Jerry Hammer, director of marketing, Minnesota State Fair, Feb. 10, 1995, notes in author's possession.

23. Morgan, *Suffragists and Democrats*, 120; Stanton et al., *History* 5:xxiii; Brown, "Decisive Victory Won," 116–20, and Maud Wood Park, "The Winning Plan," 129–130—both in NAWSA, *Victory*. The five states were Arkansas (primary suffrage), Nebraska, New York, North Dakota, and Rhode Island. Legislation passed in 1917 enacting suffrage in Indiana was challenged in the courts and reenacted in 1919. The Nebraska law, also challenged, was sustained later in 1917. An Ohio referendum was defeated, but suffrage was enacted by the legislature in 1919; Park, *Front Door Lobby*, 71; NAWSA press release, Nov. 10, 1919, 10:350–52, MWSA Records; "Electoral Thermometer," 162–63, in *Victory*.

24. *Cong. Rec.*, 49th Cong., 2d sess., 1887, 18, pt. 1:1002, 63d Cong., 2d sess., 1914, 51, pt. 5:5108, 63d Cong., 3d sess. 1915, 52, pt. 2:1483–84; Carrie Chapman Catt and Nettie Rogers Shuler, *Woman Suffrage and Politics: The Inner Story of the Suffrage Movement* (New York: Charles Scribner's Sons, 1923), 495–96; Stanton et al., *History* 5:629.

25. "Vote on Suffrage Committee Resolution," Sept. 24, 1917, 2:748–50, MWSA Records. The favorable vote included 82 Democrats and 96 Republicans; the unfavorable votes were cast by 74 Democrats and 32 Republicans. Of the 142 not voting, 59 were Democrats, 81 Republicans, and two from other parties; *Cong. Rec.* 65th Cong., 2d sess., 1917, 55, pt. 7:7384–85; Park, *Front Door Lobby*, 118; Stanton et al., *History* 5:634.

26. Park, *Front Door Lobby*, 8–9.

NOTES TO CHAPTER 9

Epigraph: [Clara] Ueland, form letter to MWSA members, Aug. 30, 1918, 3:621, MWSA Records.

1. *Cong. Rec.* 65th Cong., 2d sess., 1918, 56, pt. 1:810. The stalwarts who made the extraordinary effort to attend were minority leader James R. Mann (R., Ill.), after spending six months in a Baltimore hospital; Henry A. Barnhart (D., Ind.), who was carried in on a stretcher; Robert Crosser (D., Ohio); and Thetus W. Sims (D., Tenn.), who refused to have his broken arm and shoulder set for two days so he could be sure to vote; Flexner, *Century of Struggle*, 291–92; Peck, *Carrie Chapman Catt*, 288. Twenty-three state delegations (including Minnesota) voted solidly for the amendment; Stanton et

al., *History* 5:637. When the pairs were counted, the votes to spare rose to four; only six representatives did not vote; "How the House Voted," *Woman Citizen*, Jan. 19, 1918, p. 153, 157.

2. Park, *Front Door Lobby*, 71; Flexner, *Century of Struggle*, 292–93; U.S. Congress, *Biographical Directory of the United States Congress, 1774–1989* (Washington, D.C.: GPO, 1989), 47; Morgan, *Suffragists and Democrats*, 121. Ninety percent of the representatives from suffrage states voted for the amendment; A. F. Scott and A. M. Scott, *One Half the People*, 42; Catt and Shuler, *Woman Suffrage and Politics*, 332.

3. [Clara Ueland] to [Papie L. Quayle], Jan. 16, 1918, 3:179, board of directors minutes, Aug. 4, 1917, 14:720—both MWSA Records.

4. Park, *Front Door Lobby*, 158–67.

5. Park, *Front Door Lobby*, 181–83, 190–91.

6. Park, *Front Door Lobby*, 187; [Clara] Ueland to Knute Nelson and Frank B. Kellogg, May 25, 1918, 3:345–46, MWSA Records.

7. *Cong. Rec.* 65th Cong., 2d sess., 1918, 56, pt. 11:10928–29, 10984; Park, *Front Door Lobby*, 210–11. The conversion of Woodrow Wilson, a latecomer to the cause of suffrage, apparently began with "the ardent representations of his [three] daughters"; Ray Stannard Baker, *Woodrow Wilson: Life and Letters*, vol. 4, *President, 1913–1914* (Garden City, N.Y.: Doubleday, Doran & Co., 1931), 225–26. NAWSA leaders took particular care in cultivating his support, and his final conversion can be attributed to the very considerable contributions by women both as workers and volunteers during World War I. Though Carrie Chapman Catt was in one sense a skeptic, doubting that war would make the world a better place, she recognized the need to make the patriotism of the suffragists credible. Anna Howard Shaw, NAWSA's former president, did outstanding service in her role as chair of the Woman's Committee of the United States Council of National Defense, making that committee a viable and vital instrument. William O'Neill said of her, "As a suffragist she had her faults, but as a guerrilla fighter in the corridors of power she was magnificent"; *Feminism in America*, 184–94.

8. [Clara Ueland], form letter to legislative candidates, June 1, 3:370, Ueland to Mr. C. L. Young, Oct. 8, 3:752—both 1918, MWSA Records.

9. [Clara] Ueland to Julius E. Haycraft, Oct. 18, 3:860–61, Ueland to Hilding A. Swanson, Oct. 19, Oct. 21, 3:865–67, 885, Swanson to Ueland, Oct. 21, 3:906–7—all 1918, MWSA Records. Swanson was

elected and expressed his appreciation for having "you women assist
me"; Swanson to Ueland, Nov. 20, 1918, 4:270–71; *Legislative
Manual*, 1919, p. 758.

10. Business secretary to [Mary F.] Bone, Oct. 2, 3:676, [Clara] Ueland to
[Lavinia A.] Gemmell, Nov. 7, 4:83, Ueland to Mrs. F. Van Houten,
Nov. 20, 4:253–54, C[harles] E. Purdy to Ueland, Nov. 1, 4:16,
Ueland, "Minnesota Bulletin," [Dec.], 10:326—all 1918, MWSA
Records; U.S. Census Office, *Thirteenth Census* 2:976.

11. [Clara] Ueland to [Irene A.] Crandall, Oct. 18, 3:855–56, Ueland to
[Lydia B.] Murdoch, Oct. 15, 3:819–20, Ueland to Murdoch, Dec. 7,
4:517—all 1918, MWSA Records; Alfred W. Crosby, *America's
Forgotten Pandemic: The Influenza of 1918* (Cambridge [England]:
Cambridge University Press, 1989), 207–15; Francis M. Carroll and
Franklin R. Raiter, *The Fires of Autumn: The Cloquet–Moose Lake
Disaster of 1918* (St. Paul: Minnesota Historical Society Press, 1990),
4. Later Clara wrote to a suffrage supporter in Slayton, "We have had
a rather discouraging time for a few weeks what with forest fires,
influenza and the Holidays, but these last days the petitions have
been coming in very well"; [Ueland] to Mrs. E. G. Minder, Jan. 14,
1919, 5:131.

12. See, for example, Clara Ueland to Henry W. Lauderdale, Jan. 2,
1919, 5:28, MWSA Records. See also *House Journal*, 1919, p. 140–41;
Senate Journal, 1919, p. 122; Ueland to J. A. A. Burnquist, Jan. 6,
5:52, Burnquist to Ueland, Jan. 8, 5:71—both 1919; Minnesota,
Governor (1915–1921: Burnquist), *Inaugural Message of Gov. J. A.
A. Burnquist to the Legislature of Minnesota* ([Minn.: s. n., 1919]), 9.
The resolution was introduced by Senator Frank E. Putnam and
Representative Theodore Christianson. The vote in the House was
100 to 28 (*House Journal*, 1919, p. 141–42) and in the Senate 49 to 7
(*Senate Journal*, 1919, p. 122).

13. [Marguerite M. Wells] to [Le Roy E. Brophey], Jan. 10, 1919,
5:89–91, [Clara] Ueland to Carl N. Nelson, Jan. 15, 1919, 5:146–47,
Ueland to [Lydia B.] Murdoch, Oct. 25, 1918, 3:946–47—all MWSA
Records. Kingsley was obviously viewed by MWSA leaders as a trou-
blemaker, but her motives were not recorded in materials reviewed
by the author. Cunningham was asked by Wells or someone—Wells
and Ueland both use the pronoun "we." The other members named
were Sarah E. Lyons, Agnes Savage, Nellie Nelson, and former legislators A. M. Peterson and Daniel P. O'Neill; see Angie V. Kingsley
for Minnesota Equal Suffrage Constitutional Amendment League to

Frank Murray, Jan. 10, 1919, 3:762, Ueland to [Sidney H.] Colton, Jan. 30, 1919, 5:390.

14. Unsigned letter to "Miss Young," Jan. 10, 1919, 5:88, MWSA Records. Charles H. Warner of Aitkin County introduced the bill, which passed by a substantial vote of 96 to 30; *House Journal*, 1919, p. 142–43. The Ueland quote is from a letter that Clara wrote to Carrie Chapman Catt; Jan. 23, 1919, 5:282. Ueland wrote both Nelson and Kellogg assuring them that the resolution was not aimed at them but should be regarded as part of the effort to strengthen the national movement; Ueland to Nelson, 5:280, and to Kellogg, 5:286—both Jan. 23, 1919.

15. [Clara] Ueland to Carrie Chapman Catt, Mar. 8, 5:659, Ueland to [Josephine] Simpson, Mar. 7, 5:657—both 1919, MWSA Records; Vivian Stanley Thorp, "A Fight within a Fight in Minnesota," *Woman Citizen*, May 10, 1919, p. 1074–75.

16. See, for example, [Clara Ueland] to Stella Smith, Jan. 23, 1919, 5:267, MWSA Records. See also executive board minutes, Feb. 1, 1919, 14:777, [Ueland] to Dorothea Spinney, Mar. 11, 1919, 5:674; *House Journal*, 1919, p. 700–701; *Senate Journal*, 1919, p. 516–17, 887–88; *St. Paul Dispatch*, Mar. 21, 1919, p. 1. The motion was made by Sen. James E. Madigan and was defeated by 40 to 21; Ueland to [Josephine] Simpson, Mar. 7, 1919, 5:657.

17. Stanton et al., *History* 6:325; [Clara] Ueland, report, Mar. 19, 1919, 14:781, MWSA Records; *St. Paul Daily News*, Mar. 24, 1919, p. 1.

18. *St. Paul Daily News*, Mar. 25, 1919, p. 6; Hattie S. Bordewich to [Clara] Ueland, Mar. 29, 1919, 5:753, MWSA Records.

19. Park, *Front Door Lobby*, 214, 236, and "Winning Plan," in NAWSA, *Victory*, 138; Stanton et al., *History* 5:641; *Cong. Rec.*, 65th Cong., 3d sess., 1919, 57, pt. 3:3062.

20. Stanton et al., *History* 5:643; A. F. Scott and A. M. Scott, *One Half the People*, 44–45; "Electoral Thermometor," in NAWSA, *Victory*, 162–63.

21. Here and following paragraph, Park, *Front Door Lobby*, 244; Morgan, *Suffragists and Democrats*, 139; A. F. Scott and A. M. Scott, *One Half the People*, 163. One congressman responded "present," 33 did not vote, and there were some absentees; *Cong. Rec.*, 66th Cong., 1st sess., 1919, 58, pt. 1:93–94. The actual number of congressmen from suffrage states who voted for a federal amendment kept changing between Mar. 1914 and May 1919, but the percentage of members

from such states supporting suffrage never fell below 87.4 percent; *One Half the People*, 161.

22. Morgan, *Suffragists and Democrats*, 140–42; Park, *Front Door Lobby*, 214–16, 258–66; Stanton et al., *History* 5:641; *Cong. Rec.*, 66th Cong., 1st sess., 1919, 58, pt. 1:635; Flexner, *Century of Struggle*, 310–11. In the 1918 fall elections, NAWSA had made a strategic decision to replace two negative votes in the Senate—Republican John W. Weeks of Massachusetts and Democrat Willard Saulsbury of Delaware—with two positive votes. The association provided financial assistance to a Massachusetts suffrage organization, which mounted an energetic campaign against Weeks; both men, regarded as unbeatable, were defeated. Similar if less well orchestrated efforts were mounted in New Jersey and New Hampshire.

23. Park, *Front Door Lobby*, 270, 271; *House Journal*, 1919, p. 140–41, 700–701, 1016; *Senate Journal*, 1919, p. 122, 887–88; A. F. Scott and A. M. Scott, *One Half the People*, 168. In a 1933 letter Park embellished the list of reasons, adding—in addition to Catt's leadership— the New York state amendment victory, the work of Helen Hamilton Gardener (a member of her congressional committee who established a productive relationship with President Wilson), and the defeat of Sen. John Weeks; see Park to Inez Haynes Irwin in *One Half the People*, 159–60.

24. [Clara] Ueland to Harriet Warburton, Apr. 29, 1919, 6:93, MWSA Records. It was about this same time that the MWSA board agreed to send a letter to the Minneapolis police chief, requesting that women be among the one hundred new police officers scheduled to be added to the force; monthly meeting minutes, Apr. 19, 1919, 14:784. By 1919 these nations all had woman suffrage: Australia, Austria, Canada, Czechoslovakia, Denmark, England, Finland, Germany, Hungary, Ireland, Mexico, New Zealand (the first, in 1893), Norway, Poland, Russia, and Scotland; A. F. Scott and A. M. Scott, *One Half the People*, 36–37.

25. *Cong. Rec.*, 66th Cong., 1st sess., 1919, 58, pt. 1:93–94 (Rep. Carl Van Dyke, a confirmed supporter, died the day before the vote in 1919); *St. Paul Dispatch*, May 20, 1919, p. 1; M[arion] L. Burton to Marguerite M. Wells, June 7, 6:366, [Clara Ueland] to: Maria Sanford, June 10, 6:392, Ole O. Sageng, June 10, 6:393, Burton, June 10, 6:394, J. A. A. Burnquist, June 10, 6:395, [Anna Dickie] Olesen, June 11, 6:427, press release, June 10, 10, 6:337–38, Mabel H. Guise, "Suffrage Victory Celebration," June 9, 14:799—all 1919, MWSA Records; *Minneapolis Morning Tribune*, June 10, 1919, p. 1, 2.

26. *Minneapolis Morning Tribune*, June 10, 1919, p. 2; Thorp, "Fight within a Fight," *Woman Citizen*, May 10, 1919, p. 1074.

27. [Clara Ueland] to Marguerite M. Wells, Aug. 1, 7:1–2, press release, June 10, 10:339—both 1919, MWSA Records; Flexner, *Century of Struggle*, 312; *Minneapolis Morning Tribune*, June 10, 1919, p. 2; Catt and Shuler, *Woman Suffrage and Politics*, 353. South, described by Ueland as "attractive" and "youngish," was the daughter of William O'Connell Bradley, a Republican governor of Kentucky and that state's first Republican senator. She had been president of the Equal Rights Association of Kentucky. Shuler, NAWSA's press chair, was one of Catt's most trusted young aides and the daughter of Nettie Rogers Shuler of Rochester, N.Y., who was second in command of NAWSA's fieldwork.

28. [Clara Ueland] to [Theodora Winton] Youmans, June 26, 6:553, Ueland to Alice Stone Blackwell, July 12, 6:607—both 1919, MWSA Records. Illinois, Michigan, and Wisconsin all ratified the amendment on June 10, 1919 (Michigan in a special session). Illinois was first by a few hours, but the bill was wrongly worded by a clerk, and so Wisconsin has been credited as the first to file the ratification with the U.S. secretary of state; Flexner, *Century of Struggle*, 315; Park, *Front Door Lobby*, 272. Because the error was made in that federal office and not by the state, Illinois still claims to be number one and is ranked that way in various listings; see, for example, "Ratification Schedule," *Woman Citizen*, Feb. 21, 1920, p. 887.

29. [Clara] Ueland to Jessie E. Scott, Aug. 25, 1919, 7:173, MWSA Records.

30. Flexner, *Century of Struggle*, 287; Ford, *Iron-jawed Angels*, 244; William Henry Chafe, *The American Woman: Her Changing Social, Economic, and Political Roles, 1920–1970* (New York: Oxford University Press, 1972), 18–20. William O'Neill noted that, "Like the Pankhursts, who took credit for a suffrage bill that was actually negotiated by the constitutionalists, the American militants always believed that the 19th Amendment was solely a result of their efforts"; *Feminism in America*, 129.

31. Minnesota, Governor (1915–1921: Burnquist), *Message of Gov. J. A. A. Burnquist to the Special Session of the Legislature of Minnesota, September 1919* ([St. Paul, 1919]), 1; [Clara Ueland] to Marguerite M. Wells, Aug. 6, 7:18–19, Wells, meeting notice, [Aug. 29], 14:219, Ueland, form letter to board members, Sept. 5, 7:346, George H. Sullivan to Ueland, July 2, 6:575—all 1919, MWSA Records;

"Ratification Day in Minnesota," Sept. 27, 1919, p. 430, "The Year's Work," Feb. 21, 1920, p. 889—both in *Woman Citizen*; *Senate and House Journal*, Extra Session 1919, p. 11, 13. *St. Paul Pioneer Press*, Sept. 9, 1919, p. 7. Eleven states enjoyed unanimous ratifications by their legislatures; unanimous ratifications by one house occurred in seven states (Minnesota had eleven holdouts); nawsa press release, [1920], 10:526.

32. *Minneapolis Journal*, Sept. 9, 1919, p. 6; *St. Paul Pioneer Press*, Sept. 9, 1919, p. 1, 2; press release, Aug. 30, 1919, 7:218, Guise, "Suffrage Victory Celebration," 14:802—both mwsa Records.

33. *Minneapolis Journal*, Sept. 11, 1919, p. 1, 16.

34. *St. Paul Daily News*, Sept. 9, 1919, p. 6; Guise, "Ratification," 14:812–13, mwsa Records.

35. Irwin, *Story of the Woman's Party*, 419–29; Park, *Front Door Lobby*, 273.

36. Catt and Shuler, *Woman Suffrage and Politics*, 462–63, 477–78; Flexner, *Century of Struggle*, 318–20; A. Elizabeth Taylor, *The Woman Suffrage Movement in Tennessee* (New York: Bookman Associates, 1957; reprint, New York: Octagon Books, 1978), 104–7. Article III, Section 32 of the Tennessee constitution read: "No convention or general assembly of this State shall act upon any amendment of the Constitution of the United States proposed by Congress to the several States, unless such convention or General Assembly shall have been elected after such amendment is submitted." On June 1, 1920, the U.S. Supreme Court had ruled in an Ohio case that referenda on constitutional amendments were invalid and in conflict with constitutional provisions empowering state legislatures to ratify such amendments; Flexner, *Century of Struggle*, 320–21.

37. Taylor, *Woman Suffrage Movement*, 107–10; Catt and Shuler, *Woman Suffrage and Politics*, 422, 432; Peck, *Carrie Chapman Catt*, 329.

38. Catt and Shuler, *Woman Suffrage and Politics*, 445–50; Taylor, *Woman Suffrage Movement*, 119; Park, *Front Door Lobby*, 272–77; Mary Gray Peck, "The Secretary Has Signed the Proclamation," in nawsa, *Victory*, 149–55. Park's book is an extremely useful and modest account of the final years of the congressional campaign waged by the nawsa. Connecticut in Sept. 1920 and Vermont in 1921 joined the ranks of the ratifying states. The ten states that did not ratify were Alabama, Delaware, Florida, Georgia, Louisiana, Maryland, Mississippi, North Carolina, South Carolina, and Virginia; *Woman Suffrage and Politics*, 460–62.

39. *South St. Paul Centennial, 1887–1987: The History of South St. Paul, Minnesota,* ed. Lois Glewwe (South St. Paul: South St. Paul Chapter of the Dakota County Historical Society, 1987), 240–241; *South St. Paul Daily Reporter,* home edition, Aug. 27, 1920, p. 1, copy in collections of Dakota County Historical Society, South St. Paul. On the same day, seventy-seven women voted in Iowa's Black Hawk and Grundy counties on the establishment of a consolidated school district; Noun, *Strong-minded Women,* 261. That vote, however, was delayed a bit, and South St. Paul is generally credited with being number one.

40. Catt and Shuler, *Woman Suffrage and Politics,* 107–8.

NOTES TO CHAPTER 10

Epigraph: Minneapolis Journal, Sept. 9, 1919, p. 6.

1. [Clara] Ueland to Sara E. Brown [and other women in Hennepin and Ramsey counties outside the Twin Cities], Sept. 1, 1919, 7:241, MWSA Records.

2. *House Journal,* 1919, p. 1016; NAWSA, Jubilee Convention minutes, Mar. 1919, organizational records: published and other materials containing historical and background information, League of Women Voters of the United States Records, LWVM Records; Carrie Chapman Catt, "The Nation Calls: An Address to the Jubilee Convention of the National American Woman Suffrage Association," Mar. 24, 1919, 13:580–82, MWSA Records; Young, *In the Public Interest,* 33.

3. "Minutes of the Jubilee Convention (1869–1919) of the NAWSA," Mar. 1919, 8:538–39, MWSA Records; Edna Honoria Akre, "The League of Women Voters: Its Organization and Work," master's thesis, University of Minnesota, 1926, p. 3, in historical and background materials, and NAWSA, Jubilee Convention minutes, Mar. 1919, including regular sessions of convention and conference of Women Voters, organizational records: published and other materials containing historical and background information, League of Women Voters of the U.S. Records—both LWVM Records. The league was governed initially by a council of presidents representing those suffrage states; Young, *In the Public Interest,* 33. In 1946, a comprehensive reorganization transformed the National League of Women Voters, a federation of state leagues, into the League of Women Voters of the United

States, an organization of individual members; Louise M. Young, *In the Public Interest: The League of Women Voters, 1920–1970* (New York: Greenwood Press, 1989), 37, 45, 146–47, 151n11.

4. Young, *In the Public Interest*, 34–35.

5. Press release, June 23, 10:341, [Clara Ueland] to Mrs. H. M. Wheelock, Aug. 16, 7:62, Ueland to [Theodora Winton] Youmans, Sept. 17, 7:439—all 1919, MWSA Records; Gertrude F[oster] Brown to Ueland, Aug. 26, telegram from Ueland to Brown, Sept. 1, Ueland to Brown, Sept. 22—all 1919, state organizational meetings, correspondence and miscellaneous records, 1919 folder, state conventions, LWVM Records.

6. Here and following paragraph, Akre, "League of Women Voters," 6, 7; *Minneapolis Journal*, Oct. 21, p. 22, Oct. 22, p. 8, *Minneapolis Morning Tribune*, Oct. 22, p. 15—all 1919.

7. Akre, "League of Women Voters," 7; committee on conference and organizations minutes, Oct. 15, 16, 20, 1919, "Report on Organization—the Minnesota League of Women Voters," Mar. 10, 1920, state organizational meetings, correspondence and miscellaneous records, 1919 folder, state conventions, and *The National League of Women Voters—What Is It?*, published and other materials containing historical and background information, League of Women Voters of the U.S. Records—all LWVM Records. Copies of the printed programs were sent to the antis and NWP members "as a matter of courtesy."

8. Clara Ueland, "call" to 1919 conference, typescript, historical and background materials, LWVM Records. The invitation read in part, "Men as well as women are invited to attend these conferences and are especially urged to be present at the dinner and the mass meeting"; state organizational meetings, correspondence and miscellaneous records, 1919 folder, state conventions.

9. Unidentified clipping, 18:79, MWSA Records; "The League of Women Voters for Minnesota is to be formed in Minneapolis, Oct. 28–29, 1919," leaflet, "Organization Conference for the MN League of Women Voters, Minneapolis, Oct. 28–29, 1919"—both state organizational meetings, correspondence and miscellaneous records, 1919 folder, state conventions, LWVM Records; *Minneapolis Morning Tribune*, Oct. 29, p. 9, Oct. 30, p. 1, 8, *Minneapolis Journal*, Oct. 30, p. 21—all 1919. Of the 440 delegates, 216 were from Minneapolis, 108 from St. Paul, and 119 from other Minnesota communities. The Minnesota league's first officers were Ueland, president; Marguerite M. Wells, Minneapolis, first vice-president; Jane Humbird Burr, St.

Paul, second vice-president; Henriette T. McKnight, Minneapolis, secretary; Cornelia Lusk, St. Paul, corresponding secretary; and Helen H. Bennett, Minneapolis, treasurer. The *Tribune* reported 2,500 people attending the final event.

10. Marguerite M. Wells, "An Introduction to the League of Women Voters," Jan. 1933, p. 1–4, 6, 12, historical and background materials, LWVM Records; Young, *In the Public Interest*, 178.

11. *Minneapolis Morning Tribune*, Oct. 29, p. 9, *Minneapolis Journal*, Nov. 2, Woman's Section, 4—both 1919; Akre, "League of Women Voters," 12.

12. Course brochure, 18:30–33, NAWSA press release, Dec. 9, 1919, 10:372–73—both MWSA Records; "Report of the Executive Secretary to the Annual Convention for the Year 1920," p. 1, executive secretary reports, LWVM Records.

13. "Organizational Meetings by Congressional District 1920," state organizational meetings, correspondence and miscellaneous records, 1920 folder, state conventions, LWVM Records.

14. "Report of the Executive Secretary to the Annual Convention for the Year 1920," p. 1–2, executive secretary reports, LWVM Records; Akre, "League of Women Voters," 8.

15. *Minneapolis Morning Tribune*, Feb. 13, p. 1, Feb. 14, p. 1, *Minneapolis Journal*, Feb. 13, p. 1, Feb. 14, p. 7—all 1920; Stanton et al., *History* 5:595–96; Young, *In the Public Interest*, 37; condensed minutes of the Victory Convention, Feb. 12–18, 1920, 9:416, MWSA Records.

16. Peck, "Secretary Has Signed," in NAWSA, *Victory*, 145, and *Carrie Chapman Catt*, 322; Stanton et al., *History* 5:599; condensed minutes of the Victory Convention, 9:416, MWSA Records; *Minneapolis Journal*, Feb. 14, 1920, p. 7.

17. Condensed minutes of the Victory Convention, 9:417–18, program of Victory Convention dinners and luncheons, 18:47—both MWSA Records. NAWSA's dissolution was delayed because of nontransferable bequests; Akre, "League of Women Voters," 4. On the Minneapolis suffragists, see *Minneapolis Journal*, Feb. 13, p. 1, 15, Feb. 14, p. 1, 2, 7, Feb. 15, General News Section, 1, 10, Woman's Section, 4, Feb. 16, p. 1, 8, Feb. 17, p. 1, Feb. 22, Woman's Section, 4, *Minneapolis Morning Tribune*, Feb. 13, p. 1, 2, Feb. 14, p. 3, Feb. 15, p. 1, 8, Feb. 17, p. 20, Feb. 18, p. 1, Feb. 19, p. 1, 2, *Minneapolis Sunday Tribune*, women's sections, Feb. 8, p. 1, Feb. 15, p. 1, 8—all 1920. Two major Minneapolis papers sent reporters to cover NAWSA's celebration and the league's birthing: Lillian E. Taaffe of the *Tribune* and Aimee

Fisher of the *Journal*, whose stories gave comprehensive accounts of the events and personalities. Ulrich later left medicine and became a bookstore owner who also sold art and antiques. From 1935 to 1938 she served as first director of the Federal Writers' Project in Minnesota, which produced the popular *Minnesota: A State Guide* (New York: Viking Press, 1938; reprinted as *The WPA Guide to Minnesota* [St. Paul: Minnesota Historical Society Press, 1985]); Kenneth E. Hendrickson, Jr., "The WPA Federal Arts Projects in Minnesota, 1935–1943," *Minnesota History* 53 (Spring 1993): 176.

18. Young, *In the Public Interest*, 37, 41–42; NAWSA, Victory Convention, and League of Women Voters, First Congress, condensed minutes, Feb. 1920, p. 5, 26, organizational records: published and other materials containing historical and background information, League of Women Voters of the U.S. Records, LWVM Records; *Minneapolis Sunday Tribune*, Feb. 15, 1920, first section, 8. Park, whose first husband died in 1904, had been secretly married to Robert Hunter, an actor and New York theatrical agent, since 1908. Only a few close friends knew of the marriage; Sharon Hartman Strom, "Park, Maud May Wood," in Sicherman and Green, *Notable American Women*, 520–21. The other three officers were: Edna Fischel Gellhorn of Missouri, vice-chair; Marie Stuart Edwards of Indiana, treasurer; and Pattie Ruffner Jacobs of Alabama, secretary. In the next year, the offices of chair and vice-chair were retitled president and vice-president.

19. B. Ueland, "Clara," 428; board of directors minutes, May 11, 1920, historical and background materials, LWVM Records. Ueland may also have been influenced in her decision to step down by Catt, who hoped that leadership in the new league would come from the younger, rising group of NAWSA leaders rather than from its existing senior leadership; Young, *In the Public Interest*, 42.

20. "Portrait of a Leader," in Marguerite M. Wells, *A Portrait of the League of Women Voters* (Washington, D.C.: Overseas Education Fund of the League of Women Voters, 1962), 24–27, historical and background materials, LWVM Records; press release, May 18, 1920, 10:480, MWSA Records; B. Ueland, "Clara," 442.

21. Board of directors minutes, May 11, June 22, July 13, 1920, Nov. 11, 1921, historical and background materials, and "Report of the Executive Secretary to the Annual Convention of the Minnesota League of Women Voters," Oct. 18, 1921, p. 1, executive secretary reports—all LWVM Records. A year later, Ueland filled in for an absent executive committee member and subsequently became a permanent member.

22. Minutes, July 2, 1920–Feb. 3, 1926, Legislative Council, minutes, and Clara Ueland and Marguerite M. Wells to presidents of the member organizations of the Legislative Council, Dec. 1923, printed materials, 1923–24, scrapbooks, and Gladys Harrison, "Summary of Methods of the Minnesota League of Women Voters," June 1924, p. 11–12, executive secretary reports—all LWVM Records.

23. "Report of the Executive Secretary," Oct. 18, 1921, p. 2, executive secretary reports, LWVM Records. The pension increase raised the maximum from fifteen to twenty dollars a month for the first child and from ten to fifteen dollars for succeeding children. On the Sheppard-Towner Act, see note 33, below; on the length of the school term, see Minnesota, *Laws of Minnesota Relating to the Public School System* (Minneapolis: Syndicate Printing Co., 1919), 72.

24. B. Ueland, "Clara," 444; president's address, third annual convention, Oct. 20, 1921, p. 3, state conventions, and "Report of the Executive Secretary," Oct. 18, 1921, p. 1–2, executive secretary reports—both LWVM Records. In the aftermath of that 1921 session and in preparation for what she hoped might prove to be an even more successful legislative year in 1923, Ueland proposed that special conferences or extension courses be given for women in all parts of the state; board of directors minutes, May 5, 1921, historical and background materials.

25. B. Ueland, "Clara," 463; "Notes for Annual Report for Minnesota, 1922–23," executive secretary reports, and board of directors minutes, May 1, 1921, historical and background materials—both LWVM Records; "Legislative Summary" supplement, *Woman Voter* (Minneapolis: Minnesota League of Women Voters), May 1, 1923.

26. Young, *In the Public Interest*, 59; Cott, *Grounding of Modern Feminism*, 120–25. Others present at the meeting were: Marie Edwards, treasurer of the LWV; Lenna Yost, WCTU; Lida Hafford, General Federation of Women's Clubs; and Ethel Smith, National Women's Trade Union League. Kelley, who had been a member of the NWP's National Council, had severed her relationship with the NWP as a result of this issue.

27. Material for Nov. 21, 1922, scrapbook, 1921–23, LWVM Records. In addition to Cain, the authors were: Lucien A. Barnes of Duluth, Christopher M. Bendixen of Morgan, H. R. Berg of Rush City, Otto D. Nellermoe and Sylvanus A. Stockwell of Minneapolis, and Frank T. Starkey of St. Paul; *House Journal*, 1923, p. 487, 631–32.

28. *Minneapolis Journal*, Nov. 26, 1922, Women's Organizations sec-

tion, 1; material for Feb. 27, 1923, scrapbook, 1921–23, LWVM Records. Although rebuffed by the Republican party organization, Paige ran as an independent, which was a comfortable fit for a non-partisan legislature. Despite the party's reservation, her Republican constituents elected her to ten consecutive terms; *House Journal,* 1923, p. 631–32; Fraser and Holbert, "Women in the Minnesota Legislature," in Stuhler and Kreuter, *Women of Minnesota,* 254, 263, 283.

29. *Minneapolis Journal,* Mar. 4, 1923, General News section, 10; *Minneapolis Morning Tribune,* Aug. 27, 1925, p. 7. For five decades the views of the reformers who argued for particular legislation prevailed in Minnesota over the ERA legalists and their so-called blanket remedy. But Cain, who served only one term in office, never gave up. Testifying on behalf of ratification of the federal ERA in 1973, when changing conditions and attitudes had converted the reformers, she had the satisfaction of seeing the state legislature ratify the amendment. (Despite the acceptance of this ERA by women's groups, it failed to be ratified nationally even after the deadline for state action was extended.) See Fraser and Holbert, "Women in the Minnesota Legislature," in Stuhler and Kreuter, *Women of Minnesota,* 262–63.

30. James Truslow Adams, ed., *Dictionary of American History* (New York: Charles Scribner's Sons, 1940), 1:362; J. Stanley Lemons, *The Woman Citizen: Social Feminism in the 1920s* (Urbana: University of Illinois Press, 1973), 26–32; Paul V. Betters, *The Bureau of Home Economics: Its History, Activities and Organization* (Washington, D.C.: Brookings Institution, 1930; reprint, New York: AMS Press, 1974), 1; Young, *In the Public Interest,* 59–61, 75.

31. Young, *In the Public Interest,* 36, 43, 51, 59–60, 62, 77; Lemons, *Woman Citizen,* 55, 61n45. Unfamiliar with the work of the WJCC, Catt credited the league with the passage of the Sheppard-Towner Act in 1922. When Park replied that it had been a joint effort of the organizations affiliated with the WJCC, Catt accused her of undermining the league; Strom, "Park, Maud May Wood," in Sicherman and Green, *Notable American Women,* 521. The league had also inherited from the NAWSA a legacy of hostility to Paul's opinions and methods; Cott, *Grounding of Modern Feminism,* 122.

32. Joan M. Jensen, "All Pink Sisters: The War Department and the Feminist Movement in the 1920s," in Lois Scharf and Joan M. Jensen, eds., *Decades of Discontent: The Women's Movement, 1920–1940* (Westport, Conn.: Greenwood Press, 1983), 211–13; Young, *In*

the Public Interest, 48, 75–77; Susan Ware, "General Introduction," in *Papers of the League of Women Voters, 1918–1974*, pt. 3, series A, National Office subject files, 1920–32, compiled by Martin Schipper, guide to microfilm edition (Frederick, Md.: University Publications of America, 1986), v.

33. Young, *In the Public Interest*, 60, 95–96. Sheppard-Towner is generally acknowledged to have been the precursor of Social Security.

34. *Minneapolis Sunday Tribune*, Dec. 3, 1922, Society section, 8; Edward MacGaffey, "A Pattern for Progress: The Minnesota Children's Code," *Minnesota History* 41 (Spring 1969): 229, 232; Elizabeth Gilman, "Catheryne Cooke Gilman: Social Worker," in Stuhler and Kreuter, *Women of Minnesota*, 193.

35. *Minneapolis Sunday Tribune*, Dec. 3, 1922, Society section, 8; Adams, *Dictionary of American History* 1:362; Young, *In the Public Interest*, 96–97.

36. Joseph M. Hawes, *The Children's Rights Movement of the United States: A History of Advocacy and Protection* (Boston: Twayne Publishers, 1991), 50–51; Young, *In the Public Interest*, 96–98.

37. *House Journal*, 1925, p. 538; *Senate Journal*, 1925, p. 1109–10; *Minneapolis Morning Tribune*, Apr. 15, 1925, p. 5; board of directors minutes, May 27, 1925, historical and background materials, LWVM Records. The futile campaign continued into the 1930s, when its provisions were included in New Deal legislation; Hawes, *Children's Rights Movement*, 52–53; Young, *In the Public Interest*, 98.

38. Clara Ueland, "Ratification of the Child Labor Amendment," annual convention, Nov. 16–20, 1925, Friday morning session, Nov. 20, p. 1, 4, state conventions, LWVM Records; B. Ueland, "Clara," 453.

39. Young, *In the Public Interest*, 58; Stuhler, *Ten Men*, 81–82. Nations could adhere to the court without being members of the league.

40. Board of directors minutes, Dec. 14, 1921, historical and background materials, LWVM Records.

41. Board of directors minutes, Apr. 26, Dec. 3, 1923, historical and background materials, and executive secretary reports, Sept., Oct. 1923—all LWVM Records; *Minneapolis Morning Tribune*, Dec. 11, p. 12, Dec. 16, Society section, 12—both 1923.

42. *Minneapolis Sunday Tribune*, Aug. 23, 1925, Society section, 13; *Cong. Rec.*, 69th Cong., sess. 1, 1926, 67, pt. 3:2795–2825. In 1945 the U.S. finally accepted the World Court in its third incarnation as one of the principal organs of the newly formed United Nations.

The provision for optional jurisdiction weakened its authority as a judicial body; Stuhler, *Ten Men*, 152.

43. [Clara] Ueland to Jessie Scott, Aug. 11, 1919, 7:41, MWSA Records; B. Ueland, "Clara," 429; *Minneapolis Journal*, Sept. 6, 1920, p. 1. Hoover, who had distinguished himself in several administrative roles during World War I, was being discussed as a presidential candidate long before his election in 1928. In 1921 Ueland agreed to chair the Minneapolis committee that raised $15,000 (out of a national goal of over $1 million) for the newly established Woodrow Wilson Foundation, which would provide support for individuals or groups making efforts on behalf of world peace; *St. Paul Pioneer Press*, Mar. 2, p. 3, *Minneapolis Morning Tribune*, Mar. 2, p. 2—both 1927.

44. *Minneapolis Journal*, Oct. 5, 1924, Women's Organizations section, 1. The percentage of women who failed to vote was only slightly higher than the percentage of men who failed to vote. The national average was based on a study of forty-two of the forty-eight states and may be suspect because voting data was based on "scattered secondary sources"; Kristi Andersen, "Women and Citizenship in the 1920s," in Tilly and Gurin, *Women, Politics, and Change*, 186. Robertson's political campaign slogan was "Christianity, Americanism and Standpattism"; Young, *In the Public Interest*, 52n8; Angie Debo, "Robertson, Alice Mary," in James, *Notable American Women* 3:177–78.

45. Marguerite M. Wells to board members and fifty-six others, Nov. 28, 1921, scrapbook, 1921–23, board of directors minutes, Dec. 14, 1921, historical and background materials—both LWVM Records.

46. The ratification of the Nineteenth Amendment occurred after the deadline for filing in 1920; *Legislative Manual*, 1923, p. 462, 464. Kaercher (later Davis) served twenty-eight years as a state office-holder, a term that has been unequaled in length; *Manual*, 1923, facing p. 452; Patricia C. Harpole, comp., "Brief Biographies of Other Minnesota Women," in Stuhler and Kreuter, *Women of Minnesota*, 329; Toensing, *Minnesota Congressmen*, 28. Paige later confessed to running for office because other women were apparently unwilling to do so: "I could see that the League of Women Voters was not succeeding in its aims if no women went into public office"; Paige, untitled and undated typescript, 4 p., speeches and miscellaneous manuscript material, Mabeth Hurd Paige Papers, MHS.

47. Andersen, "Women and Citizenship," in Tilly and Gurin, *Women, Politics, and Change*, 184; Davis, *Moving the Mountain*, 187; Johnson,

"Anna Dickie Olesen," in Stuhler and Kreuter, *Women of Minnesota*, 235–41; Stuhler, *Ten Men*, 78–79.

48. Report of executive secretary to fifth annual convention, Nov. 9, 1923, state conventions, LWVM Records.

49. Board of directors minutes, Oct. 11, Nov. 5, 1923, historical and background materials, LWVM Records.

50. *Minneapolis Morning Tribune*, Sept. 3, p. 15, Nov. 4, p. 4, *Minneapolis Journal*, Oct. 19, City Life section, 4, *Minneapolis Sunday Tribune*, Oct. 26, Society section, 7—all 1924; Mildred Fearrington Hargraves, *The First Fifty Years* (St. Paul: League of Women Voters of Minnesota, 1969; copy in MHS), 4, 15; Richard T. Hargreaves obituary, *Spokane Daily Chronicle*, Mar. 7, 1939, p. 14.

51. *Minneapolis Journal*, Women's Organizations sections, May 25, 1924, p. 1, Aug. 2, 1925, p. 3; board of directors minutes, Nov. 13, 1924, historical and background materials, LWVM Records. Norton was an impressive woman, a dedicated champion of the working woman and an advocate of equal pay for equal work. She was a supporter of women in politics but, like many women who lived in the era of protective legislation, she did not support the Equal Rights Amendment; Young, *In the Public Interest*, 85; Carmela A. Karnoutsos, "Norton, Mary Teresa Hopkins," in Sicherman and Green, *Notable American Women*, 511–12.

52. *Minneapolis Morning Tribune*, Mar. 16, 1926, p. 1, 2; *Minneapolis Journal*, May 1, 1927, Women's Organizations section, 1, 2; program, eighth annual convention, Oct. 7–9, 1926, state conventions, LWVM Records. Clara Ueland spoke on public welfare in a session on the legislature that she chaired.

53. Young, *In the Public Interest*, 48, 52, 73–74, 85.

54. *Minneapolis Sunday Tribune*, Aug. 23, Society section, 13, *Minneapolis Morning Tribune*, Aug. 27, p. 7, *Minneapolis Journal*, Aug. 26, p. 15—all 1925.

55. Executive committee minutes, and board of directors minutes, 1920–27, historical and background materials, LWVM Records.

NOTES TO CHAPTER 11

Epigraph: Thorp, "Ratification Day," *Woman Citizen*, Sept. 27, 1919, p. 430.

1. *Minneapolis Journal*, Mar. 2, 1927, p. 6.

2. *Minneapolis Morning Tribune*, Mar. 1, 1927, p. 1, 12; B. Ueland, "Clara," 490–91.

3. B. Ueland, "Clara," 491–2; executive committee minutes, 1919–22, historical and background materials, LWVM Records.

4. B. Ueland, "Clara," 492–94, italics added. Information about the accident with few variations also appears in A. Ueland, *Recollections*, 224; S. Ueland, "Sense and Senility," 44; and B. Ueland, *Me*, 226–28. See also *Minneapolis Morning Tribune*, Mar. 2, 1927, p. 1, 2.

5. *Minneapolis Morning Tribune*, Mar. 2, p. 1, Mar. 3, p. 5—both 1927.

6. B. Ueland, *Me*, 226–27, and "Clara," 480–81.

7. B. Ueland, "Clara," 485, 489–90.

8. B. Ueland, *Me*, 227.

9. *Minneapolis Morning Tribune*, Mar. 2, p. 1, 2, Mar. 3, p. 5, *Minneapolis Journal*, Mar. 2, p. 1, 2, Mar. 3, p. 18, *St. Paul Pioneer Press*, Mar. 3, p. 6, *Minneapolis Sunday Tribune*, Mar. 6, first section, 2—all 1927; Cheney, *Story of Minnesota Politics*, 67. Clara's note containing instructions for her funeral was not found until some eight months later. Addressed "To my Children," it had been written some time earlier after the death of a young neighbor. She requested organ music but no singing. The service should be Episcopalian (or similar), but the minister should preferably be Unitarian. There were to be *"no remarks,"* and "I want my body cremated." A notation on the envelope from Andreas read, "Opened by me, Nov. 27, 1927"; B. Ueland, "Clara," 446–47. Three close associates were designated by the legislature to represent its members at the funeral: Mabeth Paige, Sumner T. McKnight, and Hannah Kempfer; *Minneapolis Morning Tribune*, Mar. 5, 1927, p. 1.

10. *Minneapolis Journal*, Mar. 3, 1927, p. 18.

11. *Minneapolis Sunday Tribune*, Mar. 20, second section, 2, *Minneapolis Morning Tribune*, Mar. 21, p. 1, 2, *Minneapolis Journal*, Mar. 21, p. 6, *St. Paul Pioneer Press*, Mar. 21, p. 1—all 1927; Vivian Stanley Thorp in *Minnesota Woman Voter*, Mar. 1927, p. 3.

12. *Minneapolis Morning Tribune*, Mar. 21, 1927, p. 1; Ole O. Sageng, "Extracts from Addresses," *Minnesota Women Voter*, Mar. 1927, p. 5.

13. Here and following paragraph, *Minnesota Woman Voter*, Mar. 1928, p. 1, 3; William Anderson to Marguerite [M.] Wells, Apr. 11, 1927, L[otus] D. Coffman to Wells, Apr. 14, 1927, Louise C. Zonne and Wells to Coffman, June 1, 1928—all Clara Ueland memorial funds, financial records, LWVM Records. In the years since 1930, more than sixty Clara

Ueland Fellowships have been awarded. Some of the recipients have been: Jane Shields Freeman, former national president of the Girl Scouts of the U.S.A.; Dorothy Houston Jacobson, former assistant secretary for international affairs, U.S. Department of Agriculture; Janet McCart Sigford, a former vice-president of the League of Women Voters of Minnesota and president of the Abortion Rights Council (now the Minnesota National Abortion Rights Action League); and Dorothy R. Dodge, professor of political science (former chair), Macalester College; see "Recipients of the Clara H. Ueland Memorial Fellowship, 1930–1967," typescript, Clara Ueland Fellowship file, Department of Political Science, University of Minnesota.

14. B. Ueland, Me, 220, 256–58; Theodore C. Blegen, review, Minnesota History 10 (June 1929):192.

15. Here and following paragraph, A. Ueland, Recollections, 229, 259; B. Ueland, Me, 301–2.

16. Josephine Sarles Simpson, "Early Years and Work," Minnesota Woman Voter, Mar. 1927, p. 4, 6.

17. B. Ueland, Me, 229.

18. Marguerite M. Wells, "Introductory Address," ninth annual convention, Minnesota League of Women Voters, Nov. 29–Dec. 3, 1927, state conventions, LWVM Records. Although they never knew their mother-in-law, both Harriet and Margaret Ueland recalled that their husbands (Sigurd and Rolf, respectively) "adored" their mother. Andrea Brainard had similar memories of the love and regard expressed by her father, Arnulf. Brenda's daughter, Gabrielle McIver, was quick to note that she had never heard anything critical ever said about her grandmother; conversations with the author, 1989–93, notes in author's possession.

19. President's report, 1918–19, May 13, 15:520, [Clara] Ueland to [Josephine] Simpson, Mar. 7, 5:656–57—both 1919, MWSA Records; Susan Ware, Beyond Suffrage: Women in the New Deal (Cambridge: Harvard University Press, 1981), 31; D. Schneider and C. Schneider, American Women, 189. McDonald was then president of the Hennepin County Woman Suffrage Association, the successor to Ueland's Equal Suffrage Association of Minneapolis. Perkins served as secretary of labor under President Franklin D. Roosevelt from 1933 to 1945.

20. [Clara] Ueland to [Gertrude Foster] Brown, Sept. 30, 1919, state organizational meetings, correspondence and miscellaneous records, 1919 folder, state conventions, LWVM Records.

NOTES TO CHAPTER 12

1. *Minneapolis Journal*, Mar. 3, 1907, News Section, 4; Hurd, "Brief History of the Minneapolis Political Equality Club," 23, in club records, MHS; *St. Paul Pioneer Press*, Jan. 31, 1915, section 3, p. 6. Suffragist Helen Thomas Flexner shared their assessment, warning that "every reform suffers from the fundamental psychological tendency of its advocates to claim too much for it, and from the consequent inevitable reaction against it after it has been carried through"; quoted in O'Neill, *Feminism in America*, 66. Flexner was associated with the New York Collegiate Equal Suffrage League, which sponsored a scholarly study of the effects of woman suffrage in Colorado. The results of that study prompted her remark.

2. *Minneapolis Sunday Tribune*, Aug. 23, 1925, Women's Clubs section, 12.

3. Cott, *Grounding of Modern Feminism*, 100. Elisabeth Israels Perry noted that suffrage ambitions did not extend to winning policy-making power; see "Image, Rhetoric, and the Historical Memory of Women," introduction to *Cartooning for Suffrage*, by Alice Sheppard (Albuquerque: University of New Mexico Press, 1994), 12.

4. The enrollment decline was from 47.3 percent to 43.7 percent; in 1940 there were only 0.4 percent more women in the professions than there had been in 1920. See Chafe, *American Woman*, 58, 90–92.

5. DuBois, *Feminism and Suffrage*, 18.

6. Cott described the period between the two world wars as one with "very probably the highest proportion of women engaged in volunteer associational activity in the whole history of American women"; see "Across the Great Divide: Women in Politics before and after 1920," 166, 167; see also Lebsock, "Women and American Politics," 42—both in Tilly and Gurin, *Women, Politics, and Change*.

7. Here and following paragraph, material about these Minnesota women—except where otherwise noted—is taken from the Minnesota Biography Project Files, MHS, and Foster, *Who's Who among Minnesota Women*. See also Peck, *Carrie Chapman Catt*, 409–10, 449; Young, *In the Public Interest*, 124; Charles DeBenedetti, *Origins of the Modern Peace Movement, 1915–1929* (Milkwood, N.Y.: KTO Press, 1978), 96; *St. Paul Pioneer Press*, May 21, 1922, Fourth Section, 7; C. Ueland, "While We Wage War."

8. Brainard, "Charter Members," 10.

9. Klein, *Gender Politics*, 86; Chafe, *American Woman*, 58; Evans, *Born for Liberty*, 260. In an essay written in 1964, Alice S. Rossi noted, "For the first time in the history of any known society, motherhood has become a full-time occupation for adult women"; see "Equality between the Sexes," in Sochen, *New Feminism*, 93.

10. Cott, *Grounding of Modern Feminism*, 3, 13–16; Pennington, "Woman the Helpmate," 14:244, MWSA Records.

11. Evans, *Born for Liberty*, 282 (Carmichael quote), 283; Davis, *Moving the Mountain*, 22–25.

12. Davis, *Moving the Mountain*, 34–38, 50–52, 211–18; Minnesota Governor's Commission on the Status of Women, *Interim Report* (St. Paul: The Commission, 1964), 1, 2, 5; material on Hymes, Minnesota Biography Project Files, MHS; Blegen, *Minnesota*, 579–80, 585; Minnesota, *Anti-Discrimination Laws of Minnesota: 1962 Compilation* ([St. Paul, 1962]), 5, 15.

13. Buechler, *Women's Movements*, 56–57.

14. Buechler, *Women's Movements*, 93; Black, *Social Feminism*, 61; Davis, *Moving the Mountain*, 29, 30 (Snitow quote), 32; Evans, *Born for Liberty*, 192–94.

15. Buechler, *Women's Movements*, 85–129, 221 (quote).

16. Faludi, *Backlash: The Undeclared War against American Women* (New York: Crown Publishers, 1991), 256; Sherrye Henry, *The Deep Divide: Why American Women Resist Equality* (New York: Macmillan Publishing Co., 1994), 16.

17. Wolf, *Fire with Fire: The New Female Power and How It Will Change the Twenty-first Century* (New York: Random House, 1993), 59, 132. In a book theorizing about feminism, Christina Hoff Sommers contrasts "gender" feminism with "equity" feminism as if women—with all their differences—could be expected to fit into one or the other mold; *Who Stole Feminism?: How Women Have Betrayed Women* (New York: Simon & Schuster, 1994).

18. Klein, *Gender Politics*, 29–30; Faludi, *Backlash*, 457; Mary Frances Berry, *Why ERA Failed: Politics, Women's Rights, and the Amending Process of the Constitution* (Bloomington: Indiana University Press, 1986), 45–85; Carl N. Degler, *At Odds: Women and the Family in America from the Revolution to the Present* (New York: Oxford University Press, 1980), 446.

19. "Sex Differences in Voter Turnout," Aug. 1994, fact sheet by the Center for the American Woman and Politics (CAWP), Eagleton

Institute of Politics, Rutgers University, New Brunswick, N.J., copy in author's possession; Mary E. Bendyna and Celinda C. Lake, "Gender and Voting in the 1992 Presidential Election," in *The Year of the Woman: Myths and Realities*, ed. Elizabeth Adell Cook, Sue Thomas, and Clyde Wilcox (Boulder, Colo.: Westview Press, 1994), 238–39, 251; Linda Witt, Karen M. Paget, and Glenna Matthews, *Running as a Woman: Gender and Power in American Politics* (New York: Free Press, 1994), 170. Since 1980, in thirty-five Senate and gubernatorial races involving women, the voting rate of women exceeded that of men by 1.3 percent in contests with Republican women candidates and by 2.2 percent in elections where Democratic women were running; *Washington Post*, national weekly edition (Washington, D.C.), Nov. 30–Dec. 1, 1992, p. 36.

20. *Legislative Manual, 1981–82*, p. 61–62, *1991–92*, p. 71–72, *1993–94*, p. 54, 57–58; "Women Break All Congressional Election Records," *Women's Political Times* (Washington, D.C.: National Women's Political Caucus), Winter 1992–93, p. 1, 3. A cautionary note: Women won in these high numbers because of the unusually large number of open seats. In the House, only two women defeated incumbents in the general election. Among the Senate women, one winner defeated the incumbent in the primary election, another won over a short-term gubernatorial appointee to the Senate seat. In a special election in 1993 Kay Bailey Hutchison (Republican, Texas) was elected to the U.S. Senate, bringing the total to seven. The election of Olympia Snowe (Republican, Maine) in 1994 increased the number to eight. See Witt et al., *Running as a Woman*, 177; "Women in the U.S. Senate 1922–1995," Dec. 1994, CAWP fact sheet, and *CAWP News & Notes*, Winter 1994, p. 1—copies in author's possession. Ruth Mandel of the Center for the American Woman and Politics commented after the 1994 elections: "women returned to their familiar position—pushing forward here, stalling a bit there, chalking up political firsts or near-firsts for gender politics. . . . the trend line for women in politics is uninterrupted and upwardly inclined"; *CAWP News & Notes*, Winter 1994, p. 6.

21. Henry, *Deep Divide*, 392; Garry Wills, "Hillary's No Eleanor Roosevelt," *Washington Post*, national weekly edition, Nov. 1–7, 1993, p. 24. In 1993 more than 66 percent of female college freshmen reported that they planned to earn advanced degrees. This represents a tripling in twenty-five years of the percentage of women seeking such degrees. David Merkowitz of the American Council on Education echoed Garry Wills's assessment: "If you want a long-term

indicator of major social change, this is one"; Mary Jordan, "A Matter of Degree," *Washington Post,* Feb. 7–13, 1994.

22. Akre, "League of Women Voters," 12, historical and background materials, LWVM Records.

BIBLIOGRAPHY

BOOKS, ARTICLES, AND UNPUBLISHED PAPERS

Akre, Edna Honoria. "The League of Women Voters: Its Organization and Work." Master's thesis, University of Minnesota, 1926. Copy in League of Women Voters of Minnesota Records, Minnesota Historical Society.

Andersen, Kristi. "Women and Citizenship in the 1920s." In Louise A. Tilly and Patricia Gurin, eds., *Women, Politics, and Change*. New York: Russell Sage Foundation, 1990.

Anderson, William, and Albert J. Lobb. *A History of the Constitution of Minnesota, with the First Verified Text*. University of Minnesota Research Publications, Studies in the Social Sciences, 15. Minneapolis: University of Minnesota, 1921.

Bell, Marguerite N. *The Lives and Times of Just Molly: An Autobiography*. Minneapolis: Golden Valley Press, 1980.

Bendyna, Mary E., and Celinda C. Lake. "Gender and Voting in the 1992 Presidential Election." In Elizabeth Adell Cook, Sue Thomas, and Clyde Wilcox, eds., *The Year of the Woman: Myths and Realities*, 237–54. Transforming American Politics series. Boulder, Colo.: Westview Press, 1994.

Berry, Mary Frances. *Why ERA Failed: Politics, Women's Rights, and the Amending Process of the Constitution*. Everywoman: Studies in History, Literature, and Culture; Susan Gubar and Joan Hoff-Wilson, general editors. Bloomington: Indiana University Press, 1986.

Bingham, Marjorie. "Keeping at It: Minnesota Women." In Clifford E. Clark, Jr., ed., *Minnesota in a Century of Change: The State and Its People since 1900*. St. Paul: Minnesota Historical Society Press, 1989.

Black, Naomi. *Social Feminism*. Ithaca, N.Y.: Cornell University Press, 1989.

Bolt, Christine. *The Women's Movements in the United States and Britain from the 1790s to the 1920s*. Amherst: University of Massachusetts Press, 1993.

Brainard, Andrea. "Charter Members: Lavinia Gilfillan, Clara Ueland, Alice Winter, and Florence Carpenter." Paper presented at Peripatetics meeting, Minneapolis, October 16, 1989. Copy in author's possession.

Buechler, Steven M. *Women's Movements in the United States: Woman Suffrage, Equal Rights, and Beyond*. New Brunswick, N.J.: Rutgers University Press, 1990.

Catt, Carrie Chapman, and Nettie Rogers Shuler. *Woman Suffrage and Politics: The Inner Story of the Suffrage Movement*. New York: Charles Scribner's Sons, 1923.

Chafe, William Henry. *The American Woman: Her Changing Social, Economic, and Political Roles, 1920–1970*. New York: Oxford University Press, 1972.

Chambers, Clark A. "Ueland, Clara Hampson." In Edward T. James, et al., eds., *Notable American Women, 1607–1950: A Biographical Dictionary*. 3 vols. Cambridge: Belknap Press of Harvard University Press, 1971.

Chrislock, Carl H. *The Progressive Era in Minnesota: 1899–1918*. St. Paul: Minnesota Historical Society, 1971.

———. *Watchdog of Loyalty: The Minnesota Commission of Public Safety during World War I*. St. Paul: Minnesota Historical Society Press, 1991.

Colley, Linda. "Women and Political Power." *Wilson Quarterly* 16 (Spring 1992): 50–58.

Cott, Nancy F. "Across the Great Divide: Women in Politics before and after 1920." In Louise A. Tilly and Patricia Gurin, eds., *Women, Politics, and Change*. New York: Russell Sage Foundation, 1990.

———. *The Grounding of Modern Feminism*. New Haven, Conn.: Yale University Press, 1987.

Davis, Flora. *Moving the Mountain: The Women's Movement in America since 1960*. New York: Simon & Schuster, 1991.

DuBois, Ellen Carol. *Feminism and Suffrage: The Emergence of an Independent Women's Movement in America, 1848–1869*. Ithaca, N.Y.: Cornell University Press, 1978.

———. "Making Women's History: Activist Historians of Women's Rights, 1840–1940." *Radical History Review* 49 (Winter 1991): 61–84.

Ebersole, J. F., ed. *Papers and Proceedings of the Eighth Annual Meeting of the Minnesota Academy of Social Sciences*. General topic: "Women and the State." Publications of the Minnesota Academy of Social Sciences, vol. 8, no. 8. [Mankato, Minn.]: Published for the Academy by the Free Press Printing Co., 1915.

Ericson, Kathryn. "Triple Jeopardy: The Muus vs. Muus Case in Three Forums." *Minnesota History* 50 (Winter 1987): 298–308.

Evans, Sara M. *Born for Liberty: A History of Women in America*. New York: Free Press, 1989.

Faludi, Susan. *Backlash: The Undeclared War against American Women*. New York: Crown Publishers, 1991.

Flexner, Eleanor. *Century of Struggle: The Woman's Rights Movement in the United States*. Cambridge: Belknap Press of Harvard University Press, 1959.

Folwell, William Watts. *A History of Minnesota*. 4 vols. St. Paul: Minnesota Historical Society, 1921–30. Corrected eds. published 1956–69.

Ford, Linda G. *Iron-jawed Angels: The Suffrage Militancy of the National Woman's Party, 1912–1920*. Lanham, Md.: University Press of America, 1991.

Foster, Mary Dillon, comp. *Who's Who among Minnesota Women: A History of Woman's Work in Minnesota from Pioneer Days to Date, Told in Biographies, Memorials and Records of Organizations*. N.p.: Privately published, 1924.

Fowler, Robert Booth. *Carrie Catt: Feminist Politician*. Boston: Northeastern University Press, 1986.

Fraser, Arvonne S., and Sue E. Holbert. "Women in the Minnesota Legislature." In Barbara Stuhler and Gretchen Kreuter, eds., *Women of Minnesota: Selected Biographical Essays*. St. Paul: Minnesota Historical Society Press, 1977.

Genealogical information about Andreas and Clara Ueland's children. October 13, 1987. Copy in author's possession.

Gluck, Sherna, ed. *From Parlor to Prison: Five American Suffragists Talk about Their Lives*. New York: Vintage Books, 1976. Reprint. New York: Octagon Books, 1976.

Griffith, Elisabeth. *In Her Own Right: The Life of Elizabeth Cady Stanton*. New York: Oxford University Press, 1984.

Hargraves, Mildred Fearrington. *The First Fifty Years*. St. Paul: League of Women Voters of Minnesota, 1969.

Harper, Ida Husted. *A Brief History of the Movement for Woman Suffrage in the United States*. New York: National American Woman Suffrage Association, 1914.

Harpole, Patricia C., comp. "Brief Biographies of Other Minnesota

Women." In Barbara Stuhler and Gretchen Kreuter, eds., *Women of Minnesota: Selected Biographical Essays*. St. Paul: Minnesota Historical Society Press, 1977.

Haynes, John E. "Reformers, Radicals, and Conservatives." In Clifford E. Clark, Jr., ed., *Minnesota in a Century of Change: The State and Its People since 1900*. St. Paul: Minnesota Historical Society Press, 1989.

Heilbrun, Carolyn G. *Writing a Woman's Life*. New York: W. W. Norton, 1988.

Henry, Sherrye. *The Deep Divide: Why American Women Resist Equality*. New York: Macmillan Publishing Co., 1994.

Hurd, Ethel Edgerton. *Woman Suffrage in Minnesota: A Record of the Activities in Its Behalf since 1847*. Minneapolis: Published for Minnesota Woman Suffrage Association by Inland Press, 1916.

Irwin, Inez Haynes. *The Story of the Woman's Party*. New York: Harcourt, Brace & Co., 1921.

James, Edward T., et al., eds. *Notable American Women, 1607–1950: A Biographical Dictionary*. 3 vols. Cambridge: Belknap Press of Harvard University Press, 1971.

Jensen, Joan M. "All Pink Sisters: The War Department and the Feminist Movement in the 1920s." In Lois Scharf and Joan M. Jensen, eds., *Decades of Discontent: The Women's Movement, 1920–1940*. Contributions in Women's Studies, no. 28. Westport, Conn.: Greenwood Press, 1983.

Jones, Judy Yaeger. "Nellie F. Griswold Francis." In *Women of Minnesota: Biographies and Sources*, 12–15. [St. Paul: Minnesota Women's History Month, 1991].

[Jones, Richard?]. "Labor's Position on Woman Suffrage." *New Republic*, March 11, 1916, p. 150–52.

Klein, Ethel. *Gender Politics: From Consciousness to Mass Politics*. Cambridge: Harvard University Press, 1984.

Kraditor, Aileen S. *The Ideas of the Woman Suffrage Movement, 1890–1920*. New York: Columbia University Press, 1965. Reprint. Garden City, N.Y.: Doubleday & Co., 1971.

Lebsock, Suzanne. "Women and American Politics, 1880–1920." In Louise A. Tilly and Patricia Gurin, eds., *Women, Politics, and Change*. New York: Russell Sage Foundation, 1990.

Lemons, J. Stanley. *The Woman Citizen: Social Feminism in the 1920s*. Urbana: University of Illinois Press, 1973.

Leonard, John William, editor in chief. *Woman's Who's Who of America: A Biographical Dictionary of Contemporary Women of the United States and Canada: 1914–1915*. New York: American Commonwealth Co., 1914.

Lerner, Gerda. *The Majority Finds Its Past: Placing Women in History.* New York: Oxford University Press, 1979.

Lief, Julia Wiech. "A Woman of Purpose: Julia B. Nelson." *Minnesota History* 47 (Winter 1981): 302–14.

Lounsbury, Linda. "The Woman Suffrage Movement in Minnesota." 1982. Unpublished manuscript in private collection.

Ludcke, Jeannette. *You've Come a Long Way, Lady!: The Seventy-five Year History of the Woman's Club of Minneapolis.* [Minneapolis]: The Club, [1982?].

Lunardini, Christine A. *From Equal Suffrage to Equal Rights: Alice Paul and the National Woman's Party, 1910–1928.* New York: New York University Press, 1986.

McDonagh, Eileen Lorenzi. "The Significance of the Nineteenth Amendment: A New Look at Civil Rights, Social Welfare, and Woman Suffrage Alignments in the Progressive Era." *Women and Politics* (1990), vol. 10, no. 2, p. 59–94.

MacGaffey, Edward. "A Pattern for Progress: The Minnesota Children's Code." *Minnesota History* 41 (Spring 1969): 229–36.

Martin, Theodora Penny. *The Sound of Our Own Voices: Women's Study Clubs 1860–1910.* Boston: Beacon Press, 1987.

Minnesota. Governor (1915–1921: Burnquist). *Inaugural Message of Gov. J. A. A. Burnquist to the Legislature of Minnesota.* [St. Paul, 1919].

———. ———. *Message of Gov. J. A. A. Burnquist to the Special Session of the Legislature of Minnesota, September 1919.* [St. Paul, 1919].

———. House of Representatives. *Journal.*

———. [Minnesota] Commission on the Economic Status of Women. *Minnesota Women in the Twentieth Century.* St. Paul: The Commission, 1990.

———. Minnesota Governor's Commission on the Status of Women. *Interim Report.* St. Paul: The Commission, 1964.

———. Secretary of State. *Legislative Manual.*

———. Senate. *Journal.*

Morgan, David. *Suffragists and Democrats: The Politics of Woman Suffrage in America.* [East Lansing]: Michigan State University Press, 1972.

National American Woman Suffrage Association. *Victory, How Women Won It: A Centennial Symposium, 1840–1940.* New York: H. W. Wilson Co., 1940.

Noun, Louise R. *Strong-minded Women: The Emergence of the Woman-Suffrage Movement in Iowa.* Ames: Iowa State University Press, 1969.

O'Neill, William L. *Feminism in America: A History.* 2d rev. ed. New Brunswick, N.J.: Transaction Publishers, 1989.

Park, Maud Wood. *Front Door Lobby*. Edited by Edna Lamprey Stantial. Boston: Beacon Press, 1960.

Peck, Mary Gray. *Carrie Chapman Catt: A Biography*. New York: H. W. Wilson Co., 1944.

Peripatetics [Club]. *The Peripatetics of Minneapolis*. [Minneapolis: The Club, 1990].

——. *Yearbook*. 1920–21.

Pruitt, Mary Christine. "'Women Unite!' The Modern Women's Movement in Minnesota." Ph.D. diss., University of Minnesota, 1987. Microfilm edition.

Rosenberg, Rosalind. *Divided Lives: American Women in the Twentieth Century*. American Century Series; Eric Foner, consulting editor. New York: Hill & Wang, 1992.

Rossi, Alice S. "Equality between the Sexes: An Immodest Proposal." In June Sochen, ed., *The New Feminism in Twentieth-Century America*. Problems in American Civilization; Edwin C. Rozwenc, editorial director. Lexington, Mass.: D. C. Heath & Co., 1971.

Schneider, Dorothy, and Carl J. Schneider. *American Women in the Progressive Era, 1900–1920*. New York: Facts on File, 1993. Reprint. New York: Anchor Books, 1994.

Scott, Anne Firor. *Making the Invisible Woman Visible*. Urbana: University of Illinois Press, 1984.

——. *Natural Allies: Women's Associations in American History*. Urbana: University of Illinois Press, 1991.

——. "On Seeing and Not Seeing: A Case of Historical Invisibility." *Journal of American History* 71 (June 1984): 7–21.

——. and Andrew MacKay Scott. *One Half the People: The Fight for Woman Suffrage*. America's Alternatives series. Philadelphia: Lippincott, 1975. Reprint. Urbana: University of Illinois Press, 1982.

Sheeran, Marte. "Woman Suffrage and the Minnesota Legislature, 1907–1919." [1975?]. Copy in Minnesota Historical Society.

Sicherman, Barbara, and Carol Hurd Green, eds. *Notable American Women: The Modern Period*. Cambridge: Belknap Press of Harvard University Press, 1980.

Stanton, Elizabeth Cady, et al. *History of Woman Suffrage*. 6 vols. Rochester, N.Y.: Susan B. Anthony; New York: National American Woman Suffrage Association, 1881–1922.

Sterling, Dorothy. *Ahead of Her Time: Abby Kelly and the Politics of Antislavery*. New York: W. W. Norton & Co., 1991.

Stuhler, Barbara, and Gretchen Kreuter, eds. *Women of Minnesota: Selected Biographical Essays*. St. Paul: Minnesota Historical Society Press, 1977.

Subialka, Carol A. "The Ideology of Minnesota's Woman Suffrage Movement: 1910–1920." Senior thesis, Department of History, University of Minnesota, 1987.

Swisshelm, Jane Grey. *Crusader and Feminist: Letters of Jane Grey Swisshelm, 1858–1865*. Edited by Arthur J. Larsen. St. Paul: Minnesota Historical Society, 1934.

———. *Half a Century*. 3d ed. Chicago: Jansen, McClurg & Co., 1880.

Taylor, A. Elizabeth. *The Woman Suffrage Movement in Tennessee*. New York: Bookman Associates, 1957. Reprint. New York: Octagon Books, 1978.

Toensing, W. F., comp. *Minnesota Congressmen, Legislators, and Other Elected State Officials: An Alphabetical Check List, 1849–1971*. St. Paul: Minnesota Historical Society, 1971.

Ueland, Andreas. *Recollections of an Immigrant*. New York: Minton, Balch & Co., 1929.

Ueland, Brenda. "Clara Ueland of Minnesota." 1967. Copy in Minnesota Historical Society.

———. *Me*. New York: G. P. Putnam's Sons, 1939. Reprints. St. Paul: Schubert Club, 1983. Duluth: Holy Cow! Press, 1994.

———. *Strength to Your Sword Arm: Selected Writings*. Duluth: Holy Cow! Press, 1993.

Ueland, Clara. "The Advantages of Equal Suffrage." In J. F. Ebersole, ed., *Papers and Proceedings of the Eighth Annual Meeting of the Minnesota Academy of Social Sciences*. General topic: "Women and the State." Publications of the Minnesota Academy of Social Sciences, vol. 8, no. 8. [Mankato, Minn.]: Published for the Academy by the Free Press Printing Co., 1915.

———. "While We Wage War." *Woman Citizen*, October 27, 1917, p. 413.

Ueland, Margaret L. "The Ueland Family and Their Homes on Interlachen Terrace, Minneapolis." Paper presented at Linden Hills Community meeting, Minneapolis, August 9, 1988. Copy in author's possession.

Ueland, Rolf, and Margaret L. Ueland, comps. "The Lineal Ancestors, Descendants and Other Relatives of Anne, Elsa, Brenda, Sigurd, Arnulf, Rolf and Torvald Ueland." 1973–76. Copy in author's possession.

Ueland, Sigurd. "Sense and Senility: (A Commonplace Biography)." 1971. Copy in Minnesota Historical Society.

U.S. Congress. *Congressional Record*.

Upham, Warren, and Rose Barteau Dunlap, comps. "Minnesota Biographies, 1855–1912." *Collections of the Minnesota Historical Society* 14 (1912): 1–892.

Wellman, Judith. "The Seneca Falls Women's Rights Convention: A Study of Social Networks." *Journal of Women's History* 3 (Spring 1991): 9–37.

Wells, Marguerite M. *A Portrait of the League of Women Voters.* Washington, D.C.: Overseas Education Fund of the League of Women Voters, 1962. Copy in League of Women Voters of Minnesota Records, Minnesota Historical Society.

Witt, Linda, Karen M. Paget, and Glenna Matthews. *Running as a Woman: Gender and Power in American Politics.* New York: Free Press, 1994.

Wolf, Naomi. *Fire with Fire: The New Female Power and How It Will Change the Twenty-first Century.* New York: Random House, 1993.

The Woman Suffrage Year Book: 1917. Edited by Martha G. Stapler. New York: National Woman Suffrage Publishing Co., 1917.

Woman's Club of Minneapolis. *Yearbooks.*

Woman's Journal (Boston and Chicago). Extracts of Minnesota interest. Typescript, copy in Minnesota Historical Society.

Wood, Stella Louise. "History of the Kindergarten Movement in Minnesota." In *History of the Kindergarten Movement in the Mid-Western States and in New York: Presented at the Cincinnati Convention, Association for Childhood Education, April 19–23, 1938,* p. 42–46. Copy in Macalester College Archives.

Young, Louise M. *In the Public Interest: The League of Women Voters, 1920–1970.* Contributions in American Studies, no. 96; Robert H. Walker, series editor. New York: Greenwood Press, 1989.

MANUSCRIPTS

All manuscripts are in the collections of the Minnesota Historical Society, St. Paul.

Jaeger, Luth and Nanny Mattson. Papers.

League of Women Voters of Minnesota. Records.

Mattson, Hans, and Family. Papers.

Minnesota Biography Project Files.

Minnesota Equal Franchise League. Papers.

Minnesota Woman Suffrage Association. Records (microfilm edition).

Paige, Mabeth Hurd. Papers.

Peripatetics [Club]. Records.

Political Equality Club of Minneapolis. Records.
Political Equality Club of St. Paul. Papers.
Sageng, Ole O. Papers.

PERIODICALS

Labor Review (Minneapolis), later *Minneapolis Labor Review*.

Minnesota Bulletin (Minneapolis and Red Wing: Minnesota Woman Suffrage Association).

Minnesota Woman Voter, formerly *Woman Voter* (Minneapolis and St. Paul: Minnesota League of Women Voters), including Clara Ueland memorial issue, March 1927.

The Suffragist (Washington, D.C.: Congressional Union for Woman Suffrage/National Woman's Party).

Woman Citizen (New York: National American Woman Suffrage Association).

INDEX